101 Careers in Healthcare Management

Leonard H. Friedman, PhD, MPH, FACHE, is Professor of Health Services Management and Leadership and Director of the Master of Health Services Administration degree program at The George Washington University. Prior to arriving at The George Washington University in 2008, he was a faculty member at Oregon State University beginning in 1992. Dr. Friedman's scholarly work has concentrated on the mechanisms of organizational change and strategic decision making in health service organizations. Dr. Friedman's research has explored building the resilience of healthcare organizations to respond to environmental jolts, using systems approaches to reduce medical errors and, most recently, helping understand the roots of organizational excellence in healthcare. His teaching responsibilities have included graduate and undergraduate classes in healthcare management, organization theory and behavior in healthcare, healthcare law and regulation, strategic management, and leadership in healthcare organizations. His work has been published in a variety of healthcare management journals. He is the coeditor of *Essentials of Management and Leadership in Public Health* and is the coeditor of *Advances in Health Services Management*. Dr. Friedman has been the chair of the Healthcare Management Division of the Academy of Management and Association of University Programs in Health Administration. Dr. Friedman is a fellow of the American College of Healthcare Executives.

Anthony R. Kovner, MPA, PhD, is Professor of Public and Health Management at NYU Wagner, Graduate School of Public Service, where he teaches Healthcare Management, the Governance of Non-Profit Organizations, Caring Dilemmas: Learning from Narrative, and the Capstone in Healthcare Management. Professor Kovner has written 9 books (including co-editing *Health Care Delivery in the United States*, now in its 10th edition [Springer Publishing Company, 2011]), 43 articles on healthcare management, and has published 40 case studies. In 1999, Kovner was awarded the Gary L. Filerman Prize for Educational Leadership from the Association of University Programs in Health Administration. Kovner was director of the graduate program in health policy and management at New York University (NYU) for 20 years, and currently directs the Executive MPA in Management: Concentration for Nurse Leaders at NYU.

Dr. Kovner has extensive management experience in healthcare as well. He has been a senior manager in two hospitals, a nursing home, a group practice, and a neighborhood health center, and senior healthcare consultant for a large industrial union. He has served as a consultant to the New York Presbyterian Hospital and Healthcare System, the Robert Wood Johnson Foundation, the W. K. Kellogg Foundation, Montefiore Medical Center, and the American Academy of Orthopedic Surgeons, among others. He was a board member of Lutheran Medical Center in Brooklyn for 25 years.

Professor Kovner is a world leader in evidence-based management in healthcare. With Richard D'Aquila and David Fine, he authored *Evidence-Based Management in Healthcare*; additionally, he authored numerous articles or cases about evidence-based management in the *Oxford Handbook of Evidence-Based Management*, *Frontiers of Health Services Management*, and the *Harvard Business Review*. He is a founding member of the Advisory Council of the Center for Evidence-Based Management, headquartered in the Netherlands.

101 Careers in Healthcare Management

LEONARD H. FRIEDMAN, PhD, MPH, FACHE

ANTHONY R. KOVNER, MPA, PhD

SPRINGER PUBLISHING COMPANY
NEW YORK

Springer Publishing Company, LLC
11 West 42nd Street
New York, NY 10036
www.springerpub.com

Acquisitions Editor: Sheri W. Sussman
Composition: Newgen Imaging

ISBN: 978-0-8261-9334-6
E-book ISBN: 978-0-8261-9335-3

12 13 14/ 5 4 3 2 1

Library of Congress Cataloging-in-Publication Data
Friedman, Leonard H.
101 careers in healthcare management / Leonard H. Friedman, Anthony R. Kovner.
p. ; cm.
One hundred one careers in healthcare management
One hundred and one careers in healthcare management
101 careers in health care management
Includes index.
ISBN 978-0-8261-9334-6 — ISBN 978-0-8261-9335-3 (e-book)
I. Kovner, Anthony R. II. Title. III. Title: One hundred one careers in healthcare management. IV. Title: One hundred and one careers in healthcare management. V. Title: 101 careers in health care management.
[DNLM: 1. Career Choice—United States. 2. Health Services Administration—United States. W 21]

362.1068—dc23 2012033692

Printed in the United States of America by Bang Printing.

To All Our Students: Past, Present, and Future

CONTENTS

FOREWORD

One of life's greatest blessings is having meaningful work. Having a wonderful family and good health and supportive friends is critical. But remember that you will potentially spend 40 hours a week for 40 years working at a job. So it is worth every minute you spend figuring out what you want to do for a living. It is amazing how many adults report that one of their greatest regrets is they didn't like their profession or their job. But it can be hard to figure out what your actual job options are once you pick a profession. And it can be hard to understand what people in those jobs actually do all day long. The purpose of this book is to help answer those questions. What jobs are there for people with healthcare management degrees? What do people in those jobs do all day long?

Several years ago, a pediatrician came to speak in a class I was teaching at Ohio State's healthcare management program. Dr. Lindsey Grossman explained that she saw an MD degree as a generalist degree—much like a BA or BS. While the public thinks that being a doctor is a specific profession, Lindsey said that an MD is a foundational degree that provides the platform for the physician to then specialize. She said that being an emergency room doctor is completely different from being a physician working in a lab to develop new cancer drugs, which is completely different from being a physician working for the Centers for Disease Control and Prevention managing an HIV program in Botswana. I had never thought of a medical degree in that context.

Over the years, I have thought of an MHA as a specific degree—as opposed to a MBA, which is more of a generalist degree. Only recently have I come to realize that what Lindsey said about being a physician is also true for those in healthcare administration, because having a healthcare administration degree opens up a whole world of opportunities that are strikingly different.

One of my colleagues started out thinking she would be a hospital administrator but early in her career as a consultant, an opportunity came up in pharmacy benefits management. Despite the fact that the field was nascent and that she knew little about what pharmacy benefits management firms did, she had the essential skills from her graduate education in healthcare management and she became wildly successful. Today she is an executive with one of the largest medical supply companies in the world. Little did she realize that her career would take her in that direction when she started in her MHA program. Many healthcare administrators would say the same thing—that they knew nothing about the jobs that they do today and that they never imagined the opportunities that would come their way when they selected healthcare administration as their major.

But what binds the healthcare administration professional is a desire to contribute to society or to a community. When I was in graduate school, my classmates and I went to the American College of Healthcare Executives annual meeting in Chicago. I connected with a high school classmate who was living the high life in Chicago with a great apartment and fabulous lifestyle. She was so excited to be working for an advertising agency on the Keebler cookie account. She spoke with such great enthusiasm for the elves and what the firm's plans were to advertise and sell more cookies. It was a bewildering experience to try to understand how someone could get so excited about selling cookies. When I reported this to my classmates, one of them responded, "But don't you see? What binds us together is our mutual desire to do more with our lives for the common good than to promote products or build a better mousetrap." People discover healthcare administration as a profession from a variety of avenues, but they have that innate sense that they want their lives to be about doing good for others.

This book is intended to help you on your journey exploring healthcare administration as a career. Careers are made up of a series of jobs that provide you with an opportunity to further develop your skills, explore your interests and talents, and potentially broaden your scope of impact. Good luck on your journey.

Janet Porter, PhD
Chief Operating Officer
Dana-Farber Cancer Institute

PREFACE

In the combined 60-plus years that the two of us have been teaching healthcare management, we have seen numerous changes throughout our careers. Blackboards, chalk, and overhead projectors have morphed into smart classrooms with real-time access to the Internet and electronic submission of student writing expected in almost every class. Strict lecture/discussion classes with the professor as the "sage on the stage" have shifted into case-based classes, service learning, and the professor as the "guide on the side." Our students who had at one time been primarily White males are now primarily women, with an ever-growing number of ethnic and racial minorities along with international students. Our programs that had once been almost exclusively dedicated to teaching people to manage hospitals now have expanded to include multiple organizations within the health sector, including long-term care, physician practices, commercial insurance, consulting firms, pharmaceuticals, medical devices, information technology, and biotechnology. In short, our students, the way in which they are prepared, and the world that they are preparing to enter have changed dramatically.

However, there are two factors that have remained constant over the years. The first is the relative invisibility of our programs and our discipline. If you ask prospective students to name possible health-related careers, it is highly unlikely that healthcare executive will come to mind. Students can mention numerous types and variations of clinical professionals but rarely, if ever, will they note the persons responsible for management and administration of public or private healthcare organizations. Besides, the only time students see healthcare administrators in the media is when they are portrayed as being heartless bureaucrats who stand in the way of heroic physicians and nurses trying to save the lives of their patients.

There is a second constant, the importance of which supersedes everything else. That is the dedication and devotion of our students who all want to make healthcare better. By and large, our students and graduates will never touch a patient but, in the end, their job is to create and sustain the systems that allow clinicians to do their very best work. Our students know that healthcare management is a relationship-based business that requires them to have exceptional interpersonal skills and a real passion for wanting to create organizations that touch people during some of the most vulnerable times of their lives. Our students and graduates know that they make a real difference, and it has been an honor and a privilege to work with them over the years as they embark on their career journeys. We have had the opportunity to make a difference in several generations of healthcare leaders and we invite all of you to join us on that voyage of discovery.[1]

Leonard H. Friedman, PhD, MPH, FACHE
The George Washington University
School of Public Health and Health Services

Anthony R. Kovner, MPA, PhD
New York University
NYU Wagner, Graduate School of Public Service

[1] Job descriptions contained in the book are representative of the jobs with those particular titles. Information was gathered from the job descriptions containing that title from at least two different organizations in order to ensure consistency. Professional association websites pointed us to organizations that had job openings and had posted job descriptions.

ACKNOWLEDGMENTS

I would like to acknowledge here three unforgettable mentors who have advanced my career as a healthcare manager, teacher, and researcher. These include my father Sidney J. Kovner, for his honesty, love, and intelligence; Conrad Seipp, for his kindness to me and personal devotion to equity in healthcare; and to Robert Eilers, for his personal example as a mentor, scholar, teacher, husband, and father, and for career advice.

During my over 30 years tenure at New York University/Wagner, Graduate School of Public Service, I have worked with numerous colleagues who share my enthusiasm for advising and teaching graduate students in healthcare management and helping our alumni with career development. Among them, I would like specifically to thank the following: in administration, Dean Ellen Schall, Associate Dean for Administration Tyra Liebmann, and David Schachter, Assistant Dean and Director of Student Services; on the faculty, John Billings, Steve Finkler, Jim Knickman, Roger Kropf, John Donnellan, Victor Rodwin, and Charlotte Wagenberg. Alumni who have been helpful in advising me and the program include Sofia Agoritsas, Claudia Caine, Barbara Green, David Kaplan, Peter Karow, Sherine Khalil, Jon Sendach, Robert Shiau, and Jacob Victory. Numerous others have helped our students, and to you I am grateful as well.

A special word of thanks to the most wonderful couple in healthcare management education: Len Friedman (who has been a pleasure to work with as senior coauthor) and Lydia Middleton. And to my key academic influences on the topic and friends—John Griffith, Ken White, Gary Filerman, Steve Mick, and Steve Loebs.

My family are more distinguished in academia and real life than I am—wife Chris Kovner, and daughters Sarah and Anna Kovner

(PhDs all)—and we all are expecting great things from our beloved grandchildren Zachary, Ava, Lily, and Stella.

Anthony R. Kovner, PhD
NYU Wagner, Graduate School of Public Service

This book is at its core inspirational. I often tell my students that being an effective healthcare leader requires a high level of courage and passion for this work. It has been an honor and a privilege to be associated for so many years with so many exceptional healthcare leaders across the country, who have reminded me that the work I do in the classroom and in my research really matters. Among the most visionary of those leaders is Dr. Larry Mullins, President and CEO of Samaritan Health Services in Corvallis, Oregon. He has provided me with so many opportunities to see how a truly excellent healthcare organization should operate. Another person who has profoundly influenced my teaching is Quint Studer. Every time I hear Quint speak at one of his seminars, I am reminded that purpose, worthwhile work, and making a difference are at the center of everything I do.

My career at two universities has spanned the country, and I would be remiss if I did not acknowledge my friends and colleagues at Oregon State University and at The George Washington University. While at Oregon State, Anthony Veltri and Chunhuei Chi have been dear friends and some of the most amazing colleagues anywhere. Thank you to the 10 doctoral students at Oregon State (David Kailin, Ted Ficken, Seth Wolpin, Brian Churchill, Jennifer McCarthy, Nancy Seifert, Mark King, Jan Buffa, Steve Self, and Rose Tian) who trusted me to guide their education and career development.

During my tenure at The George Washington University, I have been surrounded by colleagues who all share my enthusiasm for healthcare management education. Thank you to our chairman Bob Burke and to Doug Anderson, Phil Aspden, Brian Biles, Kurt Darr, Bianca Frogner, Al Hamilton, Tom Jazweicki, Pete Marghella, Leah Maselink, Sheila McGinnis, and Joy Volarich. The support and encouragement from the alumni at the Department of Health Services Management and Leadership are a joy to witness and I would like to acknowledge the more than 3,300 alums of our program.

I must express my thanks and appreciation to all of the persons who so graciously shared with us their thoughts and reflections on their experience as healthcare leaders. I have been honored to have taught many of these persons, and I can honestly tell them that I am a better teacher and have a more profound appreciation for this field as a result of having known them and have been allowed to help them on their careers. Special thanks go to my former students Mohamed Alyajouri, Rob Bauer, Paul Brashnyk, Dennis Delsile, Mike Eppeheimer, Taqueena Hall, Leon Harris, Kelly Kaiser, Stefanie Kirk, Megan Melvin, Josh Niehaus, Ryan Oster, Jeremy Stubson, Kory Termaine, Lauren Wixted, Dana Wolf, and Joe Yoder, who have shown me what it takes to be a healthcare leader.

This book would not have been possible without the hard work and dedication of a number of graduate students in the Department of Health Services Management and Leadership at The George Washington University. James Shimer assumed the lead role in helping to craft and organize the content of the book. Thanks as well to Am'Asa Baldwin, Ayla Baughman, Praneet Bopari, Debra Davidson, Matt Joslin, Andrew Kanoff, Jonathan Morgan, Tony Ng, and Bronson Smith. I so appreciate all of your help.

Thank you to Sheri W. Sussman and everyone at Springer Publishing Company for your guidance and patience as this book moved forward. Despite the bumps in the road that life sometimes throws at you, everyone at Springer has been wonderful and has made this a truly remarkable and memorable experience.

Thanks so much to my coauthor Tony Kovner. I have known Tony since I first entered this business in 1992 and have looked up to him as a prolific writer, a true scholar, and as a trusted friend. It has been a pleasure working with Tony on this project.

Finally, an effort of this magnitude required the unconditional love and support of my amazing family. Words are inadequate to express my love and appreciation to my wife Lydia. Without her, none of this would be possible. Thank you to my daughters Lynn and Allison, and to my stepsons Spencer, Teddy, and Will. The six of you make my life complete.

Leonard H. Friedman, PhD, MPH, FACHE
The George Washington University
School of Public Health and Health Services

I ■ INTRODUCTION TO HEALTHCARE MANAGEMENT

1 ■ WHAT IS HEALTHCARE MANAGEMENT?

The point of this question is to focus the reader on what is needed to learn to get a job and succeed at a job in healthcare management. Healthcare management is a vast field. Over 17% of the nation's gross national product is from healthcare. This means that one out of every six jobs in the United States is in the healthcare field. There are over 200,000 healthcare managers. They come with many different degrees and even with no degrees. Licensure is not required other than in the field of nursing home management in some states. What kinds of skills and experience are required to get a job in healthcare management? In essence, these include: knowledge of statistics, ability to do quantitative analysis; communications skills (this includes reading and writing); willingness to work hard; and ability to get along with other people. Assuming that all job applicants have these abilities, the question becomes "What are you expected to know about healthcare management to get a job in healthcare organizations?"

The first part of the question is "What is management?" Management involves working with others in organizations to achieve goals. Many of the functions of managers are taught in business schools or schools of management. These functions include finance, human resources, information management, operations management, marketing, and strategic planning. You can approach an answer to this question in a different way by asking "What is *not* management?" Typically, one answer is "policy." One definition of "policy" is making guidelines that are adopted by governments (and organizations) that constrain decision making and action, and limit subsequent choices. Policy influences managers, although it is not what most managers do most of the time. Similarly, as policymakers influence managers, managers can influence policymakers.

In healthcare, what is *not* management includes the clinical occupations such as physician, nurse, social worker, and so forth. Whereas in former times, managers were expected to provide support for frontline clinicians, increasingly managers are now involved also in managing healthcare to ensure patient safety and quality. Managers currently work with clinicians and support staff in increasingly larger and more complex healthcare organizations.

Entry-level jobs in management typically involve improving quality and containing cost by standardizing and improving work processes, increasing revenues through fundraising, and improving customer service by implementing shorter waits through open-access appointment systems.

"What is *healthcare management?*" This is hard to precisely define. It can perhaps best be answered (as was "What is management?) in terms of how healthcare organizations *differ* from other organizations. Healthcare organizations are obviously not manufacturing organizations, or finance organizations, or educational organizations. Drug companies manufacture products but they do not provide healthcare as do doctors and nurses. Some banks lend primarily to healthcare organizations. Universities educate the healthcare workforce and often are in the healthcare delivery business but under a separate auspice. Within universities, there are separate schools of health professions. Within or independent of such schools, there are graduate and undergraduate programs of healthcare management that are located in schools of business, public health, allied health professions, or in other schools. Of course, *healthcare* serves people who are sick or prevents them from getting sick and includes training people to provide these services.

But what is different about "healthcare management" as opposed to other kinds of management? Why go to a program of healthcare management rather than pursuing a general business degree in a school with no coursework in healthcare per se? This question is being asked by students wanting to get a job in healthcare management. It is also asked by employers in terms of "Why should we hire someone from an *accredited graduate or certified undergraduate healthcare management program* rather than someone graduating from a business school, graduate or undergraduate, without a healthcare management program?" Or, "Why shouldn't we hire someone without a master's degree (or without an undergraduate degree), if the person is qualified, such as someone who possesses a clinical degree and who can easily pick up management, if that person is smart and a good person?"

In practice, organizations increasingly are looking for persons with healthcare management training or providing or arranging to provide such extra training to persons already hired or to be hired. This additional training is made necessary because of the unique managerial and leadership challenges that healthcare organizations routinely face. This is because employers may be persuaded by other skills and experience a job candidate has, often including work experience in the organization, relative to job candidates who already have healthcare management training. We would like to explore in this short chapter what kind of training in healthcare is desirable for all managers seeking to work in healthcare organizations. There is certainly no expressed agreement about this in the field that we know of at present. We would start with the training required in our own accredited graduate programs in healthcare management. We include the following topics in our curriculum, in addition to the standard management functions—financial management, marketing, operations research, and so forth—previously mentioned. These *health* topics are: health policy, population health, medical care delivery, and support for medical care delivery.

This is the body of knowledge that differentiates healthcare management from other occupations in others kinds of organizations.

Health Policy. This includes learning about the past, present, and future U.S. healthcare system (stakeholders and interests), health reform, healthcare financing, and comparative health systems. Prerequisites include an understanding of American government and how policy is made at federal, state, and local levels.

Population Health. This includes medical and population health models of healthcare delivery, public health, how behavior influences health status, health and behavior, and access to medical care.

Medical Care Delivery. This includes the organization of medical care, integrative models and performance, high-quality healthcare, healthcare costs and value, and comparative effectiveness.

Support of Medical Care Delivery. This includes governance, management, and accountability of healthcare organizations, health workforce, and health information management.

How these topics are organized varies among curricula in undergraduate and graduate programs of healthcare management. What is distinctive about healthcare organizations is the nature of the services they provide (some services are for life-threatening diseases and accidents), how the organizations are paid for the services they provide (largely by third parties), the labor-intensive and fragmented nature of the healthcare workforce, and the uneven performance of healthcare organizations as to the costs and quality of care.

The culture of healthcare organizations generally involves a high commitment to "the patient comes first," and to high-quality and personalized service. Currently, there is pressure from the taxpayers and the government to contain the increase in healthcare costs, as well as charges of huge amounts of waste in healthcare organizations, resulting, in large part, from the way providers are paid, based on fee-for-services that results often in more services than are medically necessary, and greater incomes and revenues than are necessary for providers and healthcare organizations.

LETTER TO A YOUNG MANAGER

Of course, Clara, you are a project manager in an academic medical center. You have asked me for help in managing your career. I am a longtime professor in healthcare management. You were my student last semester in a course on this subject. You graduated from Cornell University and after college worked in a consulting firm as a senior associate. You are 28 years old, female, single, and intend to start a family some day.

You don't know exactly what you think you want to do. In response to my question, you would aspire to be a chief operational officer (COO) in a large healthcare organization. Why not aspire to be a chief executive officer (CEO)? Because you are shy or not presumptuous? But, you are ambitious. That's how and why you got to where you are and why you ask me the question. You don't expect a precise answer but just want to learn something by questioning me. I expect to learn something by answering you. It is part of my job answering this question. I get asked about it many times. I'm not that sure that I do a good enough job in my response.

I pride myself in asking the right question. This is one of the basic steps in evidence-based management. Is what you have posed an answerable question? Should the question rather be "How do I get the next job?" Certainly if you wait, Clara, the next job is not going to come to you. Not that this hasn't happened in real life to somebody else, but I believe in making your own luck. If you don't ask, you don't get. Another question, Clara, which you certainly aren't going to ask, is "How am I going to find a husband, have children, and pursue my career aspirations when I am already working 60 hours a week? Yes, I am saving money, because I haven't really got much time to spend it."

There certainly isn't anything wrong with aspiring to be a COO. One of the very best managers I know is a COO, who has no desire to be a CEO. He doesn't like the ceremonial aspects of the CEO job, going to so many boring meetings, and talking all the time about what the organization is doing rather than about how they are doing the work—producing results and helping patients. So, we're on the same wavelength. And, you can get off the trajectory to COO obviously at any step along the line. There are probably two stops between project manager and COO. First, you have to become the manager of a department, and then you have to become a manager of several departments.

Clara, you can get the next job in several ways. First, build your own resume, and the reality behind your record of accomplishment. Managers are promoted primarily because of their track records. Your track record spotlights results you have achieved, with others, of course—improving quality, containing costs, improving access, reducing voluntary turnover, raising revenues, ensuring safety, and improving patient satisfaction. You have done none of these things by yourself, but it is fine to say that you accomplished these results with others. Rising higher in the organization assumes integrity, working as a member of the team and as a leader of the team.

Integrity means that others trust you. I trusted you right away in class, Clara, because you were quiet, laughed at my sarcastic humor, which means you took it the right way, not that I was making fun of others, but rather understanding that I care deeply about doing the right thing, and suffer because of frequently encountered human mindlessness and self-interested behavior. I believe in calling things by their right names. Some people get insulted when I do so. And, of course, I can only get myself in trouble by speaking ill of others. This is why I am a professor rather than a manager. But I trust you, Clara. I know that you are consistent in your behavior and that you will consistently do the right thing, the careful thing, and the kind thing. This is what I believe about you. This is part of why I want to help you successfully manage your career.

Clara, if you want to move up in the organization, it helps to have a sponsor. The ideal mentor is experienced, has and wants to make the time to advise and help you. Often your own boss doesn't want to lose you and wants to take credit for your accomplishments. She feels she is responsible for your successes (after all, she hired you or kept you). You should be grateful to her for everything you have, rather than seeking a new position. And, this organization is financially successful and provides job security.

At some point in your job tenure (you haven't reached this point yet), Clara, you will feel that you aren't learning enough that is new, or that your boss is giving you too many projects to achieve the results you used to achieve in one project. Or she may take the best project away from you before the results are finally achieved. Of course, some hospitals consider all projects as team projects, where executive team members stay in these positions for 10 years or even longer.

What do you want out of the job anyway? How many Americans have meaningful jobs that they look forward to everyday? You are making enough money. It is difficult to find a man who will commit himself to marriage and parenthood with a successful woman. Perhaps you will find such a mate in the academic medical center, a doctor if not a manager. How do you find a sponsor/mentor if you don't have one to begin with, Clara? Why should any senior manager want to have the time to properly help you? The easiest way to start on this path is by working on projects for higher level executives or people who work with them and share what you can do. These opportunities come along or you can make these opportunities. One way of making these opportunities is by acquiring special skills—process management, marketing, fundraising, financial analysis, information management, human resources development, and others. Some of these skills can be acquired in executive education programs. Or they may be learned by working with functional experts such as internal auditors, quality improvement, human resources and finance staff, and speechwriters. New opportunities also arise in growing organizations.

Various kinds of networking can help you learn of job opportunities or of best practice. Start with networks in your own organizations. This includes persons with jobs like yours or persons at higher levels who are often willing to share their experience and give advice. Then, there are professional networks, alumni groups, and volunteer opportunities. You should take pleasure from every contact in networking, as you are learning how others see you and about what you like and don't like, can and cannot do in other jobs or in meeting management challenges. You should develop a compelling narrative of your own job history and accomplishments. And think through, Clara, what you want now in your next job or how you want to expand on what you do in your current job.

You should always plan in advance concerning what conditions you would no longer wish continue to work in your present job (e.g., a new incompetent or overbearing boss), and develop a Plan B as to what you might do next or how you would go about finding another job in this or another organization.

I would now like to go through some of the mistakes persons in your position commonly make in managing their career. Try and avoid them.

1. Not focusing sufficiently on results in your current job. This includes negotiating measurable objectives in advance and reporting on progress quarterly, and then, if you cannot achieve your objectives, either changing your tactics or your objectives.

2. Switching jobs for the wrong reasons, such as more money or higher title rather than a better opportunity to produce results and help others, which is why you got into healthcare management in the first place.

3. Switching jobs for the right reasons but insufficiently scouting out the new job, which turns out to be different from what the boss and human resources promised it would be. The organization is in worse financial shape than you thought it would be. The situation has changed during your transition time. For example, your new boss is leaving to take an exciting new job somewhere else or he gets sick or dies.

4. Ineffective managing of yourself in your relationship with your current boss. No manager wants to get fired, scapegoated, or shunned. You can avoid this fate, obviously, by performing well. "Performing well" is, of course, subject to various interpretations, which is why it makes sense to have measureable objectives and review the progress achieved regularly. The boss should perceive you, Clara, as loyal to her interests. This may include her taking credit for your ideas or work results as her own.

5. Ineffective managing of yourself. This includes thinking before you say anything whether what you are going to say is good for you. Telling the truth to power is generally not going to advance your interests. Your boss may view this as a personal attack, even if it isn't meant that way. Because otherwise, she would already have done something about what you are telling her because that is her job. Now you are actually telling her what to do or what not to do. And she doesn't like the way you are telling it to her. It also counts how you manage your time and how you manage your presence. You have to be seen as working hard, yet always available.

My main advice is not to forget why you chose to do this work, and be able to find pleasure in the work that you do each day and the company of the persons with whom you work. "The patient comes first" is a noble mission and we all should be privileged to work toward that end. Cheerfulness and the ability to deal with the solitude that each of us find ourselves inevitably facing as part of the job helps a lot. Managers need to be competent and it helps to be lucky. To an extent, we make our own luck. Why shouldn't you do well, Clara, in managing your career? You have everything going for you—health, integrity, youth, intelligence energy, and focus. Go for it![1]

[1] This is a fictional letter written by one of us to a real manager in the healthcare program who never asked for this help. We believe that this has relevance for many younger managers under similar circumstances.

2 ■ EDUCATION IN HEALTHCARE MANAGEMENT

In the previous chapter, we noted that the practice of healthcare management has undergone a number of significant changes over the past 50 years. Perhaps the most important of those has been the growing professionalization of the field. The need for increased professionalization of management has been driven by a number of factors including: changes in reimbursement from primarily out-of-pocket payment for services to largely third-party payment, the development of medicine as a sovereign profession (Starr, 1984), the increasing complexity and sophistication of medical diagnosis and treatment, federal and state regulations, and the ever-increasing numbers of elderly adults who require treatment for illness and disease. In the early days of healthcare management, hospitals were run by nuns (in the case of faith-based facilities) or physicians, and physician practices had virtually no management other than perhaps a bookkeeper or at best an office manager.

As healthcare management has grown in scope and sophistication, the need for formal education in the profession has also evolved. While a number of persons holding healthcare management positions have clinical training and were moved into management roles, the trend has been for those wishing to work in management to have specific training in the field. Beginning with the first graduate program in health administration at the University of Chicago in 1934, the field of healthcare management education has blossomed. At the present time, for students who wish to either enter the field or for those already in healthcare who want to develop their skills, there are four primary education opportunities: bachelor's, master's, doctoral, and executive education.

BACHELOR'S DEGREES IN HEALTHCARE MANAGEMENT

In Chapters 4 to 16, we will see that many healthcare management jobs require a bachelor's degree as the entry-level credential. While mid-level and senior leadership positions typically require a master's degree, the Bachelor of Arts/Bachelor of Science (BA/BS) in Healthcare Management is a very useful degree to hold for those seeking entry-level positions in this field.

A number of colleges and universities offer a BA/BS degree in Healthcare Management or Administration. In addition, many Schools of Business provide a BS in Business Administration with a concentration in Healthcare Management. While there are more than 200 schools that provide a BA/BS in Healthcare Management or some variation thereof, students should look for a program that is fully certified by the Association of University Programs in Health Administration (AUPHA). AUPHA provides a link to every certified and candidate undergraduate program in North America. All certified undergraduate programs require that students receive academic preparation in a liberal arts foundation (computation, communication, critical thinking, and social and cultural context), 19 content areas specific to healthcare management, and an experiential/applied learning component containing a minimum of 120 hours in an internship. For students interested in undergraduate study in healthcare management, it is helpful if they have outstanding verbal and written communication skills, good computational ability, and demonstrated leadership experience.

MASTER'S DEGREES IN HEALTHCARE MANAGEMENT

Unlike many other graduate professional fields that have but one well known and widely accepted degree, healthcare management does not fit this norm and is a potential area of confusion for prospective students. There are two important considerations that students need to keep in mind: the name of the degree and the home of the graduate program.

Perhaps the best known and most common master's degree in Healthcare Management is the Master of Health Administration (MHA). In addition, the Master of Science (MS), Master of Business Administration (MBA), Master of Public Health (MPH), Master of Public Administration (MPA), Master of Health Services Administration (MHSA), and Master of Science in Health Administration (MHSA) can all provide students with the highly focused academic preparation needed to assume mid-level and senior management roles in healthcare management organizations.

In addition to the specific degree, prospective students need to pay attention to the location of the healthcare management program. As one might expect, a healthcare-focused MBA will be in a school of business and will have a very strong emphasis on business principles. Similarly, a healthcare management MPH degree will be housed in a school of public health and those students should expect to hear about population health, epidemiology, and environmental health and safety. In reviewing the breadth of the field, healthcare management programs are also located in schools of public administration, nursing, medicine, allied health, and many others. The important thing to remember is that the location of the program is always linked to the focus of the educational preparation of the student.

As is the case in undergraduate healthcare management education, there are more than 200 schools offering master's degrees in the discipline. A large number of those programs are members of AUPHA, but in this case, graduate programs are accredited by the Commission on Accreditation of Healthcare Management Education (CAHME). Information about currently accredited graduate healthcare management programs is available on CAHME's and AUPHA's web pages. The 2012 criteria for CAHME accreditation require all programs to have a curriculum that is aligned with the program's mission and types of jobs that graduates typically enter. In addition, each accredited program is required to develop student competencies in the following: communications and interpersonal effectiveness; critical thinking, analysis, and problem solving; management and leadership; and professionalism and ethics. Students should expect to spend a minimum of 2 years full-time study in their master's degree program. There are a handful of programs that require students to complete a yearlong administrative residency at the conclusion of the 2 years of courses.

MHA OR MBA?

One of the most commonly asked questions is whether a student should seek a straight MBA degree or an MHA (or equivalent) degree. The simple answer depends on what sort of career path the student plans to pursue. The MBA is a rather generic business degree (granted, there are varying degrees of rigor and prestige depending on the school and the alumni) that can be applied into almost any business environment. Students who already have a BA/BS in Healthcare Management would be wise to consider an MBA since they already have a good background in healthcare. In general, students who are committed to a career in healthcare management should seriously consider an MHA or equivalent. Healthcare organizations are fundamentally different than virtually any other business, and persons who wish to be effective in a management role need to have a fine-grained understanding of the healthcare context that is possible only in MHA-type programs.

DOCTORAL DEGREES IN HEALTHCARE MANAGEMENT

For most professional roles in healthcare management, a doctoral degree is not necessary. However, for those who wish to enter an academic or research career, a doctoral degree is a necessity. There are comparatively few schools that offer focused doctoral preparation in healthcare management but those can be found through the AUPHA web page. Most university faculty members who teach in healthcare management have doctoral degrees in fields other than health management but their academic work allows them to apply their theoretical and research specializations to the context of the healthcare sector.

COMBINED DEGREE PROGRAMS

There are a number of universities that offer healthcare management degrees combined with other academic degrees. The most common additional degrees are in business, law, medicine, and public administration.

EXECUTIVE HEALTHCARE MANAGEMENT PROGRAMS

A growing trend is toward executive education in healthcare management. In many organizations, persons who have skill and education in a particular discipline such as medicine, nursing, medical technology, social work, and others, and who are competent in their work are frequently promoted to management roles. The issue here is that management represents a set of skills and competencies over and above what they currently possess. The other consideration is that for persons already working full time in a healthcare-related profession, they typically cannot dedicate 2 years of full-time study to earn their degree in management. It is for this group of adult learners who are already working in the field that the executive education programs have been developed. Most executive students have a minimum of 3 years experience in the field, and classes are taught in some combination of face-to-face and online delivery formats. In order to be CAHME-accredited, executive master's programs require a minimum of 120 face-to-face hours. While most executive programs are designed for master's-level education, there are a few executive doctoral programs available. The latter are structured for senior executives who wish to earn a doctoral degree while still maintaining their work responsibilities. AUPHA maintains a comprehensive listing of executive master's or doctoral healthcare management programs.

ONLINE HEALTHCARE MANAGEMENT PROGRAMS

Another growth area is pure online degree programs. In contrast to executive programs that require several years of professional experience and have a face-to-face course delivery component, most online programs can be taken by students with no field experience and are taught exclusively in an online format. Both bachelor's and master's online degrees are available from a variety of schools. At the present time, there are no pure online programs that have yet obtained AUPHA certification and totally online master's programs are not eligible for CAHME accreditation.

PAYING FOR YOUR EDUCATION

Undergraduate or graduate education can be an expensive endeavor, regardless of where you choose to go to school. One way to think of this is that you are making an investment in yourself and your future. Taking out loans through the school's financial aid office is a common method of paying for school. Some students decide to work full time or part time in order to finance their education. Some programs require that students go to school full time and do not permit outside work arrangements. Others permit part-time employment but recommend that work be limited to no more than 20 hours or so a week. Other programs are structured to accommodate the needs of working adults. The best advice here is to chat with the program director and ask about working and going to school.

Another opportunity to help finance an undergraduate or graduate education is through scholarships or grants that are made available through the department, college, or university. Again, ask the program director about eligibility for these scholarships. Many graduate programs have available research assistantships that help offset the cost of tuition. There are also outside scholarships exclusively available to healthcare management students.

REFERENCE

Starr, P. (1982). *The social transformation of American medicine*. New York, NY: Basic Books.

3 ■ FINDING JOBS IN HEALTHCARE MANAGEMENT

There are a number of ways for you to find a job in healthcare management. Some of those methods will be traditional and others will be a bit more creative. However, regardless of the path that you choose, there are three important things to keep in mind. First, outstanding educational preparation is a necessary condition but it is not sufficient. Virtually every employer is also looking for experience in the field. That experience can come from full- or part-time employment in a healthcare organization, volunteer work in a hospital or clinic, or clinical training. Employers are also looking for leadership experience in almost any setting. Holding an officer position in a fraternity or sorority, playing intercollegiate sports, active participation in a community organization, or significant volunteer experience can make an important difference for persons seeking their first job in the field. Students who come in with an undergraduate or graduate degree (coupled with a strong grade point average [GPA]) plus work experience and holding leadership roles will have a much better chance of finding a job than someone with an equally strong education but without any previous leadership roles.

The second important point to consider is that healthcare management is, at its heart, a relationship-based business. Persons who are successful in this field know that human relationships are absolutely vital in order to achieve the goals of providing safe, effective, and efficient healthcare. Given the importance of relationships to career success, we frequently use the phrase "Network or no work." It is essential that you go out and meet people in the industry; be able to talk about yourself, your talents, and why you want to enter this business; and, in a word, "sell" yourself. While many jobs in healthcare management are advertised in traditional formats, a large number of entry-level positions come about as a result of networking, talking with human resource managers, and connecting with the faculty at your school, who frequently are the first to know about job opportunities.

We have a third and frequently not always obvious consideration when searching for either your first job in healthcare management or one that takes you to the executive suite. It is embodied in the ancient wisdom, "Know thyself." Why is it important to know who you are before you seek a position in our field? The reason is that, in most cases, healthcare sector organizations want people whose personal values closely align with those of the organization. Stated another way, you need to fit within the culture of the organization rather than make the culture adjust to you. In order to help determine the goodness of fit, you need to be highly aware of your personal values and the things that matter most to you. If you know those attributes, you can then determine how well you fit within the values and culture of the organization.

One final thought before we enumerate the ways to find jobs in this field—keep your ego in check. Your first job, whether with an undergraduate or graduate degree, will almost certainly not be in middle management or higher. We have seen too many students return to us and ask why they failed at securing a job. More often than not, the student set unreasonable demands, had unrealistic expectations, or otherwise came across as arrogant and unwilling to be a team player. Higher level jobs with increasing levels of responsibility will come to those who prove themselves willing to pitch in, get their hands dirty, follow through on what they have promised, and admit what they don't know.

TRADITIONAL PATHWAYS

Prior to starting a search for a job, two documents are absolutely essential—the resume and cover letter. There are a large number of different templates you can use for both, but regardless of whether you use a precrafted template or just go ahead and write your own, keep in mind a few simple rules:

1. You have one opportunity to make a good first impression. Both the cover letter and resume must be absolutely perfect in terms of construction and composition. That means no spelling and grammar errors anywhere in the documents. Avoid the temptation to use fancy and overly ornate type fonts. The 10- to 12-point standard fonts such as Times New Roman, Arial, Calibri, or Tahoma are generally good.
2. Your resume should never be more than two pages long, unless you have extensive professional experience. If you have previous professional experience, make sure that you document your accomplishments in concise and honest metrics.

3. Your cover letter needs to be personalized for the organization. You need to adjust your cover letter to speak to the particular requirements found in the position description of the job for which you are applying. Also, take the time to learn as much about the organization as you can from their web page and write about the alignment of the organization's values with your own. Include specific examples of your own leadership accomplishments and link them to the job for which you are applying.

We also recommend that you work through a number of drafts of your cover letter, seeking to make each draft better than the last. Be sure to ask persons who are comfortable giving you critical feedback to carefully read and critique your cover letter and resume. Once the resume is done and you have the main parts of your cover letter thought out, you can now begin the hard work of looking for a job in healthcare management.

There are some very fortunate persons who are hired into a full-time position directly out of school without having to go through a search process. We recommend familiarizing yourself with the breadth of career opportunities available in healthcare management. Some good websites for this purpose include the following:

- Explore Health Careers is a good starting point with many excellent resources (http://explorehealthcareers.org/en/Field/13/Health_AdministrationManagement)
- U.S. Department of Labor Bureau of Labor Statistics contains up-to-date information on employment, job outlook, wages, and links to other relevant websites (http://www.bls.gov/oco/ocos014.htm)

The search for jobs in healthcare management should be started using the web links from a number of the larger healthcare associations. The associations and the scope of their jobs include the following:

- American College of Healthcare Executives (ACHE; www.ache.org) has a current membership of over 35,000 persons in hospitals, health systems, and other healthcare organizations. As a member of ACHE, you can search job opportunities and post your resume.
- Medical Group Management Associations (MGMA; www.mgma.com) has a membership of over 22,000 persons whose role is focused in managing physician practices. MGMA makes available a comprehensive career center for both job seekers and employers.

- Health Information Management System Society (HIMSS; www.himss.org) represents 38,000 members whose work is in the area of health information technology. Their web page has a link to their complete career services pages.
- Healthcare Financial Management Association (HFMA; www.hfma.org) is the leading professional association for over 37,000 healthcare financial management professionals. Their job bank allows members to review job listings and post their resumes.
- American College of Health Care Administrators (ACHCA; www.achca.org) is the leading professional association for leaders in the long-term care field. Their web page includes a link to a comprehensive career page, both listing job opportunities and permitting job seekers to post their resumes.
- American Public Health Association (APHA; www.apha.org) provides a career development center that offers job listings and career tips specifically for persons interested in federal, state, and local public health organizations.

The listing above is a sample of some of the larger dedicated healthcare management professional associations who include career services as part of their member benefits. In addition to the professional associations, most large healthcare organizations have human resource (HR) departments, and if the HR department is large enough, they will post their job vacancies on their web page.

Additional opportunities for graduates of healthcare administration programs are active duty in the military and the U.S. Public Health Service (USPHS) Commissioned Corps. The Medical Service Corps operates branches within the U.S. Army, Navy, and Air Force. Members of the Medical Service Corps hold important managerial roles in military hospitals in the United States and around the world. Persons thinking about the Medical Service Corps must possess a bachelor's or master's degree in healthcare management and are commissioned as an officer in the Army, Navy, or Air Force with the requisite service obligation.

The USPHS Commissioned Corps provides managerial and leadership opportunities for persons possessing a master's degree from a Commission on Accreditation of Healthcare Management Education (CAHME)-accredited program. Members of the USPHS Commissioned Corps wear uniforms and have military-type rank. They have opportunities to serve in government agencies in the United States and overseas.

NONTRADITIONAL PATHWAYS

Earlier in this chapter, we introduced the concept of "network or no work." Owing to the importance of relationships in healthcare management, frequently job opportunities will be known first to people who know other people, who know other people. The question then is how do you get to be in this information and knowledge loop? We have a number of very practical suggestions. First and foremost, you need to take an active role in one or more professional associations. Frequently, they offer reduced membership dues for students or persons early in their careers. Find the association that is best aligned with your personal career goals and aspirations. Most of these associations have local or state officers. Arrange a meeting with these people to introduce yourself and seek their input as to how you should structure a job search. Every one of these associations has an annual meeting with thousands and sometimes tens of thousands of persons attending. Go to the annual meeting and, if possible, to local/regional meetings in order to meet persons in the field and introduce yourself to those in the field. While these meetings involve an investment of time and money, it is crucial to attend and meet the persons who are in a position to bring in new management talent.

Another related suggestion is to arrange for informational interviews with healthcare leaders in your local community. We suggest that you not open the conversation by asking if they have any jobs in their organization. Start by finding out about them, how they got into this business, and what suggestions they have for persons who want to obtain a job in healthcare management. You might ask if they know of neighboring organizations that are looking to fill administrative vacancies.

Finally, you might think about taking a full- or part-time job in the organization that might seem to you to be something far below your education and aspirations. The reasons for this are twofold. First, most organizations advertise job vacancies first to their current employees and give hiring preference to those already working there. The second (and perhaps most important) consideration is that you give yourself ready access to managers throughout the organization and have the opportunity to prove yourself and your willingness to accept responsibility and consistently do a good job. You also get the opportunity to know and experience the culture of the organization first hand. You might be surprised at how often very competent frontline workers are quickly moved into managerial or supervisory roles.

II ■ HEALTHCARE MANAGEMENT CAREERS

4 ■ CAREERS IN ACUTE CARE HOSPITALS[1]

Name:
DENNIS R. DELISLE
Title: Operational Excellence Manager and Lean Master
Organization: Thomas Jefferson University Hospitals

1. **Briefly describe your job responsibilities.**
   Manage strategic organizational initiatives utilizing the Lean Principles and tools.
   Manage multidisciplinary teams on balanced scorecard projects.
   Responsible for training, certifying, and coaching of Lean facilitators.
   Provide consultation to operational administrators regarding performance improvement approaches and problem-solving strategies.

2. **Please give an example of what you would consider to be a "typical" day for you.**
   High degree of variation due to the nature of work; I lead and managed multiple teams and projects. Portions of my day may be spent in planning/team meetings or doing observations in the departments where the improvement projects are taking place. Throughout the week, half of my time is spent in meetings (both project and strategic), the remaining portions are dedicated to observations and office time (to get work done).

(*continued*)

[1] The practitioners who contributed their thoughts and perspectives for this book represent a convenience sample of the breadth of active healthcare practitioners. All of the practitioners in the book are either known by the editors or were recommended by someone known by us. The salary information contained in the position descriptions can vary widely depending on the size of the organization, ownership status, the geographic location of the organization, and the years of experience of the person.

Name: DENNIS R. DELISLE *(continued)*

3. What education or training do you have? Is it typical for your job?

What I have: Master of Health Services Administration (MHSA), Certified Lean Master from Breakthrough Management Group International (BMGI), Certified Project Management Professional (PMP) through the Project Management Institute (PMI), trained in General Electric's Change Acceleration Process and Work-Out Methodologies.

What is typical: Master's degree, Certified Lean Master or Master Black Belt (Six Sigma), preferred PMP certification.

4. What is the most challenging part of your job?

When working with multidisciplinary teams, the most challenging aspect is each individual's calendar. The hospital environment is demanding and dynamic, making something as seemingly simple as scheduling difficult.

5. What do you consider to be the best part of your job?

Lean emphasizes empowering the employees who do the work, typically on the front line. Facilitating improvement events with staff eager to make an impact, and realizing success through hard work and collaboration is incredibly rewarding.

6. What path did you take to get to the job you are in today?

Applied for and accepted a 1-year Administrative Fellowship position during the final year of my MHSA degree. The Fellowship offered a comprehensive level of depth and breadth to hospital operations and provided innumerable opportunities to network with senior leaders down through frontline employees. During the Fellowship, I joined several Lean Six Sigma project teams, which piqued my interest and led to my pursuit of Lean Master certification.

7. What advice do you have for someone who is interested in a job such as yours?

Get involved on a project team utilizing Lean, Six Sigma, or other approaches for performance improvement. Reach out to practitioners and read the literature (plenty of good books out there).

1. BUDGET ANALYST

JOB DESCRIPTION

A hospital's budget analyst is responsible for a wide range of activities relating to the financial operations and fiscal health of the hospital. These activities include maintaining budget and cost-accounting databases, collecting and monitoring budget variance reports, preparing productivity and various analysis reports, and helping in the preparation of the annual operational and capital budget for the hospital. Other responsibilities can include calculating contractual allowances for third-party reimbursement, working with external auditors, and performing strategic financial analysis under the direction of the Chief Financial Officer (CFO) and other senior hospital leaders.

EDUCATION AND EXPERIENCE

A bachelor's degree is a minimum expectation for most budget analyst positions. Educational background should be in finance, accounting, or another related field. Other credentials including a CPA/Master's in Business Administration (MBA) are extremely helpful. Prior experience related to financial management, especially in a hospital, is important. Many employers expect budget analysts to have at least 5 to 7 years of relevant prior experience.

CORE COMPETENCIES AND SKILLS

- Excellent interpersonal and organizational skills
- Professional computer skills, especially with Microsoft Excel
- Excellent quantitative and analytical ability
- Strong knowledge of financial operations, hospital policies/procedures, and organizational structure
- Knowledge of 10-key by touch
- Typing 40+ correct words per minute (CWPM)
- Ability to work in a fast-paced environment and under a deadline
- Ability to prioritize and handle multiple projects at once

COMPENSATION

The majority of budget analysts make between $50,000 and $90,000 annually. They can also make as much as $130,000. Budget analysts with broader responsibilities at larger hospitals will likely earn a higher salary. Similarly, those working in a busier, urban area, stand to make more than someone living in a rural setting.

EMPLOYMENT OUTLOOK

As the number of hospitals in the United States decreases slightly over the next several years, the demand for hospital budget analysts will decrease slightly as well. However, the outlook for these jobs remains high as the healthcare market in general continues to grow.

FOR FURTHER INFORMATION

- Healthcare Financial Management Association (HFMA; www.hfma.org)

2. CHIEF COMPLIANCE OFFICER

JOB DESCRIPTION

The Chief Compliance Officer (CCO) serves as the point person for all hospital compliance activities. The CCO needs to be a person of high integrity, and any other duties the CCO has should not be in conflict with the compliance goals of the hospital. Coordination and communication are the key functions of the CCO with regard to planning, implementing, and monitoring the compliance program.

EDUCATION AND EXPERIENCE

Many CCOs at larger hospitals possess a law degree, although a master's degree in business administration or health administration is frequently seen. CCOs typically have 5 or more years of experience in healthcare compliance.

CORE COMPETENCIES AND SKILLS

- Outstanding interpersonal skills including the ability to effectively communicate with persons throughout the organization, including clinicians
- Excellent verbal and written communication skills
- Experience with Center for Medicare and Medicaid Services (CMS) conditions of participation for acute care hospitals and CMS survey processes
- In-depth knowledge of external clinical quality reporting requirements
- Current knowledge of Joint Commission, state, and federal guidelines, regulations, and standards

- Must have coordinated, prepared, and participated in state, Joint Commission, and CMS surveys within past 3 years
- Current statistical knowledge and skill in developing statistical data displays
- Experience in the use of statistical and quality assessment software
- Ability to analyze and resolve complex issues

COMPENSATION

CCOs earn in the range of $90,000 to $136,000. With incentives and bonus pay added on, the salary can be as much as $150,000.

EMPLOYMENT OUTLOOK

The employment outlook for CCOs in large hospital settings is generally good. Smaller hospitals typically cannot afford a CCO and that responsibility is distributed among other staff members.

FOR FURTHER INFORMATION

- Health Care Compliance Association (http://www.hcca-info org/)
- American Association of Colleges of Nursing (http://www.aacn.nche.edu)

3. CHIEF EXECUTIVE OFFICER

JOB DESCRIPTION

The Chief Executive Officer (CEO) is responsible for (a) managing the day-to-day operations of the hospital and its entities; (b) establishing a system for ensuring that high-quality care is provided; (c) ensuring the sound fiscal operation of the hospital, while promoting services that are produced in a cost-effective manner; (d) ensuring compliance with regulatory agencies and accrediting bodies, while continually monitoring the organization's service and delivery system; (e) ensuring optimal fulfillment of the institutions charter, mission, and philosophy in response to the identified needs of the community; and (f) responding to medical staff, employees, and patients. In addition, the CEO will work closely with the Board of Directors and leadership of the organized medical staff in developing the strategic direction and major policies of the institution. The CEO reports directly to the Board of Directors.

EDUCATION AND EXPERIENCE

Most acute care hospital CEOs possess a master's degree in health administration, although master's degrees in business administration, public administration, management, or similar training is frequently seen. Persons in this role typically have at least 5 years of senior-level healthcare management experience as either a CEO or Chief Operating Officer (COO).

CORE COMPETENCIES AND SKILLS

- Outstanding interpersonal skills including the ability to effectively communicate with persons throughout the organization, including clinicians
- Excellent verbal and written communication skills
- Ability to understand multiple types of financial and legal documents
- Ability to motivate diverse groups of employees to accomplish the goals and objectives of the hospital
- Commitment to creating and sustaining high-quality healthcare delivery
- Ability to hold subordinates accountable for organizational goals
- Ability to make difficult decisions

COMPENSATION

Most hospital CEOs earn between $121,500 and $231,500 although the top end can go as high as $1,000,000. However, this figure varies depending on a number of variables, including the size of the hospital and the region of the country in which the hospital is located. CEOs of smaller hospitals in more rural areas tend to earn less than their counterparts at large, urban hospitals.

EMPLOYMENT OUTLOOK

The overall outlook for hospital CEO jobs is expected to continue a slow but steady decline. The reason for the decline is due to the reduction in the number of acute care hospitals in the United States. There continues to be a number of hospitals that are closing particularly in rural communities and urban hospitals that are either merging with competitors or are closing altogether. The average hospital CEO remains in the position for approximately 5 years, so there is a regular turnover of persons in these positions.

FOR FURTHER INFORMATION

- Visit local universities offering the Master of Health Administration (MHA) degree or equivalent. A list of these university-based programs can be found at the Association of University Programs in Health Administration (www.aupha.org)
- American College of Healthcare Executives (www.ache.org)
- Department of Labor, Bureau of Labor Statistics (http://www.bls.gov/oco/cg/cgs035.htm)

Name:
MANNY BERMAN
Title: Chief Operating Officer
Organization: Tuality Healthcare

1. **Briefly describe your job responsibilities.**
   Currently responsible for departments at both Tuality and Tuality Forest Grove Hospitals: Operations Support (Sterile Processing, Transportation, Materials Management, and Pharmacy); Facilities Support (Environmental Services, Bio-Med, Engineering, Security, Food Service, and Construction); Employee Support (Human Resources [HR], Volunteers, Library, Education, and Tuality Health Education Center); Clinical Support (Diagnostic Imaging Departments, Laboratory Services, and Pharmacy); Patient Safety Advocate (Risk Management); Medical Staff Coordination; and Clinical Information Services (implementation for the Cerner Electronic Medical Record).

   Additional Operational Responsibilites:
   Corporate Operational Policies; Liability Insurance; Professional Contracts; Raines Dialysis JV with Fresenius; Risk Management; Tuality/OHSU Cancer Center, LLC; Virginia Garcia Memorial Health Center; TMS/TMES President.
   Participation in community organizations and healthcare professional organizations.

2. **Please give an example of what you would consider to be a "typical" day for you.**
   Would be involved in 3 to 4 meetings; making rounds on patients or staff; working 1 to 2 hours on projects, business issues, or educational learning; drafting 100 e-mails; interacting with physicians or problem solving; and dealing with any emergent issues that arise.

Name: MANNY BERMAN

3. What education or training do you have? Is it typical for your job?
Bachelor's degree in Business and Accounting and a Master's in Healthcare Administration. Fellow at the American College of Hospital Administrators. Ongoing educational opportunities. I would see this as typical for my job.

4. What is the most challenging part of your job?
Having sufficient time to do strategic planning, advance planning, market development to minimize emergent issues, and grow business.

5. What do you consider to be the best part of your job?
I never have 2 days the same. Always different activities/issues/problems.

6. What path did you take to get to the job you are in today?
Undergraduate degree and summer internship at a hospital during undergraduate degree to ensure this was the field I desired. Master's degree in Hospital Administration. Transition to different growth positions in the field for job opportunities. Being active at the American College of Health Care Administrators and participation in the Hospital Association. Visibility among peers in healthcare.

7. What advice do you have for someone who is interested in a job such as yours?
Try to find opportunities to observe or participate as a volunteer when young to learn what the job entails, network as much as possible, regularly participate in educational opportunities, and ensure that you have the appropriate educational background/diploma.

4. CHIEF FINANCIAL OFFICER

JOB DESCRIPTION

The CFO is responsible for all the functions related to the financial operations of a hospital. These responsibilities include the accounting, insurance, financial systems, and auditing of all medical departments. CFOs gather and analyze all the financial data and information to make sure the hospital is operating within budget and to determine how to allocate funds to various areas. These officers create detailed reports of their findings and must explain to department heads and boards of directors why these financial decisions are being made. The CFO is typically a member of the senior leadership team of the hospital.

Additionally, the CFO:

- Is responsible for the operating and capital budgets, including revenue and expense budgets, cash forecasts, profit planning, and programs for capital investments and financing
- Facilitates communication among staff, management, vendors, and other financial resources within the organization
- Manages the cost-reporting process and understands financial impacts
- Provides assistance to the organization's CEO, and leadership and guidance to designated departments to ensure the financial stability of the organization and that the delivery of patient/resident and healthcare service programs continues to respond to the needs of both patients and the community at-large
- Provides guidance to capital equipment purchases

EDUCATION AND EXPERIENCE

CFOs of most acute care hospitals require a bachelor's degree in accounting, finance, or a related field. A master's degree in health/hospital administration, business administration, or related field is highly desirable. Hospital CFOs typically possess a minimum of 5 years of experience with increasing responsibilities for financial reporting, financial planning, and personnel management.

CORE COMPETENCIES AND SKILLS

- Outstanding interpersonal skills including the ability to effectively communicate with persons throughout the organization, including clinicians and governing board members
- Excellent verbal and written communication skills
- Knowledge of the principles and skills needed to provide fiscal control for a diverse set of healthcare services

- Knowledge of systems design and development processes, including requirements analysis, feasibility studies, software design, programming, pilot testing, installation, evaluation, and operational management
- Oversee the management and coordination of all fiscal reporting activities for the hospital
- Proven ability to link and apply complex financial instruments to business strategies
- Experience in negotiating contracts with vendors, contractors, and others
- Ability to analyze and resolve complex issues, both logical and interpersonal

COMPENSATION

Most hospital-based CFOs earn salaries in the range of $150,000 to $330,000 per year. However, this figure varies depending on a number of variables including the size of the hospital and the region of the country in which the hospital is located. CFOs of smaller hospitals in more rural areas tend to earn less than their counterparts at large, urban hospitals.

EMPLOYMENT OUTLOOK

The overall outlook for hospital CFO jobs is expected to be stable or be slightly reduced over the coming years. The reason for this projection is that the overall number of hospitals is decreasing slightly and a growing number of hospitals are deciding to become part of ever-growing number of multihospital chains.

FOR FURTHER INFORMATION

- HFMA (www.hfma.org)
- Department of Labor, Bureau of Labor Statistics (http://www.bls.gov/oco/cg/cgs035.htm)

5. CHIEF INFORMATION OFFICER

JOB DESCRIPTION

The Chief Information Officer (CIO) provides technology vision and leadership in the development and implementation of the hospital-wide information technology (IT) program. The CIO will lead the organization in planning and implementing enterprise information systems to support both distributed and centralized clinical and business operations and achieve more effective and cost-beneficial enterprise-wide IT operations.

Additionally, the CIO:

- Provides strategic and tactical planning, development, evaluation, and coordination of the information and technology systems for the hospital
- Facilitates communication among staff, management, vendors, and other technology resources within the organization
- Oversees the back office computer operations of the affiliate management information system, including local area networks and wide-area networks
- Is responsible for the management of multiple information and communications systems and projects, including voice, data, imaging, and office automation
- Designs, implements, and evaluates the systems that support end users in the productive use of computer hardware and software
- Develops and implements user-training programs
- Oversees and evaluates system security and backup procedures
- Supervises the network administrator

EDUCATION AND EXPERIENCE

Most acute care hospitals' CIOs require a bachelor's degree in computer science, business administration, or a related field, or equivalent experience. A master's degree in health/hospital administration, public health, or business administration, or a related field is highly desirable. Minimum of 3 years of experience with increasing responsibilities for management and support of healthcare information systems and IT, direct management of a major IT operation is preferred. Significant experience in a healthcare setting is desirable, specifically in technology and information systems planning to support business goals.

CORE COMPETENCIES AND SKILLS

- Outstanding interpersonal skills including the ability to effectively communicate with persons throughout the organization, including clinicians
- Excellent verbal and written communication skills
- Significant experience in data-processing methods and procedures, and computer software systems

- Knowledge in systems design and development processes, including requirements analysis, feasibility studies, software design, programming, pilot testing, installation, evaluation, and operational management
- Ability to oversee the management and coordination of all fiscal reporting activities for the hospital
- Familiarity with the design, management, and operation of health IT systems
- Proven ability to link and apply complex technologies to business strategies
- Experience in negotiating contracts with vendors, contractors, and others
- Ability to analyze and resolve complex issues, both logical and interpersonal

COMPENSATION

Most hospital-based CIOs earn salaries in the range of $80,000 to $300,000 per year. However, this figure varies depending on a number of variables, including the size of the hospital and the region of the country in which the hospital is located. CIOs of smaller hospitals in more rural areas tend to earn less than their counterparts at large, urban hospitals.

EMPLOYMENT OUTLOOK

The overall outlook for hospital CIO jobs is expected to increase over the coming years. The reason for the increase is due to need for hospitals to make health technology an increasing part of clinical and administrative operations. There remain a number of federal financial and regulatory incentives to vigorously move into health IT. CIO is a relatively new occupation and it is difficult to assess turnover, but anecdotal reports indicate that CIOs turnover at a brisk pace to accept roles with increasing salary and responsibility.

FOR FURTHER INFORMATION

- Visit local universities offering the MHA degree or equivalent, particularly those who offer concentrations in health IT (www.aupha.org)
- Health Information Management System Society (www.himss.org)
- Department of Labor, Bureau of Labor Statistics (http://www.bls.gov/oco/cg/cgs035.htm)

Name:
CHRISTINE CANDIO, RN
Title: Chief Executive Officer
Organization: Inova Alexandria Hospital

1. **Briefly describe your job responsibilities.**
   My responsibilities are to lead, direct, and ensure our operations are consistent with our mission, philosophy, and objectives in serving our patients and community with safety and the highest quality of care.

2. **Please give an example of what you would consider to be a "typical" day for you.**
   Although no 2 days are the same, there are important responsibilities and oversight that I strive to ensure are part of my typical day. These include rounding on the inpatient units and departments throughout the hospital; meeting with senior staff, whether as a formal group for strategic or operational matters and/or individually for functional responsibilities; employee and physician relations; community, and legislative relations (local and state); quality and financial measures; program development; and system strategic initiatives.

3. **What education or training do you have? Is it typical for your job?**
   I hold a Bachelor of Science in Nursing and a Master's in Public Health Administration with a concentration in healthcare management. In general, the industry has seen an increased number of individuals with clinical backgrounds obtaining postgraduate degrees in healthcare and/or business management programs.

Name: CHRISTINE CANDIO, RN

4. What is the most challenging part of your job?

Today the healthcare industry is presented with many challenges. Primary among these is the delicate balancing of maintaining high-quality, affordable healthcare services to meet patient and community needs in an environment of rising healthcare costs, decreased reimbursement to providers, increased numbers of uninsured and underinsured, an aging population, and uncertainties associated with healthcare reform. The impact is significant to all concerned; that is, patients, community, healthcare facilities, and physicians. As such, CEOs must face these challenges as opportunities in the reevaluation of our strategic vision, while remaining nimble and ready to adjust/course correct based on patients'/community needs.

5. What do you consider to be the best part of your job?

The best part of my job is providing a helping/guiding hand in creating the type of services and environment expected of us from our patients and community. Chief among this is interacting with our patients, families, and working with staff and physicians to ensure positive experiences to all we serve.

6. What path did you take to get to the job you are in today?

I began my healthcare career as a registered nurse (RN) at the bedside. Management was always of great interest to me. I realized that in order to progress on my career path, as well as to continue my education, it was necessary to obtain my master's degree. Over the course of several years, I held progressive leadership positions: Manager of Ambulatory Services, Administrative Director of Women's and Children's Services, System Director of Women's and Children's Services, Vice President (VP) Patient Services/Chief Nurse Executive, Executive VP, CEO.

(*continued*)

Name: CHRISTINE CANDIO, RN *(continued)*

7. What advice do you have for someone who is interested in a job such as yours?

It is very important to have focus and a true passion for the profession. Always keep the patient at the center of everything you do. Embrace ongoing education and lifelong learning. Our professional association, the American College of Healthcare Executives, is the premier organization to assist us in our ongoing educational journey.

6. CHIEF LEARNING OFFICER

JOB DESCRIPTION

The Chief Learning Officer (CLO) is a new position in hospitals. The goal of the CLO is to help facilitate and accelerate learning throughout the organization. The CLO directs the organization's education, training, and development programs to empower staff and ensure their maximum effectiveness and contribution to meet organizational goals.

As part of the senior leadership team, the CLO will:

- Partner with organizational leaders to identify needs for training and organizational development, develop and implement new training as needed
- Advise senior leadership regarding initiatives and activities that promote maximum staff effectiveness and create a positive impact on service quality
- Develop and evaluate employee development programs and ensure that programs do have a beneficial impact on service delivery
- Plan, launch, monitor, and act on long-range learning initiatives that are aligned with the organization's strategic goals
- Design and establish benchmarks that measure the impact and effectiveness of organizational development programs on the organization's overall performance
- Forge relationships with internal and external stakeholders, including, but not limited to, universities/colleges, public schools, and government entities

EDUCATION AND EXPERIENCE

Hospital-based CLOs require a master's degree, doctoral degree preferred, in education, organizational development, human resources, or comparable fields of study and a minimum of 5 years of leadership experience, preferably in the areas of human resources management, academic and/or professional development, or comparable areas.

CORE COMPETENCIES AND SKILLS

- Outstanding interpersonal skills including the ability to effectively communicate with persons throughout the organization, including clinicians
- Excellent verbal and written communication skills
- Significant experience in data-processing methods and procedures, and computer software systems
- Knowledge in systems design and development processes, including requirements analysis, feasibility studies, software design, programming, pilot testing, installation, evaluation, and operational management
- Oversee the management and coordination of all fiscal reporting activities for the hospital
- Familiarity with the design, management, and operation of health IT systems
- Proven ability to link and apply complex technologies to business strategies
- Experience in negotiating contracts with vendors, contractors, and others
- Ability to analyze and resolve complex issues, both logical and interpersonal

COMPENSATION

Most hospital-based CIOs earn salaries in the range of $80,000 to $300,000 per year. However, this figure varies depending on a number of variables, including the size of the hospital and the region of the country in which the hospital is located. CIOs of smaller hospitals in more rural areas tend to earn less than their counterparts at large, urban hospitals.

EMPLOYMENT OUTLOOK

The overall outlook for hospital CIO jobs is expected to increase over the coming years. The reason for the increase is due to the need for hospitals to make health technology an increasing part of clinical and administrative operations. There remain a number of federal financial and regulatory incentives to vigorously move into health IT. CIO is a relatively new occupation and it is difficult to assess turnover, but anecdotal reports indicate that CIOs turnover at a brisk pace to accept roles with increasing salary and responsibility.

FOR FURTHER INFORMATION

- Visit local universities offering the MHA degree or equivalent particularly those who offer concentrations in health IT (www.aupha.org)
- Health Information Management System Society (www.himss.org)
- Department of Labor, Bureau of Labor Statistics (http://www.bls.gov/oco/cg/cgs035.htm)

7. CHIEF MEDICAL INFORMATION OFFICER

JOB DESCRIPTION

The Chief Medical Information Officer (CMIO) is a new position in hospitals. The goal of the CMIO is to help facilitate and accelerate the clinical use of IT throughout the organization and serve as the bridge between the clinical staff and IT department. The CMIO directs the effective use and implementation of IT, particularly as it applies to physicians, nurses, and other clinical staff.

As part of the senior leadership team, the CMIO will:

- Serve as a liaison between medical and technical departments and executive leadership
- Head studies for the design and integration of IT systems and infrastructure in the medical department
- Study trends in health informatics to develop applications that increase efficiency in patient care
- Develop standards and "rules" in medical terminology and application to increase efficiency in patient care
- Advise steering committees on subject of health informatics and policymaking within the organization

EDUCATION AND EXPERIENCE

Hospital-based CMIOs generally require a master's degree, although some smaller hospitals might employ an advanced practice nurse in this role. It is also expected that the CMIO have experience in medical informatics.

CORE COMPETENCIES AND SKILLS

- Outstanding interpersonal skills including the ability to effectively communicate with persons throughout the organization, including clinicians
- Excellent verbal and written communication skills
- Knowledge of the process and tools for capturing, organizing, and using individual and departmental intellectual assets, such as competencies, best practices, and so on.
- Ability to work collaboratively to create meaningful use of health IT
- Familiarity with the legal and regulatory elements of health IT
- Outstanding project management skills
- Ability to educate and influence other clinicians around the adoption of health IT
- Familiarity with the full spectrum of electronic medical records systems
- Ability to analyze and resolve complex issues

COMPENSATION

CMIOs earn in the range of $50,000 to $400,000, although many of these persons do continue to practice medicine. Small hospitals would typically not be able to employ a CMIO, so these positions would be expected to be found at large, urban hospitals or academic health centers.

EMPLOYMENT OUTLOOK

A growing number of hospitals are expanding their traditional information systems roles to include persons whose primary training and experience is in medicine or nursing. Most traditionally trained CIOs do not have the clinical expertise, which makes the CMIO role particularly important as healthcare organizations grow and develop their IT infrastructure.

FOR FURTHER INFORMATION

- Health Information Management Systems Society (www.himss.org)
- CMIO (www.cmio.net)

Name:
TODD M. COHEN
Title: Director, Special Projects
Organization: MedStar Health/
Montgomery General Hospital

1. Briefly describe your job responsibilities.

I manage capital projects at a medium-sized community hospital that had been newly integrated into a regional health system. A sizable initial investment during the acquisition of this formerly independent hospital has afforded me the opportunity to design, construct, implement, and change a growing campus and hospital. The hospital sits on a 45-acre campus and has been identified by the health system to grow new programs and spaces that have regional strategic significance. I oversee an array of projects, including larger construction projects, introduction of new technology, and help with physician alignment in the design and renovation of medical office spaces. In my first 3 years of managing capital projects and construction, I have designed, built, or overseen projects totaling $75 million, including a new state of the Emergency Department, a 6-story bed tower, a new Radiation Oncology Linear Accelerator and Infusion Center, DaVinci Robotic Surgery Program, Cardiac and Pulmonary Diagnostic Center, multiple backfill renovation projects centered on conversion of inpatient rooms to private rooms, three academically affiliated medical practices and surgical clinics with Georgetown University Hospital, and various physical plant upgrades. I coordinate Certificate of Need submissions and quarterly monitoring, and interface with local regulatory agencies on land use and zoning matters.

2. Please give an example of what you would consider to be a "typical" day for you.

There really isn't a typical day. Some days are focused on strategic and master planning of clinical programs and campus development,

Name: TODD M. COHEN

others are spent on the design of clinical spaces in the inpatient and outpatient environments. I prioritize capital planning and oversee pro forma business plans for market entry or differentiating service lines/projects. Other days are focused on construction management on a macro and micro level on active job sites in the clinical, ancillary, and support services spaces. I lead a weekly senior management discussion on space planning, where typically conversions center on conceiving new programs or projects for growth and in line with our corporate and local vision. That typically evolves from a concept and moves to contracting and partnerships with design firms, ultimately through the steps of formal capital allocation and design development of tangible spaces and products. My teams perform business analytics and modeling for creation of business plans, including pro forma volume and cash flow analyses, and return on investment for new programs and technology introduction. A large part of my time is in the built environment, where I design spaces with retained architectural and engineering firms—we help with operational and clinical integration of new technology, expansion of space, and infrastructure upgrades to the physical plant. I oversee complex projects with a focus on change management, program implementation and construction, and work with end users on postoccupancy evaluations for future standardization of space to ensure functionality.

3. What education or training do you have? Is it typical for your job?

I have an MHSA degree, a master's certificate in Health Information Technology, a Bachelor of Science degree in Family Studies with an emphasis on Crisis Intervention, and various certifications in healthcare construction, project management, and a national credential usually taken by members of the design community for evidence-based design assessment of renovated or newly constructed clinical spaces. Many people in my position at other facilities are trained in the disciplines of architecture or engineering, but I think my interest and formal study of strategic planning and general management, coupled with a strong foundation in finance and

(*continued*)

Name: TODD M. COHEN *(continued)*

project management, and previous 15 years of clinical and social work experience allow me to integrate well with the administrative staff, clinical leadership, and end user teams with various players in the healthcare sector. I lead teams focused on tomorrow's next idea, while reacting to nuances of organizational behavior and change management at a facility with an aging workforce. We perform with an ever-watchful eye on an evolving regulatory climate, while learning tomorrow's convoluted health policy and focusing on patient-centered care delivery models and processes focused on outcomes, safety, and efficiency.

4. What is the most challenging part of your job?

Prioritization of many projects where competing interests want to place one project prominently on a hierarchy for implementation and/or construction can be challenging. Everyone thinks their projects are "must-funds"—our job is to help place them along a logical hierarchy and sequence for implementation—weighing urgency in the market place, patient safety, organizational financial status, and capital access as most critically assessing operational risk and exposure for the organization.

5. What do you consider to be the best part of your job?

My teams follow a simple philosophy. We think, build, create, and implement programs and spaces by keeping the patient at the center. We move behind the scenes so that our clinicians can take care of our patients. To that end, we believe that patients come first, but we move and live for the first patient. I get excited and consider the best part of our projects to be the moment when our first patient enters a new space after opening or launching a new project.

6. What path did you take to get to the job you are in today?

I spent 10 years at the bedside as a patient care technician and later a social worker doing discharge planning and case

Name: TODD M. COHEN

management. Later, I spent some time performing clinical and public health research on the epidemiology of trauma/violent death. I think my interest in human behavior academically, with a clinical understanding from acute care clinical roles, and an overarching interest in management have prepared me well. The last 6 years have been focused on formal management graduate work and an early career in managing large capital projects administratively with a focus on clinical and operational integration.

7. **What advice do you have for someone who is interested in a job such as yours?**
   Spend time clinically at the bedside and understand how space planning and healthcare construction affects the patient and end users. Design elements and plans on paper do not necessarily translate into successful outcomes operationally. Sometimes it takes failure in space planning or construction to see what works best for the patient. Do not be sensitive and take it personally—change affects the entire team in different ways, my job is to provide confidence and the ability to react and provide ideas that improve processes. That may be iterative and take time to perfect, which is the exciting part—cultivating and growing an idea from concept, getting it down on paper, and understanding process flow, on to construction—with the ability to change and evaluate the output so that a final outcome can be seen and used well by the intended audience or user.

8. CHIEF MEDICAL OFFICER

JOB DESCRIPTION

The Chief Medical Officer's (CMO's) responsibilities include promoting concepts and practice of quality improvement; establishing and maintaining effective working relationships with medical staff; participating in reviews of qualifications, credentials, performance, and professional competence and character of medical staff applicants and members; and working within the appropriate facility or operational leadership model to establish, monitor, and improve aggregate clinical outcomes.

EDUCATION AND EXPERIENCE

The majority of acute care hospital CMOs possess a medical doctorate or Doctor of Osteopathy degree, possess board certification or qualification and level of expertise typically gained through 5 years of experience in clinical practice, must be eligible for or hold a current state license to practice medicine, and be eligible for medical staff privileges. Persons in this capacity typically are also required to have 3 years of medical staff leadership experience.

CORE COMPETENCIES AND SKILLS

- Proven track record of partnering with medical staff to achieve desired facility-specific and organizational outcomes
- Knowledge of modern national trends in hospital technology, quality, and patient safety
- Skilled in effectively handling multiple conflicting assignments, demands, and priorities
- Skilled in influencing physician behaviors; partnering and problem solving with physicians and administrative leaders within multiple clinical areas and among members of the medical staff; navigating a highly matrixed organizational structure with skill and efficiency; analyzing complex financial/statistical data; maintaining a high level of organization with strong attention to detail in order to respond quickly to varying situations
- Proven experience implementing a continuous improvement culture

COMPENSATION

Most hospital CMOs earn between $190,500 and $245,500 per year. However, this figure varies depending on a number of variables, including the size of the hospital and the region of the country in which the hospital is located. CMOs of smaller hospitals in more rural areas tend to earn less than their counterparts at large, urban hospitals.

EMPLOYMENT OUTLOOK

Job opportunities for top level secular healthcare management will continue to soar according to the Bureau of Labor Statistics. CMOs will be in great demand for companies providing financial solutions to the healthcare industry. Greater focused energy concerning controlling costs, coupled with greater demands for accountability by insurance companies and Medicare, both a business and financial approach to finding the appropriate services, will place managers with medical backgrounds into enviable positions.

FOR FURTHER INFORMATION

- Association of American Medical Colleges (https://www.aamc.org/members/cmog/)

9. CHIEF NURSING OFFICER

JOB DESCRIPTION

The Chief Nursing Officer (CNO) is primarily responsible for providing leadership and guidance around quality patient care and other patient care services delivered in the hospital.

As part of the senior leadership team, the CNO will:

- Assume ultimate administrative responsibility for nursing standards and practice, regardless of the practice area or reporting relationship of the nurse
- Direct hospital nursing activities within the context of hospital policies and procedures
- Ensure continuous and timely nursing services to patients
- Ensure nursing standards, practices, policies, and procedures, in accordance with all applicable laws, regulatory, and accreditation requirements, are consistent with current research findings and national professional standards
- Direct nursing service performance improvement activities
- Actively participate in hospital leadership functions
- Collaborate with hospital leaders to design and provide patient care and services, including availability of sufficient, qualified nursing staff
- Develop, present, and manage budgets for nursing services

EDUCATION AND EXPERIENCE

Bachelor's degree in nursing and current RN license are the minimum clinical training required, although, in most cases, a master's degree in

Nursing, MBA, MHA, or related master's degree is preferred. A minimum of 3 to 5 years experience in nursing administration is desired.

CORE COMPETENCIES AND SKILLS

- Outstanding interpersonal skills including the ability to effectively communicate with persons throughout the organization, including clinicians
- Excellent verbal and written communication skills
- Outstanding physician relationship skills
- In-depth knowledge of external clinical quality reporting requirements
- Current knowledge of Joint Commission, state, and federal guidelines, regulations, and standards
- Demonstrated expertise in negotiation, coaching, and interpersonal skills
- Ability to develop, implement, and administer nursing services budget and expense control system
- Ability to prepare master nursing services staffing plan
- Ability to analyze and resolve complex issues
- Ability to recruit, interview, evaluate, and hire qualified personnel to meet patients' needs

COMPENSATION

CNOs earn in the range of $90,000 to $135,000, although with incentives and bonus pay added on, the salary can be as much as $150,000.

EMPLOYMENT OUTLOOK

Every hospital in the nation requires a CNO and according to the Bureau of Labor Statistics, jobs in nursing administration are likely to continue to grow rapidly.

FOR FURTHER INFORMATION

- Bureau of Labor Statistics (http://www.bls.gov/oco/ocos014.htm)
- American Association of Colleges of Nursing (http://www.aacn.nche.edu)

10. CHIEF OPERATING OFFICER

JOB DESCRIPTION

The COO is responsible for the smooth and efficient operation of the hospital, including management of the profit and loss statement for the hospital's business, as well as the related resources associated with the hospital operation. The COO reports directly to the CEO and is typically a member of the CEO's senior leadership team. In this capacity, the COO carries responsibility for integrating the strategic plan of the organization with the operations. The COO provides management oversight for the development of high-quality, cost-effective, and integrated clinical programs within the hospital. The management portfolio held by this leader is notably diverse, with corresponding broad organizational implications and complexity, characterized by substantial scope of responsibility in this respect. The COO is expected to act in the absence of the CEO. The COO will exercise management responsibility over the hospital, ensuring efficient services that are designed to meet the needs of patients, physicians, public, and staff. This will either be done directly or through delegation of responsibility to the management staff.

EDUCATION AND EXPERIENCE

Most acute care hospital COOs' possess a master's degree in health administration, although master's degrees in business administration, public administration, management, or similar training are frequently seen. Persons in this role typically have at least 5 years of senior-level healthcare management experience as either a COO or other administrative leadership role.

CORE COMPETENCIES AND SKILLS

- Outstanding interpersonal skills including the ability to effectively communicate with persons throughout the organization, including clinicians
- Excellent verbal and written communication skills
- Ability to understand multiple types of financial and legal documents

- Ability to motivate diverse groups of employees to accomplish the goals and objectives of the hospital
- Commitment to creating and sustaining high-quality healthcare delivery
- Ability to hold subordinates accountable for organizational goals
- Ability to make difficult decisions

COMPENSATION

Most hospital COOs earn between $95,000 and $200,000 per year. However, this figure varies depending on a number of variables, including the size of the hospital and the region of the country in which the hospital is located. COOs of smaller hospitals in more rural areas tend to earn less than their counterparts at large, urban hospitals.

EMPLOYMENT OUTLOOK

The overall outlook for hospital COO jobs is expected to continue a slow but steady decline. The reason for the decline is due to the reduction in the number of acute care hospitals in the United States. There continues to be a number of hospitals that are closing particularly in rural communities and urban hospitals that are either merging with competitors or are closing altogether. The average hospital COO remains in the position for approximately 5 years, so there is a regular turnover of persons in these positions.

FOR FURTHER INFORMATION

- Visit local universities offering the MHA degree or equivalent. A list of these university-based programs can be found at the Association of University Programs in Health Administration (www.aupha.org)
- American College of Healthcare Executives (www.ache.org)
- Department of Labor, Bureau of Labor Statistics (http://www.bls.gov/oco/cg/cgs035.htm)

Name:
MIKE EPPEHIMER
Title: Vice President, Department of Medicine
Organization: Christiana Care Health System

1. Briefly describe your job responsibilities.

Christiana Care Health System is large (1,000+ bed), two-hospital system located in Wilmington, Delaware. I have a system-level leadership role with responsibility for strategic planning, operational performance, and financial management of the Department of Medicine and recently created Inpatient Medicine Service Line. This role reports directly to the Chair of Medicine, with a matrixed relationship to the COO. My role has administrative operational responsibility for multiple operational and clinical areas, in addition to partnering with physician leaders to lead clinical process improvement initiatives.

2. Please give an example of what you would consider to be a "typical" day for you.

One of the best things about my role is that a "typical" day will cover many different diverse topics. Some topics that will be covered include negotiations and planning related to physician practice acquisitions, working with a team on a performance-improvement project, developing a training program for unit-based leadership teams, reviewing finances for our operational and research cost centers, and making staffing and recruitment plans for the upcoming fiscal year.

The unifying theme for all of my "typical" days is that almost all of our work in medicine is focused on creating a high-performing team that adds value to the patient experience by improving quality and lowering costs. We are doing that in many different ways by developing physician leaders, creating collaborative relationships

(*continued*)

Name: MIKE EPPEHIMER (*continued*)

across the system, and designing systems that promote efficiency and patient safety.

3. What education or training do you have? Is it typical for your job?

Education:

- Bachelor of Arts degree (double major in Theater and Communications) from the University of Maryland
- MHSA degree from the George Washington University (GWU)
- Certified Lean Six Sigma Black Belt from the American Society for Quality

My background in the creative arts is not typical for the job, but I have found it to be an asset to me as my career has progressed. In particular, my background in improvisational theater has helped me to feel comfortable giving presentations, dealing with uncertain situations, and in thinking creatively about problems. The "art" of improvisation combined with the "science" of the Lean Six Sigma methodologies has helped to create a somewhat unique educational background that has helped me to use a rigorous framework for quality and performance improvement, while also being flexible and creative in my work.

4. What is the most challenging part of your job?

We have a large department with multiple different areas of focus—residency programs, research, outpatient clinics, inpatient services, and so on—that is, within a large and highly matrixed health system. That size and complexity causes us to have many different projects and initiatives that need attention and often make it difficult to move quickly and create rapid change, particularly when multiple stakeholders need to be involved in decisions regarding strategy and resources.

5. What do you consider to be the best part of your job?

I have an exceptional opportunity to work every day with physicians, nurses, and other administrative leaders who are committed

Name: MIKE EPPEHIMER

to delivering great care to our community. I also feel fortunate to work with an exceptional leadership team, both in the Department of Medicine and across the system. My days are always fast-paced and interesting and I am constantly working on large, collaborative projects that will improve our healthcare delivery system.

6. **What path did you take to get to the job you are in today?**
   I worked in a number of different roles after graduating from the University of Maryland, including working as an actor, doing personal training, and working at the YMCA national headquarters. I started my career in healthcare with the Advisory Board Company, where I worked as a speaker in their Educational Services Department and in business development for their Physician Leadership Academy. I moved from consulting over to hospital leadership when I joined the GWU Hospital—first as Director of Physician Relations and then as an Associate Administrator with responsibility for a number of large ancillary departments.

7. **What advice do you have for someone who is interested in a job such as yours?**
   My advice for any administrator with interest in a departmental or service line leadership role is to think of yourself as an important, but supportive, member of the clinical care team. It is important to spend as much time as possible getting to know physicians, nurses, and other clinicians—go and see them doing their work, ask them about their challenges and needs, develop credibility by listening and following through on your commitments. Become an expert in operational improvement sciences—you have an opportunity to partner with those clinicians in creating a financially sound, operationally efficient environment that promotes the highest quality and safety for patients.

11. CHIEF QUALITY OFFICER

JOB DESCRIPTION

The Chief Quality Officer (CQO) is responsible for planning, administration, and monitoring of consistent readiness of all quality management, regulatory requirements, and quality-improvement processes. The CQO will oversee and coordinate all hospital efforts to monitor and maintain compliance with all regulatory, state, federal, and Joint Commission requirements. As a member of the senior management team, the CQO initiates and oversees the development of a comprehensive quality/performance improvement program. In collaboration with hospital leadership, staff, medical staff leadership, and the Board of Trustees, the CQO directs and coordinates quality/performance improvement and hospital initiatives.

EDUCATION AND EXPERIENCE

A bachelor's degree in nursing and current RN license are the minimum clinical training required. Most CQOs have a minimum of 3 years of experience in quality management.

CORE COMPETENCIES AND SKILLS

- Outstanding interpersonal skills including the ability to effectively communicate with persons throughout the organization, including clinicians
- Excellent verbal and written communication skills
- Experience with CMS conditions of participation for acute care hospitals and CMS survey processes
- In-depth knowledge of external clinical quality reporting requirements
- Current knowledge of Joint Commission, state, and federal guidelines, regulations, and standards
- Must have coordinated, prepared, and participated in state, Joint Commission, and CMS surveys within past 3 years
- Current statistical knowledge and skill in developing statistical data displays
- Experience in the use of statistical and quality assessment software
- Ability to analyze and resolve complex issues

COMPENSATION

CQOs earn in the range of $90,000 to $136,000 although with incentives and bonus pay added on, the salary can be as much as $150,000.

EMPLOYMENT OUTLOOK

The employment outlook for CQOs in large hospital settings is generally good. Smaller hospitals typically cannot afford a CQO and that responsibility is distributed among other staff members.

FOR FURTHER INFORMATION

- Bureau of Labor Statistics (http://www.bls.gov/oco/ocos014.htm)
- American Association of Colleges of Nursing (http://www.aacn.nche.edu)

12. CLINICAL DEPARTMENT MANAGER

JOB DESCRIPTION

Clinical Department Managers typically have responsibilities in one department and therefore have matching experience in the respective field. The person in this position will work with clinicians and administrative staff to ensure optimization of departmental goals. Clinical Department Managers will develop and implement policies, plans, and procedures that aim to meet departmental objectives. They will develop and evaluate key financial reports, while maintaining the respective departmental budget. The person in this position is further responsible for reporting these findings to top management, as well as educating medical staff during operational transition periods. Clinical Department Managers must also hire necessary staff and develop a team geared toward achieving departmental goals.

EDUCATION AND EXPERIENCE

A bachelor's degree is acceptable for entry-level departmental positions in smaller facilities. As the facility, department, and responsibilities associated with the position grow, a master's degree becomes more prominent. Background education should be in healthcare administration, long-term care administration, health sciences, public administration, business administration, or a relatable field to the respective department.

Background experience varies as it relates to the department, but usually 2 to 5 years is required.

CORE COMPETENCIES AND SKILLS

- Proven ability to drive staff's top management toward department's goals
- Superior interpersonal and communication skills, as this position requires educating clinicians about new departmental objectives and policies
- Superior analytical skills with gathering and evaluating data, reports, and budgets
- Demonstrated ability to hire, train, and manage staff
- Background knowledge and relevant experience working with the respective department
- Familiarity with health IT systems
- Excellent written skills

COMPENSATION

Most Clinical Department Managers earn between $50,000 and $140,000 per year, with the middle 50% falling between about $60,000 and $105,000. Earnings for this position are dependent upon the location and type of facility, as well as the type of department. For example, Clinical Department Managers at general medical hospitals earn nearly $90,000, while managers at nursing care facilities would only make about $70,000.

EMPLOYMENT OUTLOOK

The need to optimize efficiency and achieve departmental goals has never been more important in healthcare facilities. Clinical Department Managers will continue to play a crucial role in helping departments meet necessary objectives in the rapidly evolving industry of healthcare. From 2008 to 2018, this position is expected to grow 16%, which is much faster than most fields. Opportunities will be plentiful in relation to other fields, especially for those who already have relevant experience in healthcare.

FOR FURTHER INFORMATION

- American College of Healthcare Executives (http://www.ache.org)
- Department of Labor, Bureau of Labor Statistics (http://www.bls.gov/oco/ocos014.htm)

Name:
REBECCA J. FISCHER
Title: Associate Executive Director
Organization: Bellevue Hospital Center, New York, New York

1. **Briefly describe your job responsibilities.**
As Budget Director, I am responsible for the $750 million budget of New York's Bellevue Hospital Center, the nation's oldest public hospital.

2. **Please give an example of what you would consider to be a "typical" day for you.**
I review the hospital's year-to-date spending and revenue and create forecasts of where the budget will be at the end of the fiscal year. I meet with various departments within the hospital—both medical and support functions—to discuss their current year staffing and spending needs.

3. **What education or training do you have? Is it typical for your job?**
In my experience, most Senior Finance Staff in the New York City Health and Hospitals Corporation have advanced degrees. I earned a master's degree from NYU's Robert F. Wagner Graduate School of Public Service in Health Policy and Management. My undergraduate degree is from the Cornell University College of Arts and Sciences, where I double majored in History and Government. Twenty years ago, my first job after graduating from college was in the Budget Office at the New York City Parks and Recreation Department. Then, I worked at the Mayor's Office of Management and Budget for 6 years, managing the unit responsible for overseeing the Health and Hospitals Corporation.

4. **What is the most challenging part of your job?**
The hardest part of my job is having to say "no" to requests because the Hospital does not have unlimited resources.

(*continued*)

Name: REBECCA J. FISCHER (*continued*)

5. What do you consider to be the best part of your job?
The opportunity to be an integral part of an organization whose mission is very important to me.

6. What path did you take to get to the job you are in today?
Twenty years ago, I worked in the Budget Office at the New York City Parks and Recreation Department. Then, I worked at the Mayor's Office of Management and Budget, where I was responsible for managing the unit that supervised the New York City Health and Hospitals Corporation. Then I went to graduate school at NYU Wagner, and I worked at Rutgers University's Center for State Health Policy while I was in school. After graduate school, I worked at Columbia-Presbyterian Medical Center and then took a position working for the CFO at Bellevue Hospital. When I first arrived at Bellevue, I was responsible for the Managed Care Department. Four years ago, I added Outpatient Revenue to my portfolio. Recently, I was put in charge of the Budget Office.

7. What advice do you have for someone who is interested in a job such as yours?
You should always follow your passion and find something that you enjoy doing every day. You spend more waking hours at work than at any other single activity. It is important to love what you do so that you can enjoy getting up each day.

13. COMMUNITY RESOURCE ADVISOR/ OPTIONS COUNSELOR

JOB DESCRIPTION

Community Resource Advisors play an integral role in providing information for services to patients during and after their inpatient stay. This position works with elderly patients 60 years and older, disabled patients 22 and older, and the respective patients' families. These advisors offer free, unbiased information so that patients and their caregivers can make informed decisions after the patient's stay. This position will make recommendations to the patient about available options for long-term care, housing services, and even home care services. Community Resource Advisors will meet patients and their caregivers at the hospital, in physician offices, rehabilitation centers, community settings, and at home.

EDUCATION AND EXPERIENCE

This position will often require a bachelor's degree in related field, such as social work or nursing. Individuals considering this position should be willing to obtain a social work license. Previous experience working as a case manager for 5 to 10 years with the elderly and disabled populations is desirable. Knowledge of home care resources and the services associated with these populations is also helpful.

CORE COMPETENCIES AND SKILLS

- Excellent communication skills, as this position requires working with patients, patients' family members, and medical staff
- Familiarity with long-term care service options and community resources
- Ability to travel to various locations within a community
- Superior writing skills to develop information packets
- Comfort with working in various medical environments
- Demonstrated ability to research relevant services for patients on websites
- Knowledge of state and federally subsidized programs and resources
- Ability to work with a multidisciplined team of doctors, nurses, and patients

COMPENSATION

Community Resource Advisors should expect to make $40,000 to $65,000. Experience and the level of responsibility will affect the position's salary. Those working in for-profit organizations will tend to make more than advisors in not-for-profit organizations.

EMPLOYMENT OUTLOOK

Community Resource Advisors can prevent nursing home placements, saving the state and federal government thousands of dollars per patient each month. Realizing these savings will be integral if these positions will continue to receive financial support.

FOR FURTHER INFORMATION

- EOEA Elder Affairs—Massachusetts Council on Aging (http://www.mcoaonline.com/content/eoea/index.php)
- Case Management Society of America (http://www.cmsa.org)

14. DIRECTOR OF BUSINESS DEVELOPMENT

JOB DESCRIPTION

The Director of Business Development is responsible for planning, developing, implementing, and evaluating new clinical outreach opportunities at the hospital in collaboration with key service line and departmental leaders. The Director provides support to leadership in strategic planning, project facilitation, productivity and operations improvement, strategic analysis, space planning, and other strategic activities within the hospital.

EDUCATION AND EXPERIENCE

Master's degree in health administration, business, or an analytical field is required along with 3 to 5 years of experience in healthcare planning, management, or consulting.

CORE COMPETENCIES AND SKILLS

- Outstanding interpersonal skills including the ability to effectively communicate with persons throughout the organization
- Excellent verbal and written communication skills
- Demonstrable knowledge of healthcare industry trends and hospital business structure
- Ability to build and maintain appropriate peer relationships to facilitate organizational objectives
- Ability to drive the development of major strategic and capital projects and determine volume projections for inpatient and outpatient services. Facilitate annual strategic review and goal-setting process

- Participate in hospital's master space plan development, hospital budget development, and provide data support on scheduled and ad hoc projects
- Experience in leading and motivating work teams with the intent to create and articulate a vision and direction. Ability to inspire, encourage, and influence others toward a shared vision and optimal outcomes
- Demonstrated ability to quickly understand an issue, identify alternatives, quantify and assess, and objectively present recommendations that are in the best interest of the system, the region, and the hospital
- Ability to facilitate group discussions and to work broadly with administration, hospital, and medical staff
- Capable of analyzing financial, volume, and market data

COMPENSATION

Directors of Business Development earn in the range of $75,000 to $130,000 although the total salary will vary depending on the size and location of the hospital, and the education and experience of the candidate.

EMPLOYMENT OUTLOOK

Typically, only larger hospitals and health systems can afford to have the position of Director of Business Development. It is reported that this is a position that frequently is used to develop persons who plan to move into senior management positions; therefore, the turnover of business development professionals is very brisk.

FOR FURTHER INFORMATION

- HFMA (http://www.hfma.org)
- American College of Healthcare Executives (http://www.ache.org)

15. DIRECTOR OF CLINICAL LABORATORIES

JOB DESCRIPTION

The Director of Clinical Laboratories is generally responsible for all operational aspects of the clinical laboratory. Additional duties may include ordering of supplies, scheduling patients, cross-training staff, scheduling staff, budget preparation, hiring new/open positions, as well as ensuring that services provided through the clinical laboratory are of the highest quality possible.

EDUCATION AND EXPERIENCE

Bachelor's degree in medical technology or equivalent is required along with current state licensure as a medical technologist. A minimum of 3 to 5 years of experience in supervisory position in a clinical laboratory is required. Many hospitals prefer persons with master's-level preparation in business or health administration.

CORE COMPETENCIES AND SKILLS

- Outstanding interpersonal skills including the ability to effectively communicate with persons both inside and outside the organization
- Excellent verbal and written communication skills
- Strong leadership and consensus building skills
- Must be familiar with clinical laboratories data management systems
- Demonstrated effective project management skills
- Must be able to deal with multiple project demands and tight deadlines
- Demonstrated skill in quality improvement methods as applied in the clinical laboratory
- Experience with evaluating business initiatives, departmental operations, and new services
- Demonstrated initiative, follow through, and ability to work independently
- Ability to build and manage budgets

COMPENSATION

Directors of Clinical Laboratories earn in the range of $80,000 to $120,000 although the total salary will vary depending on the size and location of the hospital, and the education and experience of the candidate.

EMPLOYMENT OUTLOOK

It is projected that there will be a continuing, stable demand for Directors of Clinical Laboratories at hospitals across the United States. These are positions that initially require training and experience as a licensed laboratory technologist. A growing number of hospitals are discovering that training and experience in the lab are not enough in order to effectively run the managerial elements of the lab and are seeking persons who have management training.

FOR FURTHER INFORMATION

- Clinical Laboratory Management Association (http://www.clma.org)

Name:
JEFFREY A. FLAKS
Title: President and CEO
Organization: Hartford Hospital

1. **Briefly describe your job responsibilities.**
I am president and CEO of Hartford Hospital, the flagship tertiary care center of Hartford HealthCare, a regional, integrated healthcare network with more than 15,000 staff members and $2 billion in net revenue. Before becoming president and CEO, I served as Hartford Hospital Executive VP and COO.

2. **Please give an example of what you would consider to be a "typical" day for you.**
The range of activities and topics that make up a typical day for me reflect the breadth and depth of work we do at Hartford Hospital. I focus on improvements in quality, safety, and operations; work with our leadership on a host of projects and programs to continually enhance our services and technology; and help lead our Board in governing the hospital with its more than 7,000 staff members, state-of-the-art research and training programs, and wide array of community projects. Every day, I engage with staff and further the cause of staff empowerment to make improvements in our processes and operations. There must be time for strategic thinking and planning, as well as dialog with the medical staff. Some aspect of community involvement is part of every day. All of this makes for a full calendar, but no matter how booked I may be, I always make time to talk with patients and families or to read their letters. An administrator must be a manager, financial analyst, mentor, advocate, strategist, and leader. Being well versed in clinical matters is a must. But, ultimately, we are providing care to our communities, and that's job one.

Name: JEFFREY A. FLAKS

3. What education or training do you have? Is it typical for your job?
I have a master's degree in health services administration from the GWU [George Washington University] and a Bachelor of Science from Ithaca College. Because of the growing complexity of the work, healthcare executives increasingly are trained and credentialed in healthcare-specific graduate programs. For me, the graduate work I completed, together with my administrative fellowship, were the foundations of my career. I continue to have a strong relationship with the faculty and administration at GWU. In fact, I served on the Board of Trustees and, in 2006, was honored with the Distinguished Alumni Service Award.

4. What is the most challenging part of your job?
Staying on track is the most significant practical challenge. Careful time management means having enough time to address the wide range of activities that are part of the job—especially staying close to patients, staff, and the community. It's important that my calendar and my priorities match up. From a broader perspective, it's about balancing the present and the future. This means exceeding the expectations of all of our stakeholders on a day-to-day basis, while positioning the organization for the future.

5. What do you consider to be the best part of your job?
Hartford Hospital is a place where miracles happen every day, and it is deeply fulfilling to be part of that. Also, it's very gratifying to help staff members grow and develop as people and professionals. In addition, the launching of three related initiatives has been very satisfying: (a) How Hartford Hospital Works (H3W) (now renamed How Hartford HealthCare Works to reflect its system-wide status) was launched 4 years ago following the Baldrige process to remove variation, generate ideas, improve performance, and engage and recognize staff. To date, this process has produced more than

(*continued*)

Name: JEFFREY A. FLAKS (*continued*)

5,000 staff ideas with more than 1,500 already implemented. (b) HH2020 (Hartford Hospital 2020) was launched more than 2 years ago as the master facility plan to create a world-class campus to match and support the culture of innovation and vision to deliver the latest in care services. (c) The restructuring of the hospital's traditional academic departments into subspecialty models and patient-centered institutes has just started. Engaging the staff in institutional transformation—and seeing dramatic results in staff and patients satisfaction and in clinical quality—has been exciting and rewarding for me.

6. What path did you take to get to the job you are in today?

My administrative fellowship at Detroit Medical Center was an essential building block of my career. It was in Detroit where I learned in detail about large, complex, mature, academic medical centers as an administrative fellow reporting to then-CEO, David Campbell. Since the beginning of my career, my strongest desire has always been to make the greatest contribution and most positive impact I can, which the fellowship program allowed me to do. In addition, the relationships I developed during and as a result of the fellowship program became lifelong relationships. As examples, when David Campbell later became CEO of Saint Vincent Catholic Medical Centers of New York, I was one of his first hires as a VP at age 29 and was given the responsibility to integrate the services of seven hospitals. Ironically, it was also in Detroit, 16 years ago, where I met Elliot Joseph, now CEO of Hartford HealthCare and my current boss.

Ultimately, I wanted greater responsibility and the opportunity to drive the decision making—whether related to service lines, physician recruitments, financials, union negotiations, and so on—which I was able to do as EVP and COO of MidState Medical Center. There, I found myself fully aligned with the values and visions of MidState's President and CEO Lucille Janatka—especially to MidState's commitment to the Malcolm Baldrige National Quality Award criteria. Our achievements at MidState, which is part of the

Name: JEFFREY A. FLAKS

Hartford HealthCare network, led to my initial position at Hartford Hospital.

7. **What advice do you have for someone who is interested in a job such as yours?**
Be passionate about the work you are doing. Make the most positive contributions you can. Be engaged. Remain curious and a lifelong learner. Be willing to step outside your comfort zone and build on experiences. Timing is important, but consistently doing the right thing is fundamental. Be willing to be accountable. Be willing to take well-informed risks. Give back. Given the times, there is a great need for true leaders—authentic individuals who are humanistic, but who take people to places where they did not expect to go.

16. DIRECTOR OF DEVELOPMENT

JOB DESCRIPTION

The Director of Development heads the Development Department and is primarily responsible for philanthropy and fund raising in the respective not-for-profit hospital. Frequently the Director of Development is also in charge of the hospital's foundation. This position is often referred to as the Executive Director of the hospital foundation. In every case, this person is in charge of leading all fund-raising activities. There is extensive work and interaction with real and potential donors.

EDUCATION AND EXPERIENCE

A bachelor's degree in business administration is the minimum academic qualification, although a master's degree in either business or health administration is becoming the standard level of education for Directors of Development. A minimum of 5 years of progressive fund-raising responsibilities in a healthcare environment or comparable complex organization is required.

CORE COMPETENCIES AND SKILLS

- Outstanding interpersonal skills including the ability to effectively communicate with persons both inside and outside the organization
- Excellent verbal and written communication skills
- Experience working with medical visionary leaders and the corporate sector in regard to philanthropic and strategic partnerships
- Must be familiar with development program data management systems
- Must be skilled at working with volunteer groups and community leaders
- Significant experience in planned giving, annual fund campaigns, and other philanthropic activities
- Experience with the various state and federal laws surrounding fund-raising and development
- Builds and maintains a strong employee communication program
- Builds appropriate major and planned giving, annual giving, grant writing, donor stewardship, and recognition programs; gift processing and use of volunteers
- Capable of analyzing financial, volume, and market data

COMPENSATION

Directors of Development earn in the range of $79,000 to $150,000 although the total salary will vary depending on the size and location of the hospital, and the education and experience of the candidate.

EMPLOYMENT OUTLOOK

The U.S. Department of Labor projects steady growth of Directors of Development in the coming years. Job growth is projected to be good throughout the hospital industry. Virtually all not-for-profit hospitals are involved with fund-raising and development work and, given the shrinking levels of reimbursement from commercial and government payers, these professionals will play an ever important role for the foreseeable future.

FOR FURTHER INFORMATION

- Association of Fundraising Professionals (http://www.afpnet.org)

- Association for Healthcare Philanthropy (http://www.ahp.org/Pages/Home.aspx)

17. DIRECTOR OF EMERGENCY SERVICES

JOB DESCRIPTION

The Director of Emergency Services assumes 24-hour fiscal, clinical, and operational responsibility for his/her assigned area, incorporating the hospital's mission, goals, and strategic plan. The Director of Emergency Services ensures quality patient care and oversees patient flow processes within the emergency department. The Director of Emergency Services, in collaboration with the Director of Security, Fire, and Safety and Deputy Safety Officer, is responsible to provide clinical support for the Emergency Management Plan.

EDUCATION AND EXPERIENCE

Most Directors of Emergency Services are RNs who have additional education in business or health administration. Persons in this role typically have 5 or more years of emergency department nursing experience.

CORE COMPETENCIES AND SKILLS

- Outstanding interpersonal skills including the ability to effectively communicate with persons both inside and outside the organization
- Excellent verbal and written communication skills
- Strong leadership and consensus building skills
- Must be familiar with emergency services data management systems
- Ability to manage the flow of patients and information to expedite care, collaborating with physicians and healthcare professionals.
- Ensures regulatory compliance with Department of Homeland Security (DHS), Occupational Safety and Health Administration (OSHA), and all other regulatory agencies
- Proven experience in creating staffing models for both full- and part-time professional employees
- Proven abilities to build and manage budgets
- Must be able to work in a team environment and ensure high-quality, compassionate patient care
- Exceptional problem-solving skills

COMPENSATION

Directors of Emergency Services earn in the range of $55,000 to $90,000 although the total salary will vary depending on the size and location of the hospital, and the education and experience of the candidate.

EMPLOYMENT OUTLOOK

Virtually every community hospital in the United States has a functioning emergency department that requires the skill and talent of a Director of Emergency Services. This job is becoming more complex as hospitals are required to maintain high-quality emergency services 24 hours a day, 365 days a year.

FOR FURTHER INFORMATION

- Emergency Nurses Association (http://www.ena.org/Pages/default.aspx)

Name:
JODI S. JOYCE
Title: Vice President, Quality and Patient Safety
Organization: Legacy Health, Portland, Oregon

1. **Briefly describe your job responsibilities.**
   I lead the development, refinement, and implementation of our organization's strategic plan for quality and patient safety. This involves partnering with physicians, nurses, and other clinical and operational leaders and staff to identify and prioritize opportunities for improving patient care and outcomes.

2. **Please give an example of what you would consider to be a "typical" day for you.**
   7:00 a.m.: Report progress on our Quality and Safety plan, including review of our Quality Dashboard, at the Board of Directors' Quality Subcommittee
   8:30 a.m.: Notify my management team of follow-up items from the Board meeting
   9:00 a.m.: Meet with our Pain and Oversedation Process Improvement Team to review their newly developed pain management protocol, and help them refine their communication and implementation plans
   11:00 a.m.: Summarize findings and recommended actions from our Culture of Safety Survey for our CMO
   1:00 p.m.: Interview candidates for a vacant manager position in our department
   3:30 p.m.: Join our Intensive Care Unit Manager for "leadership rounds" in her unit, to talk with staff about the patient safety

(*continued*)

Name: JODI S. JOYCE (*continued*)

challenges they encounter and their ideas for making our patient care areas and our processes safer

5:00 p.m.: Send a congratulatory note to our Surgical Services team for their great work that has resulted in an 18% reduction in surgical site infections in less than 6 months

3. What education or training do you have? Is it typical for your job?

I have a Bachelor of Science in Liberal Arts, a Bachelor of Science in Nursing, and an MBA. Having an MBA is common for executive positions in large healthcare organizations like mine. A clinical background is also common for my role, but most often persons filling this position are physicians.

4. What is the most challenging part of your job?

It can be difficult to help a large, diverse organization maintain focus on what is most important. Many quality and safety issues feel "urgent," so it is easy to become "overly reactive," instead of planful in how they are addressed. In addition, the priorities of different disciplines and professions do not always appear well aligned, so sometimes there is a sense of "competing interests."

5. What do you consider to be the best part of your job?

It is incredibly rewarding to make a significant, positive difference in patients' lives. Over the past 3 years, our organization has achieved industry-leading performance by reducing inpatient mortality 28% and healthcare-associated infections by 58%.

6. What path did you take to get to the job you are in today?

I started my career as a bedside nurse in the neonatal intensive care unit (NICU). Two years later, I became the manager of a large

Name: JODI S. JOYCE

NICU. My decision to get an MBA was based on the realization that I had much to learn about leading and managing. After completing my MBA, I worked for a healthcare consulting company helping hospitals improve efficiencies and the quality of their care. My roles since then have been increasingly focused on improving quality and patient safety in large healthcare organizations.

7. **What advice do you have for someone who is interested in a job such as yours?**
   Do what you are passionate about. Don't be discouraged if your background doesn't seem a perfect fit for what interests you; tenacity, creativity, and a successful track record can open many doors. Stay humble and commit to being a lifelong learner.

18. DIRECTOR OF ENVIRONMENTAL SERVICES

JOB DESCRIPTION

The Director of Environmental Services plans, administers, and directs all activities related to environmental services, complying with the standards established by the hospital and various regulatory agencies. Leads environmental services staff and assistant managers and works to establish and maintain effective working relationships with other departments to provide a unified approach to patient care.

EDUCATION AND EXPERIENCE

Directors of Environmental Services generally possess a bachelor's degree in business administration or environmental health. To become eligible for one of these positions, the candidate must also have 4 to 6 years of hospital housekeeping experience.

CORE COMPETENCIES AND SKILLS

- Outstanding interpersonal skills including the ability to effectively communicate with persons inside the organization
- Excellent verbal and written communication skills

- Develops and maintains environmental services, in accordance with state and federal regulations, accepted standards, professional practices, and hospital policies
- Must be familiar with environmental services data management systems
- Experience at creating and maintaining job descriptions and completing annual performance reviews on all employees in a timely manner
- Working knowledge of infection control techniques
- Experience in supervising departmental personnel including: hiring; orientation; determining workload and delegating assignments; training; monitoring, scheduling, and evaluating performance; and initiating corrective and disciplinary actions
- Skilled in supporting and motivating staff at both the supervisory and hourly level
- Proficient in computer skills, including word processing and spreadsheet applications
- Ability to build and manage budgets

COMPENSATION

Directors of Environmental Services earn in the range of $60,000 to $85,000 although the total salary will vary depending on the size and location of the hospital, and the education and experience of the candidate.

EMPLOYMENT OUTLOOK

Job prospects for Directors of Environmental Services are reported to be good across the country. Every hospital must maintain a highly effective environmental services department that need to be run by persons who are dedicated to providing a safe and clean setting for patients, clinicians, and visitors.

FOR FURTHER INFORMATION

- Association for the Healthcare Environment (http://www.ahe.org)

19. DIRECTOR OF FOOD AND NUTRITION SERVICES

JOB DESCRIPTION

The Director of Food and Nutrition Services directs and integrates all aspects of food and nutrition service for patients, employees, and cafeteria customers, including clinical nutrition services, retail, and catering services. The Director provides leadership and direction and is responsible for planning, organizing, and staffing the department in accordance with the mission, values, and vision of the hospital.

EDUCATION AND EXPERIENCE

Bachelor's degree is required with a minimum of 3 years of experience in food service management or a recognized culinary diploma with a minimum of 5 years of demonstrated management experience. Most hospitals prefer someone with an RD.

CORE COMPETENCIES AND SKILLS

- Outstanding interpersonal skills including the ability to effectively communicate with persons both inside and outside the organization
- Excellent verbal and written communication skills
- Strong leadership and consensus-building skills
- Directs and integrates all aspects of food and nutrition service for patients, employees, and cafeteria customers, including clinical nutrition services, retail, and catering services
- Ensures that there are ongoing in-service and educational training programs for staff, and policies and procedures in place to guide the staff in their duties that address safety for food handling, emergency supplies, orientation for new employees, work assignments, and job descriptions
- Must be able to deal with multiple project demands and tight deadlines
- Oversees proper menu planning, purchasing of food and supplies, schedules, sanitation, and the retention of essential records
- Demonstrated initiative, follow through, and ability to work independently
- Ability to build and manage budgets

COMPENSATION

Directors of Food and Nutrition Services earn in the range of $65,000 to $110,000 although the total salary will vary depending on the size and location of the hospital, and the education and experience of the candidate.

EMPLOYMENT OUTLOOK

The employment outlook for Directors of Food and Nutrition Services is somewhat complicated. Each and every hospital must be able to meet the precise dietary requirements of all inpatients and therefore must have an operational onsite food service. Food and nutrition services for inpatient care will continue to require a Director. However, hospitals also maintain a cafeteria for employees and visitors, as well as catering for hospital events. In a number of cases, hospitals outsource their food service operations for these service lines to an outside vendor. In other cases, hospitals have actively tried to improve the quality of their food service by working to improve and upgrade internal operations. In either case, Directors of Food and Nutrition Services will continue to play an important role in all hospitals.

FOR FURTHER INFORMATION

- Association for Healthcare Foodservice (http://www.healthcare-foodservice.org)

20. DIRECTOR OF HUMAN RESOURCES

JOB DESCRIPTION

The Director of Human Resources (HR) heads the HR department in a hospital, overseeing the entire functioning of the department. This position typically reports directly to the CEO of a hospital. Recruitment of employees, training, development, setting the salaries and benefits of employees, and managing employee–employer relations are some of the primary duties of a hospital Director of HR.

EDUCATION AND EXPERIENCE

A bachelor's degree in business administration is the minimum academic qualification, although a master's degree in either business or health administration is becoming the standard level of education for

Directors of HR. Most hospitals require a minimum of 5 years of senior HR experience. Experience in working with labor unions is also critical for Directors of HR.

CORE COMPETENCIES AND SKILLS

- Outstanding interpersonal skills including the ability to effectively communicate with persons throughout the organization, including clinicians
- Excellent verbal and written communication skills
- Thorough knowledge of all aspects of HR administration, including applicable local, state, and federal regulatory requirements; Fair Employment Practices Act; the National Labor Relations Act; Title VII of the Civil Rights Act; Rehabilitation Act; and wage and hour and employee benefits-related regulations
- In-depth knowledge of external clinical quality reporting requirements
- Current knowledge of Joint Commission, state, and federal guidelines, regulations, and standards
- Must have coordinated, prepared, and participated in state, Joint Commission, and CMS surveys within the past 3 years
- Current statistical knowledge and skill in developing statistical data displays
- Experience in the use of statistical and quality assessment software
- Experience in leading and managing change

COMPENSATION

Directors of HR earn in the range of $70,000 to $150,000 although the total salary will vary depending on the size and location of the hospital.

EMPLOYMENT OUTLOOK

The employment outlook for Directors of HR is generally good. This is a position that all hospitals must fill. There is no specific information relating to turnover in this position, but Directors of HR at smaller hospitals typically move into positions with larger salaries and additional opportunities.

FOR FURTHER INFORMATION

- Society for Human Resource Management (http://www.shrm.org/Pages/default.aspx)

Name:
DAVID M. KAPLAN
Title: Vice Chairman, Administration and Finance, Department of Surgery
Organization: The Mount Sinai Medical Center

1. **Briefly describe your job responsibilities.**
   Responsible for overseeing all the financial, operational, revenue cycle, educational, research, and strategic aspects of the Department of Surgery at The Mount Sinai Medical Center.

2. **Please give an example of what you would consider to be a "typical" day for you.**
   Conduct and/or participate in multiple meetings on any given day, while managing daily "fire drills" (staffing issues, equipment issues, financial concerns, etc.), and working to mentor the senior leaders within the department on how to handle certain situations. Additionally, physicians will stop by to visit or discuss new initiatives or desired equipment/resources. Lastly, throughout the day there are significant volumes of correspondence (both e-mail and phone) that need to be managed as well.

3. **What education or training do you have? Is it typical for your job?**
   Master's in Public Administration with a focus on Health Administration and Finance. This is very typical for this type of position.

4. **What is the most challenging part of your job?**
   Dealing with a typical bureaucracy in a large academic medical center is probably the most frustrating part of this position. This requires a large amount of patience and prowess to be able to successfully navigate the system to achieve initiatives in a creative and timely manner.

Name: DAVID M. KAPLAN

5. What do you consider to be the best part of your job?

Mentoring, cultivating, and growing future leaders within the organization. At the same time, seeing how our team continues to make such a positive impact on the department and the organization as a whole.

6. What path did you take to get to the job you are in today?

I have been around the block as they say. I started my career as an academic resident back in 1995 and learned the ropes about physician billing. Soon after I was promoted to a Division Administrator in a Pediatrics Department. Following this, I learned practice operations as a Practice Manager for a large multispecialty outpatient setting. Using these skills, I was promoted to work in a Management Services Organization (MSO) as a Practice Manager. I then transitioned to be a healthcare consultant for a large nationally renowned firm, where I traveled the country working on a variety of projects such as revenue cycle redesign, physician compensation assessments, strategic planning, and complete financial turnaround projects. Following this great experience, I shifted back into industry as the Administrator for Cardiology at a large New York City Academic Medical Center.

Having received critical experience in faculty practice, school operations, I needed to round out my experience on the hospital side. To achieve this, I moved to a VP role overseeing nine departments, including trauma and emergency services, at another medical center in the New York area. After a couple of years in this role, I missed the school and faculty practice aspects and opted to shift to my current role as Vice Chairman, Administration and Finance, for the Department of Surgery at The Mount Sinai Medical Center. This time around, I have also pursued the academic mission in this role and spend a fair amount of time teaching medical and graduate students the business of medicine and have even received a faculty appointment within the medical school as Instructor of Surgery.

(*continued*)

Name: DAVID M. KAPLAN *(continued)*

7. What advice do you have for someone who is interested in a job such as yours?

Nothing too novel, but here are my top five recommendations:

(1) Network, network, network...

Meet as many people as humanly possible. This means that new candidates need to attend as many events and conferences as they can. Also, I strongly urge folks to set up as many informational interviews to make connections, and learn about different positions. Regular follow-up with network connections is also critically important to ensure name recognition.

(2) Be well rounded.

Don't get pigeon-holed too early in your career. I recommend getting exposure to many different areas within a large medical center. This will allow a certain comfort level with discussing numerous topics/subjects, when networking or interviewing for positions.

(3) Don't be afraid of change.

Lots of people, especially in this economy, have latched on for dear life to their jobs. For growth purposes, a person must be willing to take some risks, and this may require a change of scenery. The average healthcare administrator changes jobs roughly five to six times during their career, and that is ok, trust me, I can speak from experience.

(4) Be open and honest with your boss.

The relationship with your boss is critically important to your happiness and overall job satisfaction. A good boss will foster a certain level of comfort that will, in turn, foster a productive environment. Conversely, a horrible boss will create a very uncomfortable situation and stymie productivity.

To help ensure a good relationship with your boss, I often advise people to develop an open and honest rapport with their boss. A person should be able to discuss any ideas/issues good, bad, and indifferent, including job growth, job satisfaction, and, yes, this includes monetary/salary issues.

Name: DAVID M. KAPLAN

(5) Have fun!
Healthcare is extremely challenging and will become more so in the future. So this industry is not for the faint of heart, which means that to be successful a person must truly love what they do and most importantly will have fun doing it. A wise person once told me that if you love what you do, then you will never work a day in your life.

21. DIRECTOR OF INFECTION PREVENTION

JOB DESCRIPTION

The Director of Infection Prevention serves as the primary resource person for the hospital and the community in the area of infection control. This individual will provide consultation, recommend educational tools, manage staff in areas of surveillance, coordinate projects, reporting, education, regulation, and oversees outbreak investigation.

EDUCATION AND EXPERIENCE

Directors of Infection Prevention should have a bachelor of science in nursing and be currently licensed as an RN. A CIC (Certification in Infection Control) is preferred with 3 to 5 years experience in infection control along with management experience.

CORE COMPETENCIES AND SKILLS

- Outstanding interpersonal skills including the ability to effectively communicate with persons throughout the organization and in the community
- Ability to plan, direct, and evaluate staff
- Ability to think critically and provide reliable advice
- Excellent verbal and written communication skills
- Understand the area of infection control and be knowledgeable in the methods of avoiding and handling related issues
- Ability to hold subordinates accountable for organizational goals
- Ability to develop and maintain a department budget
- Understand the regulations imposed by various agencies

COMPENSATION

A Director of Infection Prevention may earn in the range of $80,000 to $110,000. However, this figure varies depending on a number of variables including the size of the hospital and the region of the country in which the hospital is located. Directors of Infection Prevention of smaller hospitals in more rural areas tend to earn less than their counterparts at large, urban hospitals.

EMPLOYMENT OUTLOOK

Every hospital or health system has a position dealing with infection control and possessing the knowledge to lead this effort is a valued skill in healthcare organizations.

FOR FURTHER INFORMATION

- Association for Professionals in Infection Control and Epidemiology (http://www.apic.org)

22. DIRECTOR OF MARKETING

JOB DESCRIPTION

The Director of Marketing for an acute care hospital is responsible for a wide range of activities, including helping to develop and execute a strategic plan for marketing the hospital's services to the community. He/she will also help market the hospital's services and activities to other groups, including patients, employees, and physicians. Guiding the hospital's interactions with the media will also be critical, as will helping to train other senior leaders within the hospital to interact with members of the media. Other responsibilities include advertising, internal communications, hospital publications, community relations, and helping to manage special events. He/she will also work closely with the hospital's senior leadership to help manage successful implementation of the hospital's vision and strategic plan.

EDUCATION AND EXPERIENCE

A bachelor's degree is a minimum expectation for most Director of Marketing positions, and a master's degree is preferred. Educational background should be in marketing, communications, public relations, journalism, or another related field. Prior experience in healthcare, hospital, or service line marketing is crucial. Many employers expect marketing directors to have at least 5 to 7 years of relevant prior experience.

CORE COMPETENCIES AND SKILLS

- Ability to use good judgment in potentially difficult political situations
- Excellent written and oral communication skills
- Excellent editing skills
- Outstanding interpersonal skills, as this position will be responsible for working with top management
- Ability to work under pressure and deal effectively with crises
- Solid understanding of computer applications (Microsoft Word, etc.)
- Should understand the impact of market forces on hospital strategy
- Should be able to promote cross-departmental collaboration

COMPENSATION

The majority of marketing directors make between $60,000 and $100,000 annually. They can make as little as $40,000 or as much as $120,000. Marketing directors with broader responsibilities at larger hospitals will likely earn a higher salary. Similarly, those working in a busier, urban area stand to make more than someone living in a rural setting.

EMPLOYMENT OUTLOOK

As the number of hospitals in the United States decreases slightly over the next several years, the demand for hospital marketing directors will decrease slightly as well. However, the outlook for these jobs remains high as the use of social media and other types of communication increases among hospitals.

FOR FURTHER INFORMATION

- American Association of Advertising Agencies (http://www.aaaa.org/Pages/default.aspx)

Name:
STEFANIE KIRK
Title: Financial Analyst, Department of Medicine, Division of Nephrology
Organization: Johns Hopkins Medicine

1. **Briefly describe your job responsibilities.**
   As the Financial Analyst for the Division of Nephrology, Department of Medicine, I work with the administrative manager, division chief, and senior leadership to plan, monitor, and reconcile the finances of the division. This includes preparing the annual budget, reprojections, and year-to-date budget analyses for Johns Hopkins Hospital, Bayview Medical Center, and community physician sites totaling $11.5 million in expenses and revenue. In addition, I develop business plans and evaluate existing programs to calculate financial performance. Lastly, I am responsible for the daily finances for the division and I manage transactions with affiliate's contracts, joint ventures, and grant spending.

2. **Please give an example of what you would consider to be a "typical" day for you.**
   My responsibilities and daily jobs tasks vary each day, so a "typical" day for me first starts at the end of the day prior where I prioritize what needs to be done the next day. An example of the activities in my day would include meeting with a faculty member to review their account balances to ensure that expected gift donations, honoraria, or reimbursements have been processed appropriately. Then, I would work on reconciling our monthly expenses and revenue to complete various reports and explain variances. If there is a lag in our faculty billing charges, I would contact the billing department to see what the issue is and work to resolve the problem.

Name: STEFANIE KIRK

Lastly, I may meet with the division management to discuss our future plans of adding clinics, changes in funding, or a new business venture we may pursue.

3. What education or training do you have? Is it typical for your job?
As a graduate of the University of Maryland Baltimore County, I earned a BS in Interdisciplinary Studies with a focus in Public Health and Biology. Typically for my job, since it is a financial position, most people have an accounting or business background; however, it is not a requirement and I do not. However, I did earn my MHSA degree at the GWU [George Washington University] so I understand the basic principles of finance and have a strong hospital operations foundation, which I think is beneficial and has set me apart from my counterparts.

Additionally, I have had wonderful residency and work experiences that have helped hone various skill sets such as being well versed in Microsoft Word, Excel, PowerPoint, Outlook, and Visio programs that are required for my role. Other transferable skills that have been useful in my role are the ability to manage several major activities simultaneously with strong organizational skills, self-motivation, and excellent problem-solving skills. Lastly, once started in my role, I had on-the-job training to learn our financial software applications, databases, and spreadsheets that are essential to my role.

4. What is the most challenging part of your job?
With every job there are challenges and from these difficulties there is the opportunity to grow and learn. In my role, I have inherited a number of bad habits that were allowed by my predecessors. My biggest challenge is to foster an environment of change that will encourage people to change previous behaviors and see things in a new way that is more efficient. This is especially hard when working to determine if there is a better way to do something without having the history of data and time to prove that the new way is actually an improvement. Also, in today's difficult financial environment, it is hard to "do more with less" and it is difficult to balance patient safety, quality, equality, and maintain a high morale with limited resources.

(*continued*)

Name: STEFANIE KIRK (*continued*)

5. What do you consider to be the best part of your job?

I enjoy my job because at the end of the day I am a problem solver. If I can help someone do his or her job easier, I feel rewarded. It is a wonderful feeling to have a team that is supportive so I work hard, so the doctors can focus on treating patients, researchers can focus on their lab work, and medical office coordinators can focus on organizing various patients' needs. In my role, I am able to ensure that we plan far in advance for changes, manage everyday issues, and provide the resources and information needed so that each person can happily continue in their role. I enjoy my role because finances are an integral part of our daily activities and although I do numerous tasks behind the scene, when the everyday operations are seamless, I feel I have accomplished my goal.

6. What path did you take to get to the job you are in today?

The path I took to get to my job was adventurous and somewhat untraditional. In undergrad, I originally had aspirations of becoming a scientific researcher but after spending time in biology labs, I decided I wanted to change paths to work with "whole people" and not microorganisms. I knew I wanted to work in healthcare management because of my internship experiences with the Centers for Medicare and Medicaid Services and Johns Hopkins Outpatient Center, where I was exposed to health policy and the implementation of policies in the hospital setting. This passion led me to obtain a master's in health services administration from GWU, where I had two experiences that greatly shaped my career path.

The first was that I was encouraged to join the National Association of Health Services Executives as a student member. As a result of this experience, I attended conferences, participated in their student case competition, and networked with senior executives, one of which became my mentor and offered me a job at his community hospital. This was my first experience

Name: STEFANIE KIRK

working in a hospital setting with administration and I loved it! I enjoyed my projects that allowed me to improve the hospital surgery department efficiency, and I was able to "test out" the management theories that I was simultaneously learning in graduate school.

My second major career path milestone was when I completed a year residency at Johns Hopkins Bayview Medical Center. This residency allowed me to learn about hospital operations on a broad level from service line management to Board of Trustees meetings. As a result of being a part of the Hopkins family, I was afforded the opportunity to work for 6 month internationally with Hopkins International Medical Center in Singapore. As my first job out of graduate school, this was an amazing experience. I worked as a project analyst to prepare the hospital for their Joint Commission International reaccreditation survey. After my international experience, I wanted to strengthen my financial knowledge which brought me to choosing my current role as a financial analyst.

7. What advice do you have for someone who is interested in a job such as yours?

Have fun learning! It is easy for an early careerist, or anyone starting a new job, to worry about all the things they do not know. This causes a lot of stress, pressure, and sometimes mistakes because of the fear of asking questions. I would advise someone interested in a job such as mine to relax, realize that you are not expected to know everything, and have fun learning, problem solving, and asking lots and lots of questions. I have realized that fear of asking a "dumb question" can lead to incorrect assumptions and, in most cases, people appreciate honesty and admitting that you do not know something and would like to learn the very basic process and then build on that foundation. Also, I would advise learning how to bake (or purchase) sweet treats to bring to meetings that you have to discuss "sensitive" topics.

23. DIRECTOR OF MATERIALS MANAGEMENT

JOB DESCRIPTION

The Director of Materials Management implements and administers the hospital supply chain function under general supervision and within corporate guidelines. The Director is responsible for purchasing, inventory control, material systems, and financial controls. Materials management works closely across hospital departments to ensure that medical technology of all types is available to clinicians and patients.

EDUCATION AND EXPERIENCE

Minimum of a bachelor's degree in business or healthcare administration or other related field is required. Five or more years of healthcare materials management experience, with at least 3 years of supervisory experience.

CORE COMPETENCIES AND SKILLS

- Outstanding interpersonal skills including the ability to effectively communicate with persons both inside and outside the organization
- Excellent verbal and written communication skills
- Analyzes and recommends policies and procedures relative to supply chain's technology practices and suppliers
- Maintains cost/revenue ratios in accordance with budget; maintains adequate inventory levels. Assists with negotiation of contracts with suppliers for the purchase of capital and noncapital products and services
- Develops and prepares reports and presentations on usage statistics, purchasing trends, and marketing data and savings relative to competitive bidding and national agreements
- Must be able to deal with multiple project demands and tight deadlines
- Creates a team environment and exhibits appropriate quality service behaviors in meeting and/or exceeding the needs of employees, customers, coworkers, and others
- Demonstrated initiative, follow through, and ability to work independently
- Ability to build and manage budgets

COMPENSATION

Directors of Materials Management earn in the range of $60,000 to $110,000 although the total salary will vary depending on the size and location of the hospital, and the education and experience of the candidate.

EMPLOYMENT OUTLOOK

The employment outlook for Directors of Materials Management is good now and into the foreseeable future. Hospitals must be technologically sophisticated in order to be competitive, and it is up to the Director of Materials Management to help guide the hospital to make the best technology-acquisition decisions possible.

FOR FURTHER INFORMATION

- Association for Healthcare Resource and Materials Management (http://www.ahrmm.org)

24. DIRECTOR OF MEDICAL RECORDS

JOB DESCRIPTION

The Director of Medical Records is responsible for maintaining the records of patients, in accordance with federal government regulations regarding patient privacy. Administration and oversight of the medical records program along with an understanding of the latest computer software and technology are key responsibilities of the position.

EDUCATION AND EXPERIENCE

A bachelor of science in health information management is a degree aimed at preparing one for a career in information and data management, among other areas. Following the completion of this degree, graduates are eligible to sit for the Registered Health Information Administrator Certification (RHIA). Although not required, a master's degree in health information management or a similar area will provide one with the knowledge and skill set needed.

CORE COMPETENCIES AND SKILLS

- Outstanding interpersonal skills including the ability to effectively communicate with persons throughout the organization, including clinicians

- Ability to plan, direct, and evaluate staff
- Ability to read, analyze, and apply laws, regulations, and procedures, as related to medical records
- Excellent verbal and written communication skills
- Ability to understand and use the latest computer software and security
- Ability to hold subordinates accountable for organizational goals
- Ability to develop and maintain a department budget

COMPENSATION

A Director of Medical Records may earn in the range of $80,000 to $120,000. However, this figure varies depending on a number of variables including the size of the hospital and the region of the country in which the hospital is located. Directors of Medical Records of smaller hospitals in more rural areas tend to earn less than their counterparts at large, urban hospitals.

EMPLOYMENT OUTLOOK

The outlook for Directors of Medical Records is expected to increase in the coming years. The consistently changing landscape of health IT will require this position to adapt and grow.

FOR FURTHER INFORMATION

- Department of Labor, Bureau of Labor Statistics (http://www.bls.gov/oco/ocos103.htm)
- American Health Information Management Association (http://www.ahima.org/Default.aspx)

25. DIRECTOR OF PASTORAL CARE

JOB DESCRIPTION

The Director of Pastoral Care develops and manages services designed to meet the religious and/or spiritual needs of patients and their families, as well as hospital team members. The Director may also be used as a resource for the hospital on questions of ethics. As a Director, progression of the department including recruitment, training, and budgeting are key duties of the position.

EDUCATION AND EXPERIENCE

A master's degree in theology, counseling, administration, or a comparable discipline is ideal. Certification by an appropriate clinical pastoral agency and ongoing advanced training in theology, management, or clinical or pastoral skills are required. A minimum of 2 years clinical pastoral experience in a healthcare setting is typically required.

CORE COMPETENCIES AND SKILLS

- Outstanding interpersonal skills including the ability to effectively communicate with persons throughout the organization and in the community
- Ability to plan, direct, and evaluate staff
- Ability to understand and work with representatives from multiple faith groups
- Excellent verbal and written communication skills
- Ability to hold subordinates accountable for organizational goals
- Ability to develop and maintain a department budget

COMPENSATION

A Director of Pastoral Care may earn in the range of $60,000 to $100,000. However, this figure varies depending on a number of variables including the size of the hospital and the region of the country in which the hospital is located. Directors of Pastoral Care of smaller hospitals in more rural areas tend to earn less than their counterparts at large, urban hospitals.

EMPLOYMENT OUTLOOK

Job prospects for Directors of Pastoral Care are reported to be good across the country as this is an important part of every hospital.

FOR FURTHER INFORMATION

- The National Association of Catholic Chaplains (http://www.nacc.org/resources/job_dirpastoralcare.asp)

Name:
STEPHANIE MEIER
Title: Administrative Director, OB/GYN
Organization: Winthrop University Hospital

1. **Briefly describe your job responsibilities.**
   I lead the department and oversee day-to-day operations of the department of OB/GYN at an academic medical center.

2. **Please give an example of what you would consider to be a "typical" day for you.**
   A typical day consists of meetings, rounds at the practice, and speaking with physicians and staff.

3. **What education or training do you have? Is it typical for your job?**
   My undergraduate degree is in business, and I hold a Master of Hospital Administration. Graduate training is typical for this position.

4. **What is the most challenging part of your job?**
   We operate in an environment of doing more with less. We are constantly challenged to meet the needs of our patient population with limited resources.

5. **What do you consider to be the best part of your job?**
   I have the ability to work on many different projects; I think the aspect that keeps it interesting is that I'm always able to do something new, with the knowledge that it is going to make a difference in a patient's life.

Name: STEPHANIE MEIER

6. What path did you take to get to the job you are in today?

I completed an administrative residency after my graduate training, which provided an excellent foundation to build upon. I started in the corporate offices of the largest nonprofit healthcare system before going to operations.

7. What advice do you have for someone who is interested in a job such as yours?

My advice is to work hard and be willing to "go the extra mile." I think a solid foundation in understand data and being able to interpret information is also very helpful. You have to understand ambiguity and paradox, which can become very challenging. It is important to keep the patient in mind in everything you do, no matter how mundane the task. I strongly believe that in order to be successful in healthcare you have to be committed to the central purpose of helping people in what is often a time of need.

26. DIRECTOR OF PATIENT ACCOUNTS

JOB DESCRIPTION

The Director of Patient Accounts is responsible for promoting and maximizing the revenue cycle throughout the organization. This includes oversight of all processes involved in the capture, management, and collection of patient revenues.

EDUCATION AND EXPERIENCE

A bachelor's degree in finance or accounting is required, but a master's degree is preferred. An experience of 3 to 5 years in healthcare accounting and finance is required.

CORE COMPETENCIES AND SKILLS

- Outstanding interpersonal skills including the ability to effectively communicate with persons throughout the organization and in the community

- Ability to plan, direct, and evaluate staff
- Ability to understand and adapt to the changing regulatory environment
- Excellent verbal and written communication skills
- Excellent understanding of hospital billing, coding, registration, and financing
- Ability to hold subordinates accountable for organizational goals
- Ability to develop and maintain a department budget

COMPENSATION

A Director of Patient Accounts may earn in the range of $80,000 to $150,000. However, this figure varies depending on a number of variables including the size of the hospital and the region of the country in which the hospital is located. Directors of Patient Accounts of smaller hospitals in more rural areas tend to earn less than their counterparts at large, urban hospitals.

EMPLOYMENT OUTLOOK

Job prospects for Directors of Patient Accounts are reported to be good across the country. This is a crucial position in maintaining and improving the financial standing of any hospital.

FOR FURTHER INFORMATION

- HFMA (http://www.hfma.org)

27. DIRECTOR OF PATIENT ADMISSIONS

JOB DESCRIPTION

A hospital's Director of Patient Admissions is responsible for overseeing many of the critical front-end processes the hospital's patients encounter when entering the hospital. He/she will lead many of the hospital's staff members in performing these functions, including front desk registration, emergency department registration, insurance verification, information desk greeters, central scheduling, and the cashier areas. The Director of Patient Admissions is responsible for planning and implementing procedures and policies for these areas, and must ensure high customer service, quality, and productivity.

EDUCATION AND EXPERIENCE

A bachelor's degree is usually the minimum expectation for most Directors of Patient Admissions. In some cases, a high school degree or equivalent will be accepted. In these cases, an associate's degree in business or some other related medical field is preferred. In general, educational background should be in business or health administration, or another related field. Prior experience in a managerial role is important, usually at least for 2 to 5 years.

CORE COMPETENCIES AND SKILLS

- Excellent interpersonal skills are critical
- Proficient in use of computer software, including Microsoft Word and Excel
- Strong organizational and analytical capabilities
- Knowledge of and ability to interpret Joint Commission on Accreditation of Healthcare Organizations (JCAHO) standards
- Demonstrated ability to teach, mentor, and manage a team of employees
- Understanding of medical terminology
- Strong written and oral communication skills
- Proven ability to work under stress and make effective decisions without being given directions

COMPENSATION

The majority of Directors of Patient Admissions make between $50,000 and $90,000 annually. They can make as little as $30,000 or as much as $110,000. Directors with broader responsibilities at larger hospitals will likely earn a higher salary. Similarly, those working in a busier, urban area stand to make more than someone in a rural setting.

EMPLOYMENT OUTLOOK

As the number of hospitals in the United States decreases slightly over the next several years, the demand for Directors of Patient Admissions will decrease slightly as well. However, the outlook for these jobs remains high as the healthcare market, in general, in the United States continues to remain strong.

FOR FURTHER INFORMATION

- American College of Healthcare Executives (http://www.ache.org)

Name:
JOSH NIEHAUS
Title: Business Development Manager
Organization: Baptist Medical Associates/Baptist Community Health Services

1. **Briefly describe your job responsibilities.**
I oversee the implementation process for newly hired physicians and physician practice acquisitions. This includes working with the legal, human resources, and finance departments, and outside consultants to ensure that all the due diligence is completed prior to employment and/or practice acquisition. I am also responsible for the preparation of the materials that go before the monthly Baptist Medical Associates Board of Directors meeting. Also, I work with executive leadership to identify and implement new business opportunities for Baptist Medical Associates and Baptist Community Health Services.

2. **Please an example of what you would consider to be a "typical" day for you.**
A typical day for me begins with catching up on e-mails and voice mails that may have come through since I last left the office. I then start working on my list of tasks that need to be completed for any practice or physician that we are in active negotiations. I spend a lot of my day on the phone and at the computer communicating with all the various departments and people who are helping me work through the process of on-boarding physicians. I usually have a couple of meeting each day that I attend that deal with anything from physician compensation, practice operations, and new facility design.

Name: JOSH NIEHAUS

3. What education or training do you have? Is it typical for your job?

I have a MHSA degree from the GWU [George Washington University]. This is typical for this job, as well as 3 to 5 years of experience.

4. What is the most challenging part of your job?

The most challenging part about my job is that I am responsible for so many different tasks for which I'm depending on others to do the work. Because most of my job is working with so many different people to get deals pushed through, tight deadlines are difficult to meet. It can be very difficult to push people whom I do not have authority or direct supervision over.

5. What do you consider to be the best part of your job?

The best part of my job is that I am involved in so many different areas. Therefore, I am still learning everyday through new experiences. One meeting I could be designing a facility for a new sports medicine program and the next meeting I'm working with executive leadership to discuss a strategy about a new market or practice acquisition opportunity. My job is never the same everyday.

6. What path did you take to get the job you are in today?

While doing my administrative residency at Baptist Healthcare System, it became apparent to me that healthcare is moving toward tighter alignment strategies between physicians and hospitals. Therefore, I chose to focus a lot of my learning activities in the area of physician alignment at Baptist Hospital East, during the end of my residency. Through the relationships I made and the opportunities that happened to open up when I was finishing my residency, I was able to secure my current position.

7. What advice do you have for someone who is interested in a job such as yours?

Get involved in a hospital's physician alignment strategy. Every hospital has a strategy to align with physicians. The strategies come

(*continued*)

Name: JOSH NIEHAUS *(continued)*

in many forms, such as joint ventures, employment, and electronic health record adoption. Not only do hospitals have such strategies, but most hospitals are dedicating a lot of resources to these strategies. Therefore, I suggest through an internship or residency, a student find a hospital that is dedicating significant resources to its physician alignment strategy. The student will probably find that there are lots of opportunities to find a position in this area because of the emphasis that hospitals are putting into this area.

28. DIRECTOR OF PHARMACY SERVICES

JOB DESCRIPTION

The Director of Pharmacy Services is responsible for the efficient operation of the hospital pharmacy. The Director establishes standards of quality, productivity, and performance, in accordance with established hospital policies and procedures and the requirements of state and federal regulatory agencies. The Director of Pharmacy Services is generally responsible to the hospital COO.

EDUCATION AND EXPERIENCE

Directors of Pharmacy Services are required to be licensed to practice pharmacy in the state in which they are working. A graduate degree in business administration or health administration is highly desirable. A minimum of 7 years of experience in hospital pharmacy practice is required.

CORE COMPETENCIES AND SKILLS

- Outstanding interpersonal skills including the ability to effectively communicate with persons both inside and outside the organization
- Excellent verbal and written communication skills
- Develops and maintains pharmacy services, in accordance with state and federal regulations, accepted standards, professional practices, and hospital policies
- Must be familiar with pharmacy services data management systems

- Experience at creating and maintaining job descriptions and completing annual performance reviews on all employees in a timely manner
- Responsible for the planning, supervision, coordination, and successful execution of all activities related to the pharmacy's operations
- Experience in supervising departmental personnel including: hiring, orientation, determining workload and delegating assignments, training, monitoring, scheduling and evaluating performance, and initiating corrective and disciplinary actions
- Coordinates pharmacy operations commensurate with the scope of services provided and the identified needs of patients
- Proficient in developing and maintaining computerized databases
- Ability to build and manage budgets

COMPENSATION

Directors of Pharmacy Services earn in the range of $120,000 to $160,000 although the total salary will vary depending on the size and location of the hospital, and the education and experience of the candidate.

EMPLOYMENT OUTLOOK

Job prospects for Directors of Pharmacy Services are reported to be excellent. Job openings will result from planned retirements of existing directors and the need to replace those who leave hospitals for other reasons.

FOR FURTHER INFORMATION

- American Society of Health System Pharmacists (http://www.ashp.org)

29. DIRECTOR OF PHYSICIAN RECRUITING

JOB DESCRIPTION

The primary responsibilities of the Director of Physician Recruiting are to recruit and retain physicians in product lines, in an effort to impact volume and growth. The Director is responsible for implementing all areas of the recruitment, screening, interviewing, and hiring process.

The Director must also be able to produce and maintain a budget for the department.

EDUCATION AND EXPERIENCE

A bachelor's degree in business, marketing, or a closely related field is required. A master's degree is preferred. A minimum of 3 years recruiting experience, with previous experience in recruitment of physicians or related healthcare professionals are required. Management and budgeting experience are required. Possessing a medical background with varied knowledge of physician specialties is preferred.

CORE COMPETENCIES AND SKILLS

- Outstanding interpersonal skills including the ability to effectively communicate with persons throughout the organization and in the community
- Ability to plan, direct, and evaluate staff
- Ability to communicate effectively with physicians and understand the various specialties
- Understand medical needs for the hospital
- Excellent verbal and written communication skills
- Ability to formulate and execute organizational strategies
- Ability to develop and maintain a department budget

COMPENSATION

A Director of Physician Recruiting may earn in the range of $80,000 to $130,000. However, this figure varies depending on a number of variables including the size of the hospital and the region of the country in which the hospital is located. Directors of Physician Recruiting of smaller hospitals in more rural areas tend to earn less than their counterparts at large, urban hospitals.

EMPLOYMENT OUTLOOK

The job market for Directors of Physician Recruiting is increasing as hospitals are employing more physicians and physician groups.

FOR FURTHER INFORMATION

- National Association of Physician Recruiters (http://www.napr.org)

30. DIRECTOR OF PHYSICIAN RELATIONS

JOB DESCRIPTION

The Director of Physician Relations directs and oversees programs designed to foster positive relations between physicians and the hospital or healthcare facility. The director promotes the organization among members of the medical community in order to establish partnerships and affiliations. Director of Physician Relations is responsible for planning and implementing outreach efforts focusing on physicians, community groups, and other potential referral sources in the hospital's target markets. The position primarily focuses on developing and improving hospital referral relationships with physicians in the service area, with the goal of maximizing referral and redirection opportunities for both inpatient and outpatient services.

EDUCATION AND EXPERIENCE

Directors of Physician Relations are required to possess a bachelor's degree in business, healthcare administration, or a related field; a master's degree is generally preferred. Most candidates for the Director of Physician Relations have 3 years of progressively responsible experience in hospital marketing or business development.

CORE COMPETENCIES AND SKILLS

- Outstanding interpersonal skills including the ability to effectively communicate with persons both inside and outside the organization
- Excellent verbal and written communication skills
- Strong leadership and consensus building skills
- Must be familiar with physician relations data management systems
- Skilled at enhancing communication between community physicians and hospital specialists
- Proven ability to monitor needs and respond to concerns of community physicians
- Demonstrated skill at relationship management promoting clinical services, programs, and facilities in order to enhance referral volume and ensure the success and growth of the hospital
- Experience at communicating with current and potential referring physicians, enhancing awareness of hospital offerings,

identifying provider issues, monitoring and reporting on referral trends, and serving as a general customer contact for referring entities
- Proficient in developing and maintaining computerized databases
- Ability to build and manage budgets

COMPENSATION

Directors of Physician Relations earn in the range of $64,000 to $124,000 although the total salary will vary depending on the size and location of the hospital, and the education and experience of the candidate.

EMPLOYMENT OUTLOOK

Managing the relationship with physicians is an important activity at every hospital. Given the changes envisioned by health reform, there is no question that effective Directors of Physician Relations are going to be in high demand in the near future.

FOR FURTHER INFORMATION

- American Association of Physician Liaisons (http://www.physicianliaison.com/default.cfm)

Name:
VANITHA PUSHPARAJ
Title: Administrative Director, Cardiac and Vascular Institute
Organization: Mount Sinai Medical Center

1. **Briefly describe your job responsibilities.**
   The Administrative Director exercises management responsibility over the business and operational activities of the department. Responsible for establishing short- and long-term goals and objectives inline with Mount Sinai Medical Center, as well as ensuring compliance with federal, state, and city regulatory agencies. I am currently responsible for over 500 staff, physicians, and ancillary providers.

2. **Please give an example of what you would consider to be a "typical" day for you.**
   A typical day involves strategic meetings with staff, physicians, and key stakeholders on operations and program development for cardiology services. Develop budgets, perform analyses on new or existing programs, and create business plans for new ventures.

3. **What education or training do you have? Is it typical for your job?**
   MPA from NYU/Wagner. Yes, a master's degree is a requirement for the position. I have had over 15 years working in hospitals both in operations and in business development.

4. **What is the most challenging part of your job?**
   Managing silos, holding staff accountable, and motivating change.

5. **What do you consider to be the best part of your job?**
   Improving systems, developing new programs, and implementing new technologies.

(*continued*)

Name: VANITHA PUSHPARAJ *(continued)*

6. What path did you take to get to the job you are in today?

I worked in hospital operations for a significant part of my career to lay groundwork for the job I currently hold. However, I made a conscious and committed change in career path to business development and created a physician network (at a prior job), as I saw how critical physician networks and strategic growth strategies were to advance a hospital's bottom line. That work taught me to work aggressively and independently to creatively build a program from the ground up.

7. What advice do you have for someone who is interested in a job such as yours?

Don't be afraid to challenge yourself to diverge from the path you originally were on; careers morph and success depends on adaptability to changing environments.

31. DIRECTOR OF REHABILITATION SERVICES

JOB DESCRIPTION

The Director of Rehabilitation Services sets and implements guidelines for programs such as physical therapy, occupational therapy, and speech therapy. The individual is responsible for the management, planning, resource allocation, and budgeting of the department.

EDUCATION AND EXPERIENCE

A bachelor's degree is required as a minimum, master's degree preferred, in either physical or occupational therapy. Experience of 3 to 5 years in clinical work along with management experience is typically recommended. CPR certification and a Physical or Occupational Therapist license are required.

CORE COMPETENCIES AND SKILLS

- Outstanding interpersonal skills including the ability to effectively communicate with persons throughout the organization and in the community
- Ability to plan, direct, and evaluate staff

- Understanding of medical needs for the hospital
- Understanding of the regulations of government and private payers
- Excellent verbal and written communication skills
- Ability to formulate and execute organizational strategies
- Ability to develop and maintain a department budget

COMPENSATION

A Director of Rehabilitation Services may earn in the range of $90,000 to $130,000. However, this figure varies depending on a number of variables including the size of the hospital and the region of the country in which the hospital is located. Directors of Rehabilitation Services of smaller hospitals in more rural areas tend to earn less than their counterparts at large, urban hospitals.

EMPLOYMENT OUTLOOK

Job prospects for Directors of Rehabilitation Services are reported to be good across the country, and in high demand at certain locations. This specific position is not present at every hospital, depending upon the services offered and organizational structure.

FOR FURTHER INFORMATION

- American Physical Therapy Association (http://www.apta.org)
- American Occupational Therapy Association (http://www.aota.org)

32. DIRECTOR OF REVENUE CYCLE MANAGEMENT

JOB DESCRIPTION

The Director of Revenue Cycle Management is responsible for the system that evaluates patient revenue optimization. This position strategically implements measurement tools, policies, and process alterations to ensure that the hospital achieves maximum patient billing, in a timely manner. Working with other hospital employees, directors, and senior management, the Director of Revenue Cycle Management will develop solutions with respective members to create a more efficient system of billing. This position must drive change through performing cost/benefit analyses, evaluating solution options, and communicating with key stakeholders to push decision making. The Director confirms that the revenue cycle is in compliance with governmental and regulatory regulations.

EDUCATION AND EXPERIENCE

Hospitals hiring Directors of Revenue Cycle Management require a bachelor's degree, with a master's degree strongly preferred. The background education should be in finance, accounting, health administration, business administration, or another business-related field. Additionally, hospitals look for a minimum of 5 to 10 years previous experience in a directly related financial role, as well as 3 years experience with management.

CORE COMPETENCIES AND SKILLS

- Direct operational experience
- Outstanding interpersonal, communication, and presentation skills
- Excellent analytical skills, as it relates to problem solving, project management, and business solutions
- Superior knowledge of revenue codes, Diagnosis Related Groups (DRGs), payment methodologies, and managed care operations
- Ability to identify, implement, and drive change management
- Manage, motivate, and educate a revenue cycle team
- Knowledge of relevant state and federal laws and regulations related to the healthcare industry

COMPENSATION

The policies and procedures that a Director of Revenue Cycle Management implements in a provider could cost or save the hospital millions of dollars annually. The position's salary well reflects the criticality of this individual's role in the hospital. The Director of Revenue Cycle Management should expect to earn a salary between $100,000 and $170,000. The variability of this position's salary is attributable to the size of the provider, the provider's geographic location, and the individual's amount of previous experience.

EMPLOYMENT OUTLOOK

The Director of Revenue Cycle Management plays a crucial role in ensuring that a hospital is reimbursed accurately for all healthcare services rendered. While it takes many years of experience working with hospital revenue cycles to become a Director of Revenue Cycle Management, this position will continue to exist in hospitals around the country for many years.

FOR FURTHER INFORMATION

- American College of Healthcare Executives (www.ache.org)
- HFMA (www.hfma.org)

Name:
JEREMY STUBSON
Title: Strategic Account Sales Executive
Organization: VHA, Inc.

1. Briefly describe your job responsibilities.

My role is to provide overall sales, service, and strategic healthcare management advisory support through a strategic partnership between VHA, Inc., based in Irving, Texas, and Providence Health & Services, based in Renton, Washington. Providence Health & Services is a Catholic-based, integrated, not-for-profit healthcare system that includes 28 acute care facilities, 217 physician group practices, senior services, a health plan, a liberal arts university, high school, and many other services that stretch across five states from California to Alaska.

2. Please give an example of what you would consider to be a "typical" day for you.

A typical day for me begins at about 5:00 a.m. when I begin to respond to e-mails. By 7:00 a.m., I am usually on teleconference calls with my virtual team that is located across the United States. While I am on the phone (hands-free of course), I commute to my office, which is located at the System Office for Providence Health & Services. I usually have several in-person and virtual conference calls with various leaders and clinicians across the system regarding the various strategic initiatives that will help increase quality care, while reducing cost.

3. What education or training do you have? Is it typical for your job?

I received my undergraduate degree in psychology from the University of Oregon in Eugene, Oregon, and went on to receive my

(*continued*)

Name: JEREMY STUBSON *(continued)*

master's degree in Healthcare Administration from Oregon State University in Corvallis, Oregon. Aside from my formal education, I have been in active healthcare leadership roles for the past 15 years in both acute, ambulatory care, and integrated delivery systems from Oregon to Montana, Colorado, and Washington.

4. What is the most challenging part of your job?

The most challenging part of my job is that I must remain objective in providing recommendations and advice regarding services and contract negotiation between the suppliers, vendors, and the member. Equally challenging is influencing a system as large as Providence Health & Services to move quickly to seize opportunities that better position them to stay ahead of the curve of change within the industry.

5. What do you consider to be the best part of your job?

The best part of my job is working with a group of very dedicated, hard-working professionals whose collective focus is to help healthcare organizations, large and small, position themselves to provide the best care at the most affordable price, while reducing unnecessary waste.

6. What path did you take to get to the job you are in today?

My career path as been a very rewarding and interesting one; I started my career as a Clinic Manager for a hospital-owned Urgent Care Clinic, Internal Medicine, and Family Practice Clinic. From there, I have managed physician-owned group practices from Obstetrics and Gynecology to Orthopedic and Spine Surgery, Gastroenterology, ASC Management, Pain Management, Plastic Surgery, Service Line Leadership for two different Integrated Delivery Systems, and now as an Executive Advisor that provides management service and strategic support for a company that supports over 1,600 hospital and health systems across the United States.

Name: JEREMY STUBSON *(continued)*

7. What advice do you have for someone who is interested in a job such as yours?

While some individuals have alternative experience in sales or supply chain management, I would strongly advise anyone wanting to work for VHA, Inc., to spend at least 5 to 7 years in direct healthcare organizations to better understand the challenges and complexities of healthcare and how health systems operate relative to industry changes and pressures. I also believe it is important to have experience in the entire healthcare continuum; from acute care to the patient-centered medical home model.

33. DIRECTOR OF SAFETY

JOB DESCRIPTION

The Director of Safety is in charge of the hospital's safety, security, and emergency management. This position is accountable for working with the organization's staff in all departments. The Director of Safety must continually collect key hospital-wide data to evaluate ways to improve safety management programs. It is this person's responsibility to make sure the hospital is in compliance with all safety and environmental regulatory and accreditation requirements. Additionally, the Director of Safety will oversee areas that include fire and life safety, hazardous materials and waste management, emergency management, infection control, and medical equipment management. This individual reviews and develops safety policies, procedures, and programs in each department and the hospital as a whole.

EDUCATION AND EXPERIENCE

Directors of Safety in a hospital typically require a bachelor's degree, while a master's degree in a related field is preferred. At least 5 years of safety experience in a hospital setting is required.

CORE COMPETENCIES AND SKILLS

- Thorough working knowledge of governmental regulations
- Ensure that the hospital is in compliance with all regulatory agencies

- Ability to manage a team that will help implement departmental and hospital-wide safety plans, policies, and procedures
- Strong analytical skills to select, evaluate, and react to safety and environmental reports, while also adhering to an annual budget
- Strong ability to communicate, especially when it relates to implementing or changing hospital safety measures
- Develop safety management performance indicators

COMPENSATION

The level of responsibility of the Directors of Safety will reflect a sizable salary. This individual should expect to make between $80,000 and $115,000. The individual's previous experience and the size and geographic location of the hospital will largely explain the range of salary.

EMPLOYMENT OUTLOOK

The Director of Safety plays a crucial role in maintaining the safety standards of the hospital. Significant experience and education are required to become a Director of Safety. This position will continue to have a future at hospitals as providers rely on these individuals to ensure they are in compliance with state and federal regulations.

FOR FURTHER INFORMATION

- American College of Healthcare Executives (http://www.ache.org)
- International Association for Healthcare Security and Safety (http://www.iahss.org)

34. DIRECTOR OF SOCIAL SERVICES

JOB DESCRIPTION

The Director of Social Services functions as the main figure within the Social Services Department, which is often in a rehabilitation center. It is this person's responsibility to identify and provide for the needs of each patient in order for the patient to reach his or her potential. While adhering to federal, state, and local guidelines and regulations, the Director of Social Services will additionally work with patients' families to ensure the smoothest possible transition beyond the hospital admission. This position will lead teams of social workers that help patients readjust to a new environment, whether it is in a rehabilitation center, a nursing home, or the patient's house.

EDUCATION AND EXPERIENCE

A bachelor's degree in social work is often the only educational requirement for becoming a Director of Social Services at smaller clinics. At larger rehabilitation centers, however, a master's in social work is the minimum. Experience in an acute or long-term care facility or a license that fulfills state and federal regulations is expected. Most Directors of Social Services have experience in management.

CORE COMPETENCIES AND SKILLS

- Outstanding interpersonal and communication skills in order to work with residents and residents' families
- Demonstrated ability to successfully council residents and assist them in achieving their maximum potential
- Familiarity with gathering and evaluating admissions reports, as well as preadmission screenings
- Excellent management skills including the ability to lead staff toward achieving the goals of the Social Services Department
- Ability to train staff when required
- Superior understand of local, state, and federal requirements
- Exceptional writing skills

COMPENSATION

The Director of Social Services is the lead of the Social Services Department. This individual should expect to receive a salary that reflects this position's leadership. Typically, the Director of Social Services will receive a salary between $80,000 and $110,000, with $95,000 being an appropriate average.

EMPLOYMENT OUTLOOK

The Director of Social Services plays a critical role in coordinating teams to offer services to the families of patients. This position is responsible for ensuring that patients and their families have a smooth discharge from the hospital. Social services workers provide information about post-admission services that could prevent readmissions, saving millions of dollars each year for the hospitals. Hospitals will continue to utilize social workers, making the director of this department a coveted position.

FOR FURTHER INFORMATION

- National Association of Social Workers (http://www.socialworkers.org)
- Society for Social Work Leadership in Healthcare (http://www.sswlhc.org)

35. DIRECTOR OF UTILIZATION MANAGEMENT

JOB DESCRIPTION

The Director of Utilization Management (UM) is in charge of meeting utilization goals and running utilization programs throughout the respective organization. This position is expected to monitor topics that include overutilization, underutilization, standardization, implementation of new technology, and assurance that hospital values are met. The Director of UM will also educate clinicians and staff on utilization findings as a way to brainstorm, promote, and implement efficient utilizations practices that are also in the patients' best interests. This individual is responsible for incorporating these practices, while monitoring the annual budgets of various departments.

EDUCATION AND EXPERIENCE

Directors of UM at hospitals are required to have a bachelor's degree, with a master's degree strongly preferred. Background education should include nursing, education, healthcare administration, or a business-related field. Directors of UM are typically expected to have 3 to 10 years experience in nursing, discharge planning, UM, or other related fields in an acute care setting.

CORE COMPETENCIES AND SKILLS

- Excellent communication and utilization skills, as this position will be required to work closely with clinicians, administrative staff, and other top management

- Superior analytical skills and experience working with reports and budgets
- Ability to manage and drive a team that will impact the entire hospital
- Proven ability to be proactive, as this person will be required to attend outside functions and programs that keep the individual up-to-date on potentially beneficial UM practices
- Outstanding education skills to help develop UM practices
- Demonstrated judgment and decision making

COMPENSATION

The Director of UM steers teams that ensure the hospital saves money through proper supply and resource use. This individual should expect to earn a salary between $75,000 and $100,000, which well reflects the position's leadership.

EMPLOYMENT OUTLOOK

Providers and health systems are constantly looking for practices that ultimately save money for the organization. This position plays a key role in developing strategies that allow the organization to run with as little waste as possible. Hospitals will continue to value the Director of UM, giving this position an optimistic future outlook.

FOR FURTHER INFORMATION

- American College of Healthcare Executives (http://www.ache.org)

Name:
JENNIFER WEISS WILKERSON
Title: Vice President, Planning and Business Development
Organization: Good Samaritan Hospital

1. **Briefly describe your job responsibilities.**
   I have direct responsibility for strategic planning and also oversee people/departments responsible for marketing, physician relations, joint replacement and spine programs, community outreach, emergency department patient navigation, retail, auxiliary and volunteers. I have 7 direct reports and another 10 people reporting through my reports. The majority of my responsibility is for Good Samaritan Hospital, although I also have some regional system strategic planning responsibility for MedStar Health's Baltimore region.

2. **Please give an example of what you would consider to be a "typical" day for you.**
   One of the things I like most about my job—but is also challenging—is that there are no typical days. I do attend a lot of meetings because much of my work is collaborative. I formally meet with physicians on a regular basis, and due to their schedules, these meetings typically take place very early in the morning or in the late evening. I meet with my direct reports (separately and/or together) on a regular basis and participate in twice weekly executive team meetings.

3. **What education or training do you have? Is it typical for your job?**
   I have an MHSA degree from the GWU [George Washington University]. As part of my education, I completed a yearlong

Name: JENNIFER WEISS WILKERSON

administrative residency at a hospital. Most people in my position have similar degrees including an MHSA or MBA.

4. What is the most challenging part of your job?
If I only had more time! Sometimes, I spend an entire day in meetings and then still have a full day's worth of work to accomplish. It is also challenging to work with physicians—many of them are independent (i.e., not employed by the hospital) so our incentives are not always aligned, and they may also work for a competitor hospital(s). We have to figure out ways to work together for mutual benefit and, most importantly, the benefit of our patients. External factors such as payment changes, new regulations or the impact of the economy can also be challenging to address.

5. What do you consider to be the best part of your job?
I enjoy working in a hospital—knowing that my work has positive impact on the lives of our patients and their families makes it worthwhile. I love that no day is the same, and that I am consistently facing new challenges. As a strategic planner, I am expected to develop new ideas and find best practices—both within our industry and others. This keeps my job interesting.

6. What path did you take to get to the job you are in today?
After college, I worked in a healthcare strategy consulting firm for 2 years as a research associate. This allowed me to develop an in-depth understanding of healthcare and strategic planning. I then decided to pursue an MHSA to further my career. I continued to work at the consulting firm, while I pursued my degree. After completing my coursework and administrative residency, I worked at another consulting firm for 2 years before going to work in a hospital again.

(*continued*)

Name: JENNIFER WEISS WILKERSON *(continued)*

7. What advice do you have for someone who is interested in a job such as yours?

Having "real world" experience before and/or during graduate school is very important. I look for this when hiring someone. This experience can be gained from full- or part-time employment, as well as internship or volunteer experiences. It is also important to understand hospital operations, regardless of whether or not you plan to work in operations as your career. Understanding the operational side of the business enables me to be more effective at developing and helping to execute strategy.

36. MANAGED CARE COORDINATOR

JOB DESCRIPTION

A Managed Care Coordinator works to coordinate referrals, authorizations, and payments for patient care services. The coordinator must ensure compliance with all guidelines and policies of the managed care organizations.

EDUCATION AND EXPERIENCE

The position requires a GED with an associate's degree preferred. Two years of experience in referral management or insurance managed care environment is preferred.

CORE COMPETENCIES AND SKILLS

- Outstanding interpersonal skills including the ability to effectively communicate with persons throughout the organization and in the community
- Ability to plan, direct, and evaluate staff
- Ability to think critically and provide reliable advice
- Excellent verbal and written communication skills
- Understand the insurance system and its rules and regulations
- Understand medical coding and terminology
- Ability to hold subordinates accountable for organizational goals

- Ability to develop and maintain a department budget
- Understand the regulations imposed by various agencies

COMPENSATION

Managed care coordinators earn in the range of $40,000 to $70,000 although the total salary will vary depending on the size and location of the hospital, and the education and experience of the candidate.

EMPLOYMENT OUTLOOK

Employment of medical and health services managers is expected to grow by 16% through 2018 according to the Bureau of Labor Statistics, faster than the average for all occupations.

FOR FURTHER INFORMATION

- HFMA (www.hfma.org)
- American Association of Health Plans (www.aahp.org)

37. OUTPATIENT CLINIC MANAGER

JOB DESCRIPTION

An Outpatient Clinic Manager is responsible for the daily operations of an outpatient care/clinic. In addition, the manager is also responsible for overseeing the efficient delivery of quality care, implementing policies, objective and procedures, evaluating personnel, developing reports and budgets, and coordinating events with managers.

EDUCATION AND EXPERIENCE

An undergraduate degree in healthcare management or business administration along with at least 2 years of administrative experience in a clinic setting is required for outpatient clinic managers.

CORE COMPETENCIES AND SKILLS

- Outstanding interpersonal skills including the ability to effectively communicate with persons throughout the organization and in the community
- Ability to plan, direct, and evaluate staff
- Ability to think critically and provide reliable advice

- Excellent verbal and written communication skills
- Ability to hold subordinates accountable for organizational goals
- Ability to develop and maintain a department budget
- Understand the regulations imposed by various agencies

COMPENSATION

Salaries for Outpatient Clinic Managers vary from one location to the next. The salaries range from $50,000 and go up to $140,000, with a median salary of $82,000 according to the Bureau of Labor Statistics.

EMPLOYMENT OUTLOOK

Job opportunities for Outpatient Clinic Managers are expected to increase faster than the average for all occupations. Job growth is expected to grow by 16% through 2018 according to the Bureau of Labor Statistics.

FOR FURTHER INFORMATION

- Managed Group Management Association (MGMA; www.mgma.com)
- National Institutes of Health (www.nih.gov)
- HFMA (www.hfma.org)

Name:
LAUREN WIXTED
Title: Manager, Surgical and Invasive Scheduling
Organization: Main Line Health

1. **Briefly describe your job responsibilities.**
   I am responsible for the day-to-day operations of the surgical scheduling department, which schedules elective surgeries for the operating rooms [ORs], surgery centers, and Electrophysiology/Catheterization labs in the system. I am also responsible for generating and reporting the surgical services data and I am an active member of systemwide OR and Department of Surgery committees.

2. **Please give an example of what you would consider to be a "typical" day for you.**
   Each day varies. I could be working on reports, analyzing data, attending meetings, fielding questions from the surgeons and their offices, working on the schedule with my staff and the OR managers, among other things.

   One thing I do everyday is review the surgical schedule at all sites for accuracy and ensure the OR teams are prepared for surgery.

3. **What education or training do you have? Is it typical for your job?**
   I received my Bachelor of Science Degree in Health Policy and Administration from the Pennsylvania State University and my MHSA degree from the GWU [George Washington University]. I completed my Administrative Fellowship at Main Line Health.

   For my position, a bachelor's degree is required.

(continued)

Name: LAUREN WIXTED *(continued)*

4. What is the most challenging part of your job?
Working to meet and exceed the needs of a variety of customers.

5. What do you consider to be the best part of your job?
Working with a variety of customers across the system.

6. What path did you take to get to the job you are in today?
After receiving my bachelor's degree, I knew I wanted to further my education in healthcare administration. I attended GW because of the program history, alumni involvement, location, and their residency requirement. Through completing a residency/fellowship, I was able to gain exposure and experience in a variety of areas. After the fellowship, I applied for and was offered my current position.

7. What advice do you have for someone who is interested in a job such as yours?
Healthcare is a wonderful field with endless opportunities. No matter what role you play, the patient and his/her safety come first.

38. QUALITY ASSURANCE COORDINATOR

JOB DESCRIPTION

The Quality Assurance Coordinator ensures the hospital is delivering high-quality and safe care to patients. Understanding the quality measures and standards is imperative to ensure the facility meets or exceeds these goals. The coordinators are in charge of the ongoing improvement of the quality assurance process, which entails analyzing statistical results and following up on any problems.

EDUCATION AND EXPERIENCE

Quality Assurance Coordinators typically have clinical experience working as an RN and therefore require the training and education to obtain that degree.

CORE COMPETENCIES AND SKILLS

- Outstanding interpersonal skills including the ability to effectively communicate with persons throughout the organization and in the community
- Ability to plan, direct, and evaluate staff
- Ability to think critically and provide reliable advice
- Excellent verbal and written communication skills
- Understand the laws, policies, and standards related to quality of patient care
- Ability to hold subordinates accountable for organizational goals
- Ability to develop and maintain a department budget
- Understand the regulations imposed by various agencies

COMPENSATION

A Quality Assurance Coordinator may earn in the range of $50,000 to $70,000. However, this figure varies depending on a number of variables including the size of the hospital and the region of the country in which the hospital is located. Quality Assurance Coordinators of smaller hospitals in more rural areas tend to earn less than their counterparts at large, urban hospitals.

EMPLOYMENT OUTLOOK

All hospitals need a Quality Assurance Coordinator and therefore this position will remain stable. With the transition of being paid for quality, the Quality Assurance Coordinators will have an even more important role in the organization.

FOR FURTHER INFORMATION

- American Health Quality Association (http://www.ahqa.org)

39. SENIOR CASE MANAGER

JOB DESCRIPTION

Senior Case Managers at hospitals have either a nursing or social worker background. This position works with doctors, nurses, caregivers, and family members, to develop a successful discharge plan for elderly and disabled patients. A Senior Case Manager closely communicates with insurance companies to ensure that hospital stays and services rendered are covered. With the assistance of the patient's medical team, the Senior Case Manager will determine when the patient is ready for discharge. When a patient requires rehabilitation or needs to stay in a nursing home, the Senior Case Manager will coordinate with the respective institution to ensure that a bed and the proper services are available.

EDUCATION AND EXPERIENCE

A bachelor's degree in social work or nursing is often the minimum requirement for this field, with a preference for a master's degree. Many healthcare providers require their Senior Case Managers to become licensed social workers or RNs. Experience of 5 to 10 years working in a hospital setting is expected. Any experience working with insurance company's contracts is also desirable.

CORE COMPETENCIES AND SKILLS

- Proven ability to work within a multidisciplined environment
- Working knowledge of various insurance plan regulations
- Superior knowledge of a hospital care setting
- Excellent communication skills, as this individual will be required to work closely with families and caregivers of patients
- Excellent writing ability
- Demonstrated ability to lead a medical team through safe patient discharge plans

COMPENSATION

Senior Case Managers should expect to earn anywhere from $50,000 to $70,000 a year. This salary is largely dependent upon experience, background education, provider geographic location, and the position's responsibilities.

EMPLOYMENT OUTLOOK

Providers rely on Senior Case Managers to facilitate elderly and disabled discharge plans. They play a key role of communicating with the medical staff, insurance companies, and the families and caregivers of patients. Hospitals will continue to look for individuals who have the right blend of skills for senior case management positions.

FOR FURTHER INFORMATION

- Case Management Society of America (http://www.cmsa.org)

40. VOLUNTEER SERVICES COORDINATOR

JOB DESCRIPTION

The Volunteer Services Coordinator is responsible for working with and overseeing volunteers of the hospital, which can range in number from tens to hundreds based on the size of the facility. Volunteers participate in a multitude of tasks throughout the hospital from patient transport to working at the front desk. The coordinator must make sure the volunteers have the proper training and the state-mandated records, conduct the interviewing and hiring process, and be the point person for these employees. The coordinator will also work to create policies, job descriptions, and funding events.

EDUCATION AND EXPERIENCE

Volunteer Services Coordinators typically have a bachelor's degree, with a minimum of 3 years of experience in nonprofit fundraising, recruiting, marketing, and leading groups of people.

CORE COMPETENCIES AND SKILLS

- Outstanding interpersonal skills including the ability to effectively communicate with persons throughout the organization and in the community
- Ability to plan, direct, and evaluate staff
- Ability to think critically and provide reliable advice
- Excellent verbal and written communication skills
- Understand the regulations associated with volunteers working within hospitals
- Ability to develop and maintain a department budget

COMPENSATION

A Volunteer Services Coordinator may earn in the range of $30,000 to $60,000. However, this figure varies depending on a number of variables including the size of the hospital and the region of the country in which the hospital is located. Volunteer Services Coordinators of smaller hospitals in more rural areas tend to earn less than their counterparts at large, urban hospitals.

EMPLOYMENT OUTLOOK

Volunteers are essential for the function of hospitals throughout the country and economic challenges increase the importance of these individuals. This position is going to remain stable and a part of all healthcare organizations.

FOR FURTHER INFORMATION

- Association for Healthcare Volunteer Resource Professionals (http://www.ahvrp.org)

5 ■ CAREERS IN PHYSICIAN PRACTICE MANAGEMENT

41. ASSOCIATE ADMINISTRATOR

JOB DESCRIPTION

The Associate Administrator serves as backup for the Chief Executive Officer (CEO)/Administrator of the clinic. Only mid to large clinics have the resources to support an Associate Administrator. The role of the Associate Administrator is similar to the CEO/Administrator in terms of their work with developing and implementing the clinic's strategic plan and for oversight of all clinic operations, including human resources (HR), finance, compliance with legal and regulatory requirements, information technology (IT), medical records, accreditation, and reimbursement by third-party payers. Depending on the size of the clinic, the Associate Administrator might be given direct responsibility for overseeing particular service lines.

EDUCATION AND EXPERIENCE

Education and experience varies depending upon the size and complexity of the physician practice. Smaller practices will frequently hire persons with a bachelor's degree in either business or (preferably) healthcare administration in the role of Associate Administrator. Large physician practices typically require a master's degree in business or healthcare administration. Most of the larger physician practices require a minimum of 3 years of physician practice management experience in a leadership role.

CORE COMPETENCIES AND SKILLS

- Outstanding interpersonal skills including the ability to effectively communicate with persons throughout the organization
- Excellent verbal and written communication skills
- Demonstrated track record of developing and maintaining collaborative relationships among diverse groups, including board members, medical staff, as well as key external stakeholders

- Ability to build and maintain appropriate peer relationships to facilitate organizational objectives
- Skill in establishing and maintaining effective working relationships with employees, policy-making bodies, third-party payers, patients, and the public
- Specific knowledge of finance, marketing, human resource management, and public relations in healthcare
- Skill in exercising a high degree of initiative, judgment, discretion, and decision making to achieve the mission of the clinics
- Ability to identify trends and motivate the workforce toward changes needed to remain competitive
- Ability to identify opportunities for improvement and change
- Ability to utilize standard computer-related applications
- Skill in analyzing financial, volume, and market data

COMPENSATION

Associate Administrators can expect to earn between $55,000 and $110,000 per year. This salary will vary depending on the size, location, and medical specialty of the practice. Small practices will typically use the CEO/Administrator to fill this role. Only mid-to large-size physician practices can afford to have their own Associate Administrator.

EMPLOYMENT OUTLOOK

The U.S. Department of Labor projects strong growth of physician practice managers with faster than average growth. A significant part of this growth is due to changes projected to occur as a result of healthcare reform that will shift the focus of care from the hospital to the physician clinic.

FOR FURTHER INFORMATION

- Medical Group Management Association (MGMA; http://www.mgma.com)
- American Medical Group Association (http://www.amga.org)

Name:
MOHAMED ALYAJOURI
Title: Director, Quality Improvement and Informatics
Organization: The Corvallis Clinic, Corvallis, Oregon

1. Briefly describe your job responsibilities.

With this new role in the organization, I am responsible for overall planning, development, and implementation of healthcare informatics programs, products, and services; addressing the clinical needs of patients; and to support the physicians and their staff. I will oversee and monitor the development and implementation of quality improvement programs and initiatives. I also have our Health Information Services department reporting to me.

2. Please give an example of what you would consider to be a "typical" day for you.

A typical day for me would start with a follow-up with any physicians and clinical staff who may have e-mailed or called me and needed me to address a specific Electronic Medical Record (EMR) workflow, issue, and/or potential need for workflow redesign. Sometimes it may be engaging them in a one-on-one training session that they may have wanted. I also make daily rounds throughout the providers' hallways and check on them and their staff. During these rounds, I will address concerns or provide immediate support with the EMR, and sometimes take major issues back to our IT staff. Later on, I will work on some ongoing reports from our billing system as well as the EMR. These reports are intended to monitor provider patterns in patient care and referrals. I also manage several operations-related projects, and thus typically manage the daily or weekly status conference calls with our vendors. These calls are usually about ongoing projects involving the clinical systems. Additionally, I am in about two to three meetings a day with different groups within our organization.

(*continued*)

Name: MOHAMED ALYAJOURI *(continued)*

3. What education or training do you have? Is it typical for your job?

My educational background is a bachelor's degree in health management and policy. I am also currently finishing up a Master's in Public Health. I was sent on several application and role-specific training courses by my organization. I represent the Corvallis Clinic at User Group and system vendor conferences. The education and training is typical for my specific job.

4. What is the most challenging part of your job?

The most challenging part of my job is not having an answer or a solution right away. People expect me to be an expert at what I do sometimes but it's not always the case. I have to do some research or digging around before I can come up with a solution to a problem. I may rely on help from my other team members or from other coworkers and that could take time. In a physician's world, time is so crucial.

5. What do you consider to be the best part of your job?

The best part of my job is my daily interactions with people. I love to meet with our providers and clinical staff and work with them on making their job easier. I love training our doctors on a new workflow or showing them a tip or trick that could save them time and allow them to go home early.

6. What path did you take to get to the job you are in today?

Six years ago, I started out as a nonpaid undergraduate intern with the Corvallis Clinic, and then was hired upon graduation to work as a Financial Analyst. Three years later, I was promoted to an Operations Analyst. Last week, I was promoted to my new job, Director of Quality Improvement and Informatics.

Name: MOHAMED ALYAJOURI

7. What advice do you have for someone who is interested in a job such as yours?

First of all get the education. For your first job, don't be afraid to take an entry-level job and get your feet in the door. You will learn so much about the organization by doing the tedious day-to-day manual tasks. Once you're in, distinguish yourself from others by taking on or helping with challenging projects. This will demonstrate your willingness to work and allows you to showcase your problem-solving skills. Organizations love to hire problem solvers who can work on their own and can show initiative.

42. BILLING MANAGER

JOB DESCRIPTION

The Billing Manager is responsible for ensuring maximization of cash flow, budget oversight, revenue cycle management, and operation of the billing department. The manager is also responsible for staffing and training of the department.

EDUCATION AND EXPERIENCE

A bachelor's degree in business administration, finance, healthcare, or a related area of study. Minimum of 5 years of management experience in private practice or hospital billing.

CORE COMPETENCIES AND SKILLS

- Outstanding interpersonal skills including the ability to effectively communicate with persons throughout the organization
- Excellent verbal and written communication skills
- Understanding of the billing and revenue cycle process
- Understanding of financial, insurance, and practice operation regulations
- Proficient in operations of computerized billing and electronic health record systems

- Promotes excellent customer service with all staff members and works to ensure customer service measures are achieved
- Ability to identify opportunities for improvement and change

COMPENSATION

The Billing Manager can expect to earn between $70,000 and $100,000 per year. This salary will vary depending on the size, location, and medical specialty of the practice.

EMPLOYMENT OUTLOOK

Billing Manager is a position needed in every physician practice and therefore will continue to be in demand. An effective Billing Manager with a great understanding of physician payments and regulations is an integral part of the long-term success of a practice.

FOR FURTHER INFORMATION

- MGMA (http://www.mgma.com)
- American Medical Group Association (http://www.amga.org)
- Healthcare Billing and Management Association (www.hbma.org)

43. CHIEF EXECUTIVE OFFICER/ADMINISTRATOR

JOB DESCRIPTION

In many physician practices, the titles CEO and Administrator are used to mean the same thing. The difference is a function of the size and complexity of the practice. Regardless of the size of the practice, the CEO/Administrator is responsible for developing and implementing the clinic's strategic plan and for general oversight of all clinic operations, including human resources (HR), finance, compliance with legal and regulatory requirements, IT, medical records, accreditation, and reimbursement by third-party payers. The CEO/Administrator represents the clinic in negotiations with other healthcare organizations and commercial payers. The CEO/Administrator reports to a Board of Directors that is typically made up of physicians currently working in the practice.

EDUCATION AND EXPERIENCE

Education and experience vary depending upon the size and complexity of the physician practice. Smaller practices are frequently managed by persons with a bachelor's degree in either business or (preferably) healthcare administration. Large physician practices typically require a master's degree in business or healthcare administration. Most of the larger physician practices require a minimum of 5 years of physician practice management experience in a leadership role.

CORE COMPETENCIES AND SKILLS

- Outstanding interpersonal skills including the ability to effectively communicate with persons throughout the organization
- Excellent verbal and written communication skills
- Demonstrated track record of developing and maintaining collaborative relationships among diverse groups, including board members, medical staff, as well as key external stakeholders
- Ability to build and maintain appropriate peer relationships to facilitate organizational objectives
- Skill in establishing and maintaining effective working relationships with employees, policy-making bodies, third-party payers, patients, and the public
- Specific knowledge of finance, marketing, HR management, and public relations in healthcare
- Skill in exercising a high degree of initiative, judgment, discretion, and decision making to achieve the clinic's mission
- Ability to identify trends and motivate the workforce toward changes needed to remain competitive
- Ability to identify opportunities for improvement and change
- Ability to utilize standard computer-related applications
- Skill in analyzing financial, volume, and market data

COMPENSATION

The CEO/Administrator can expect to earn between $64,000 and $160,000 per year. This salary will vary depending on the size, location, and medical specialty of the practice. Small primary care practices (Family Practice, Internal Medicine, Pediatrics, and Obstetrics/Gynecology) typically pay less than similar size specialty practices. The salary in larger, multispecialty practices is generally higher than in smaller multispecialty practices.

EMPLOYMENT OUTLOOK

The U.S. Department of Labor projects strong growth of CEO/ Administrators with faster than average growth. A significant part of this growth is due to changes projected to occur as a result of healthcare reform that will shift the focus of care from the hospital to the physician clinic.

FOR FURTHER INFORMATION

- MGMA (http://www.mgma.com)
- American Medical Group Association (http://www.amga.org)

Name:
PAUL BRASHNYK
Title: Clinic Manager
Organization: UW Medicine Neighborhood Clinics

1. Briefly describe your job responsibilities.

I currently manage a clinic that is part of a large healthcare system in Seattle, Washington. I managed private practices prior to working for a larger system. I have found that in both types of organizations, the practice administrator and/or clinic manager is responsible for the following: (a) In a health care system, your support in internal (i.e., HR department, a finance department, IT department, etc.). (b) In private practice, your support is external (i.e., professional associations, CPA, Independent Physicians Association [IPA], etc.). Regardless of the type of organization, a practice administrator and/or clinic manager is responsible for varying degrees of the following: business operations, financial management, HR management, information management, organizational governance, patient care systems, quality management, and risk management. I currently work for a health system, 80% of my Full Time Equivalent (FTE) is allocated to the clinic and 20% of my FTE is allocated to the network for network projects.

2. Please give an example of what you would consider to be a "typical" day for you.

A typical day can vary. In the forefront of my mind on any given day is ensuring that the clinic is running smoothly. A typical day might include moving from a morning huddle with clinic staff, conducting staff meetings, participating and/or leading a network-level meeting

(*continued*)

Name: PAUL BRASHNYK *(continued)*

on an area that I have been assigned responsibility, meeting with peer managers, interviewing staff and facilitating panel interviews, reviewing financial reports, developing strategies to meet organizational objectives, meeting one-on-one with staff for coaching. As a clinic manager, you can find yourself doing something more macro at one point in the day (i.e., budgeting, planning a new network clinic) and then end your day doing something more micro in nature, but equally important (i.e., problem solving a process issue with an employee, problem solving a patient concern, etc.). The key is bringing enthusiasm, passion, and a sincere commitment to great patient care to all.

3. What education or training do you have? Is it typical for your job?

I have a MPH in Health Policy and Management with a focus on Health Care Management from Oregon State University. I also have a BS in Psychology from the University of Oregon, as well as a BS in Health Care Administration with a minor in Business Administration from Oregon State University. I have approximately 12 years of practice management experience (10 years primary care and 2 years specialty). While living in Corvallis, Oregon, I served on the contracting committee of our local Independent Practice Association (IPA) from 2000 until my move to Seattle in 2007. I was on the management team of a $3 million, 3-year American International Healthcare Alliance (AIHA)/USAID grant, the primary objective was to establish three primary care clinics in Uzhgorod, Ukraine. I served on the board of the Oregon Medical Group Management Association (OMGMA), ultimately serving as president at the time of my move to Seattle in 2007. I graduated from the Leadership Corvallis Program in 2001 (a leadership development program) and ultimately served on the organization's board as their treasurer, until my move to Seattle. Healthcare management requires you to have a broad, well-developed skill set; it is becoming more and more common to see clinic managers with graduate degrees.

Name: PAUL BRASHNYK

4. What is the most challenging part of your job?

The healthcare environment is ever-changing and turbulent. While this pace of change can be an exciting part of your work, it can also be a challenging piece. Being able to manage organizational change is an important skill when working as a clinic manager. As a clinic manager, you must lead your organization through many changes. Some of these changes can be hard on your staff and physicians. As a manager, you are challenged to lead the way in times of change, all the while maintaining an organization with high employee morale and an unwavering commitment to quality care, and a continued commitment to putting the patient first at all times. You must be creative, enthusiastic, and genuine at all times.

5. What do you consider to be the best part of your job?

The best part of my job is the satisfaction I get from knowing that I have played an important role in a patient's overall healthcare experience. I also enjoy building teams and leading by example. People are an organization's greatest asset. As a clinic manager, you have to surround yourself with smart, capable, skilled people and you have to encourage and coach your team so that they can provide the best care possible to your patient base, every patient, every time. As a manager, you play an important role in helping your individual team members reach their own personal goals.

6. What path did you take to get to the job you are in today?

As a high school student, I worked in a doctor's office filing charts. While in college, I worked part time as a receptionist at a doctor's office. After graduating with my initial undergraduate degree in psychology, I worked part time with clients at a weight loss clinic and part time in the business office of a private physician group practice. After 3 years, I decided I wanted to pursue physician group practice management full time so I pursued a second undergraduate degree in that field as well as a graduate degree in

(*continued*)

Name: PAUL BRASHNYK *(continued)*

that field. My first job out of graduate school was managing a private primary care physician group practice. During that time, I also became active in the MGMA and the OMGMA, ultimately serving as president of the OMGMA. While in Oregon, I was also involved with the AIHA. I also worked as an adjunct healthcare administration instructor at a local college. I then relocated to the Seattle area and managed a specialty clinic. I had a strong desire to work for a large integrated health system. Through word-of–mouth, I became aware of an opportunity with my current employer and I decided to pursue it.

7. What advice do you have for someone who is interested in a job such as yours?

I think the key is to get healthcare management and/or healthcare organization experience any way you can. Set up informational interviews with individuals who have positions similar to the one you want. Listen to the advice that is given to you in these informational interviews. If you are looking for a position, do not hold out for the "perfect" job. Be willing to take a less than the perfect job, give 100% to that job, volunteer to take on extra projects that interest you, and perform well, and you will rise within that organization and/or you will develop the skills needed to take the next step. Gaining experience any way you can is key. Education is obviously important and essential, but having the real world, relevant work experience to pair with your education is very attractive to employers.

44. CHIEF INFORMATION OFFICER

JOB DESCRIPTION

The Chief Information Officer (CIO) is responsible for leading the strategic direction of the information technology (IT) resources and practices in the physician practice. The CIO will be responsible for providing overall IT leadership and for establishing IT goals within the framework of the practice's goals and objectives. This individual will collaborate with leaders at the highest level of the organization and manage a team of professionals who are accountable for the delivery of all information technology services in the practice. The CIO is responsible for the management of multiple information and communications systems and projects, including the physician electronic medical record (EMR) system.

EDUCATION AND EXPERIENCE

A bachelor's degree in healthcare management or IT is the required educational preparation with a master's degree the preferred credential. Typically, 5 years of progressively responsible experience in health IT is required.

CORE COMPETENCIES AND SKILLS

- Outstanding interpersonal skills including the ability to effectively communicate with persons throughout the organization, including clinicians and support staff
- Excellent verbal and written communication skills
- Significant experience in data processing methods and procedures, and computer software systems
- Systems design and development process, including requirements analysis, feasibility studies, software design, programming, pilot testing, installation, evaluation, and operational management
- Oversee the management and coordination of all administrative reporting activities for the clinic
- Familiarity with the design, management, and operation of health IT systems
- Proven ability to link and apply complex technologies to business strategies
- Experience in negotiating contracts with vendors, contractors, and others
- Ability to analyze and resolve complex issues, both logical and interpersonal.

COMPENSATION

CIO's in physician clinics earn salaries in the range of $80,000 to $200,000 per year. However, this figure varies depending on a number of variables, including the size of the clinic and the region of the country in which the clinic is located. CIO's of larger multispecialty clinics tend to earn more than their counterparts at smaller single specialty clinics.

EMPLOYMENT OUTLOOK

The overall outlook for CIO jobs in medium and large physician clinics is expected to increase over the coming years. The reason for the increase is due to need for clinics to make health technology an increasing part of clinical and administrative operations. There remain a number of federal financial and regulatory incentives to vigorously move into health IT. CIO's are a relatively new occupation and it is difficult to assess turnover, but anecdotal reports indicate that CIO's turn over at a brisk pace to accept roles with increasing salary and responsibility.

FOR FURTHER INFORMATION

- Medical Group Management Association (http://www.mgma.com)
- American Medical Group Association (http://www.amga.org)

45. CLINICAL RESEARCH DIRECTOR

JOB DESCRIPTION

A Clinical Research Director can have a variety of responsibilities in the physician practice management setting. Essential responsibilities include providing leadership to clinical research teams, reviewing and implementing appropriate research protocols, evaluating the safety and efficacy of research data, and helping to analyze and present research data. Another primary responsibility is preparing budgets for research activities and serving as a liaison to pharmaceutical and biotechnology companies.

EDUCATION AND EXPERIENCE

A bachelor's degree is a minimum expectation for most Clinical Research Directors, although many Clinical Research Directors are master's prepared. Educational background should be in a scientific or medical discipline, or another related field. Prior experience in clinical practice and research activities is important. Many employers expect clinical research directors to have at least 7 to 10 years of hands-on experience in clinical research.

CORE COMPETENCIES AND SKILLS

- Knowledge of aspects of clinical research and management and operations

- Knowledge of the drug development process and applicable regulatory requirements and guidelines
- Excellent interpersonal skills
- Excellent organizational skills
- Demonstrated ability to teach, mentor, and manage a team of employees
- Effective computer skills
- Strong written communication ability

COMPENSATION

The majority of Clinical Research Directors make between $60,000 and $100,000 annually. They can make as little as $40,000 or as much as $130,000. Directors with broader responsibilities at larger firms will likely earn a higher salary. Similarly, those working in a busier, urban area stand to make more than someone living in a rural setting.

EMPLOYMENT OUTLOOK

As the healthcare industry in the United States continues to grow, the employment outlook for this field continues to remain strong. New technologies and clinical breakthroughs, as well as the continued growth of the pharmaceutical industry, also continue to fuel the need for these positions.

FOR FURTHER INFORMATION

- National Institutes of Health (http://www.nih.gov)

Name:
NANCY L. FARRELL
Title: Chief Administrative Officer
Organization: Weill Cornell Physician Organization
Weill Cornell Medical College

1. Briefly describe your job responsibilities.

Principal administrative officer for the management of an 850 physician, multispecialty academic group practice

Responsible for recommending and implementing governance policies and procedures

Directs the clinical practice operations and fiscal management of the Physician Organization (PO), including billing and collection activities: $1 billion in medical services resulting in collections of $500 million

Directs the PO's adaptation to healthcare reform, including clinical transformation and new physician payment models

Directs all business development activities including strategic and operations planning and the development of new programs and practices, including business planning, design, and occupancy of the new medical office facilities

Coordinates all strategic planning and joint programs including clinical IT and facilities development with New York Presbyterian Hospital

Directs ambulatory patient care experience improvement efforts including change management and human resource (HR) development

Directs all managed care contracting and contract compliance activities

Directs investment in clinical IT

Name: NANCY L. FARRELL

2. Please give an example of what you would consider to be a "typical" day for you.

A typical day is a series of group meetings and conference calls with specific agendas to push along various projects that have been selected through the planning and governance process as priorities. The meetings are less often about current operations and financial performance that I delegate to the managers who work for me, and more often about strategy and choices of where to invest resources, improve an interorganizational or intraorganizational relationship, or how to anticipate and/or correct a problem. In between those meetings, I write and answer hundreds of e-mails, and write or review and share draft documents. I spend time in the early evenings going to professional and community meetings or events with organizations that I support or where I volunteer my time.

3. What education or training do you have? Is it typical for your job?

I have a BA degree in microbiology, an MPA in health economics, and an Master's in Business Administration (MBA) in economics. I have 35 years management experience working in an academic medical center of which more than 20 have been managing a faculty practice plan or academic multispecialty group practice, a management subspecialty in itself. Master's-level training is typical, although not necessarily two master's degrees.

4. What is the most challenging part of your job?

The most challenging part of my job given my age and female gender and the fact that I am not a physician has been to establish credibility with the academic medical center clinical faculty and leadership that good medical science and good management are positively correlated, not inversely correlated.

(*continued*)

Name: NANCY L. FARRELL (*continued*)

5. What do you consider to be the best part of your job?

The best part of the job is the interaction on a daily basis with very smart medical faculty and staff who are seeking to advance medical research, education, and patient care. There may be organizational and resource difficulties to overcome every day too, but the interactions are what keep the days stimulating.

6. What path did you take to get to the job you are in today?

I was pre-med in college and decided then that medicine was not the best choice for me. Immediately after college I worked at a medical school in a research laboratory for 3 years, while I went to graduate school in the evening for my MPA healthcare degree. When I finished the course work for my first master's degree, I switched positions to take an administrative residency at an academic medical center while continuing on in the evening to obtain an MBA. For 10 years, I was a traditional hospital administrator managing inpatient and support services. Then I switched to the medical school to manage the faculty practice plan for a decade. For 5 years, I worked for two academic medical centers doing organizational development, strategic planning, and managed care contracting, returning once again to faculty practice plan management at the medical college where I have continued to the present.

7. What advice do you have for someone who is interested in a job such as yours?

Healthcare management has become much more specialized than when I was finishing graduate school. Today, it is necessary to have a specialization or focus for the early years of a career, such as strategic planning, finance, health policy, managed care, hospital service lines, or physician practice management. A prospective faculty practice plan executive needs to learn the specific areas of practice management operations, physician billing, reimbursement and compensation, regulations and procedures, academic medical center

Name: NANCY L. FARRELL

governance, ambulatory care facility design, and HR management as well as the generalist areas of financial management, auditing, planning, project management, and change management. Most of all, the prospective executive needs to learn how academic physicians function while carrying out their mission of research, education, and patient care so as to be able to provide appropriate management infrastructure and support services. A sense of humor always helps.

46. DIRECTOR OF UTILIZATION AND CASE MANAGEMENT

JOB DESCRIPTION

The Director of Utilization and Case Management is responsible for strategic direction, leadership, planning, organization, and general management for all aspects of the Managed Care Department. The Director is responsible for ensuring effective utilization of services. Working with the clinical departments, Manager of Utilization and Case Management, and Medical Director(s), the Director directs the design, implementation, and evaluation for a standardized case management model that results in standardizing a care coordination model throughout the clinic, with ongoing metrics for evaluation and improvement of patient care. The Director is responsible for ensuring that maximum incentive payments are received for various case management programs.

EDUCATION AND EXPERIENCE

A bachelor's degree in health or business administration is required with a master's degree in one of these disciplines as the preferred educational preparation. Typically, 5 years of experience in a medical care delivery organization is required. Four years of experience in peer review with quality management responsibility is also required. Five years of nursing or patient care experience is preferred. Some clinics prefer nationally recognized certification as a Risk/Compliance Officer.

CORE COMPETENCIES AND SKILLS

- Outstanding interpersonal skills including the ability to effectively communicate with persons throughout the organization
- Excellent verbal and written communication skills

- Regularly communicates with physicians and providers regarding quality and risk management problems, issues, and potential resolutions
- Ability to assist supervisors, managers, and directors in the development, review, and revision of clinical policies and procedures
- Responds to requests for quality management intervention and provides trouble shooting assistance. Maintains strict confidentiality related to medical records and other data generated by departmental functions
- Monitors patient complaints by overseeing concerns and complaints reported through clinical staff. Addresses, resolves, and follows-up as needed
- Addresses and follows-up on alleged violations of rules, regulations, policies, procedures, and standards of conduct. Develops a program for such violations
- Experience in conducting risk assessments on potential and actual litigations and assisting insurers and counsel with defense issues
- Ability to identify trends and motivate workforce toward changes needed to adopt and remain competitive
- Promotes excellent customer service with all staff members and works to ensure customer service measures are achieved
- Ability to identify opportunities for improvement and change
- Ability to utilize standard computer-related applications

COMPENSATION

Directors of Utilization and Case Management can expect to earn between $65,000 and $115,000 per year. This salary will vary depending on the size, location, and medical specialty of the practice. Small practices will typically use the CEO/Administrator to fill this role. Only mid to large size physician practices can afford to have their own Director of Utilization and Case Management.

EMPLOYMENT OUTLOOK

The U.S. Department of Labor projects strong growth of Directors of Utilization and Case Management with faster than average growth. A significant part of this growth is due to changes projected to occur as a result of healthcare reform that will shift the focus of care from the hospital to the physician clinic.

FOR FURTHER INFORMATION

- MGMA (http://www.mgma.com)
- American Medical Group Association (http://www.amga.org)

Name:
JENNIFER N. LOCKHART
Title: Practice Administrator, Obstetrics and Gynecology
Organization: Johns Hopkins Community Physicians

1. Briefly describe your job responsibilities.

I am the Practice Administrator for a community Obstetrics and Gynecology clinic that is part the very large and ever-expanding Johns Hopkins Health System. As the Administrator, I am responsible for the daily operations and financial viability of the specialty practice. Daily operations include the following: budget management and the hiring, supervision, staffing, evaluation, and discipline of staff. In conjunction with the medical providers and staff, I work to develop and implement common priorities and goals related to providing optimal customer service, maximizing operational efficiency, ensuring financial viability, and rendering high-quality healthcare services. I also demonstrate, through leadership example, visible organizational support and a positive attitude, a positive work environment and enhance provider and staff morale. I am also responsible for fostering a positive relationship with the local community served by the health center. I supervise five medical providers (three physicians and two nurse midwives) and seven support staff (three nurses, two medical assistants, and two medical office assistants). It is not required by my job role, but I sometimes use my nursing background to help assist the support staff with triaging patients.

2. Please give an example of what you would consider to be a "typical" day for you.

Administrators tend to wear many hats, which doesn't always lend to having a "typical day." However, there are some common activities

(*continued*)

Name: JENNIFER N. LOCKHART *(continued)*

that happen almost daily. I usually begin my day by performing staff and environmental rounds to identify if there are any pertinent issues or concerns that need to be addressed. From there, I tend to any voice mails and e-mail messages that are waiting for me. I review the payroll that is submitted bi-weekly, and address any issues of lateness or absenteeism with the staff. I spend a lot of time analyzing statistics and auditing reports, such as the number of patients seen, number of patients who missed appointments, number of deliveries and surgeries, incomplete physician bills, the list goes on and on. I attend monthly meetings with the other practice administrators from the clinic sites located in our region, as well as monthly OBGYN management meetings with the regional office and medical directors to discuss current practices, documentation, planning for events, staffing needs, and how the practices can continue to grow. Our patient appointments are scheduled through a call center. Each week, I perform customer service audits on the calls being handled by the agents. Lastly, most complaints, issues, or concerns from the patients, staff, or providers are directed to me for resolution. You generally receive more complaints and criticism than accolades in my role, but I work hard to find solutions to all that is put in front of me.

3. What education or training do you have? Is it typical for your job?

I received my bachelor's degree in nursing from the University of Maryland at Baltimore, School of Nursing. I received two master's degrees from Johns Hopkins University, one from the School of Nursing in Health Systems Management and the other from the Carey Business School in Business Administration. Additionally, I received some on-the-job leadership training, while holding the position of Women's Surgery Coordinator for the Johns Hopkins Hospital.

Name: JENNIFER N. LOCKHART

4. What is the most challenging part of your job?

Managing people and initiating the "crucial conversations" is difficult for most managers. It is normal for people to make mistakes and not meet expectations, and it is my job to handle these situations as they arise. It is human nature to want everyone to like you. The fact of the matter is, when you are a manager, your staff is not going to like every decision that you make. Even the best managers encounter this issue, especially when you are the bearer of bad news. I have accepted the fact that work is not a popularity contest, it is work. And as much as I would like to be able to be a friend to my employees, I believe it is important to maintain a degree of distance so that personal relationships with individual employees do not interfere with my ability to effectively manage the staff or give off the appearance of favoring one employee over another. It's ironic, but in my experience, employees often dislike managers who try to please everyone.

Another challenge for me, as I am certain it is for other managers, is getting my staff to understand what my job duties entail. I know that they often see me in my office on the computer or heading to a meeting and do not fully understand what my job is like. A lot of what I do involves making decisions on their behalf and being held accountable for the actions of my staff, both good and bad. Because most of this takes place "behind the scenes," you are often misunderstood and seldom rewarded by the staff for your best ideas, decisions, or accomplishments.

5. What do you consider to be the best part of your job?

I am a people person and enjoy my daily interactions with the providers, staff, and patients. I enjoy being able to set and accomplish goals and knowing that I had an integral role in the changes that are made in the department. I enjoy bringing a group of individuals together and seeing them begin to function as a team. I really enjoy helping my staff reach their potential and advance in their careers through the development of their skills and abilities.

(*continued*)

Name: JENNIFER N. LOCKHART (*continued*)

My employees appreciate that I make accommodations for them to attend conferences, workshops, or seminars that are related to their job roles. I encourage them to become a part of professional organizations and to become involved with community service or volunteer groups.

6. What path did you take to get to the job you are in today?

I am not sure that my personal path to this job is what most people would take. I began my career as an operating room nurse, specializing in women's surgery. Over a 10-year period, I quickly progressed from staff nurse to charge nurse to Women's Surgery Coordinator to Operating Room Coordinator. I liked the leadership role and decided to attend graduate school for a MBA and a Master's in the Science of Nursing, focusing on health systems management. Toward the end of my master's program, I began to look for management positions that were linked to my areas of interest, women's health and surgery.

7. What advice do you have for someone who is interested in a job such as yours?

Think of the managers you have previously worked for, emulate their good qualities and try to learn from those that weren't so successful. Maintain open lines of communication with your staff. The more accessible you are to your staff, the more you will learn about them and what is happening in your work environment. I know it is easy to hide out in an office with the door closed, but it will only hinder your effectiveness as a leader in the long run. I believe that maintaining a good balance between work and your personal life is important. Being a manager can be stressful at times and having activities that can relieve stress will help you keep your sanity.

47. DIRECTOR OF CLINICAL OPERATIONS

JOB DESCRIPTION

The Director of Clinical Operations directs, supervises and coordinates all clinic operations and physician activities. This involves either direct or indirect responsibility for staffing, budgeting, fiscal planning, telecommunications and equipment purchases and maintenance, and facility development. This is carried out through daily interaction with physicians, managers, supervisors, and senior administrative personnel. The Director also supervises a staff of supervisors, clinical coordinators, medical assistants, and other clinical support to provide for the healthcare needs of clinic patients and their families. The Director works collaboratively with medical staff on patient care issues and department direction, and directs projects aimed at improving department services and overall clinic goals.

EDUCATION AND EXPERIENCE

Directors of Clinical Operations typically possess a bachelor's degree and current registered nurse (RN) license. A master's degree in healthcare or business administration is the preferred educational preparation. Most persons in this role have a minimum of 3 years experience in clinic operations.

CORE COMPETENCIES AND SKILLS

- Outstanding interpersonal skills including the ability to effectively communicate with persons throughout the organization
- Excellent verbal and written communication skills
- Demonstrated track record of developing and maintaining collaborative relationships among diverse groups, including board members, medical staff, as well as key external stakeholders
- Ability to build and maintain appropriate peer relationships to facilitate organizational objectives
- Must have an in-depth working knowledge of regulatory licensing, certification, and accreditation applicable in clinic environments
- Experience in balancing patient care priorities and department needs
- Ability to perform multiple tasks with multiple priorities
- Leads the development and implementation of annual capital and operating budgets

- Facilitate smooth operation of clinic operations by supporting policies and by the ability to act as a mentor and resource person for team members
- Motivate staff and influence positive morale
- Ability to utilize electronic medical record and related computer applications

COMPENSATION

The Director of Clinical Operations can expect to earn between $50,000 and $90,000 per year. This salary will vary depending on the size, location, and medical specialty of the practice. Small practices will typically use the CEO/Administrator to fill this role. Only mid-to large-size physician practices can afford to have their own Director of Clinical Operations.

EMPLOYMENT OUTLOOK

The U.S. Department of Labor projects strong growth of Directors of Clinical Operations with faster than average growth. A significant part of this growth is due to changes projected to occur as a result of healthcare reform that will shift the focus of care from the hospital to the physician clinic.

FOR FURTHER INFORMATION

- MGMA (http://www.mgma.com)

Name:
MEGAN MELVIN
Title: Outpatient Clinic Manager
Organization: Kaiser Permanente

1. **Briefly describe your job responsibilities.**
   I am accountable for coordinating all back office clinical functions for the healthcare teams in a medical office to achieve excellence in quality of care, service, access, resource utilization, employee/physician satisfaction, and workplace and patient safety. I also lead the critical implementation of regionally consistent practices, processes, and protocols within a clinical department to ensure a consistent care experience for our members.

2. **Please give an example of what you would consider to be a "typical" day for you.**
   The fun thing about working in operations is that there is not a "typical" day. My schedule usually starts at 7:30 a.m. ending around 6:00/7:00 p.m. My day usually has prescheduled meetings ranging from regional projects to individual one-on-one meetings with my staff and clinicians at the clinic. Often these meetings are interrupted by clinic emergencies (staffing concerns/building maintenance concerns, etc.), medical emergencies, and member needs. Every day varies and it is this constant unpredictability in the day's schedule that makes this position exciting.

3. **What education or training do you have? Is it typical for your job?**
   I have a BA in psychology and business administration, and a MPH with an emphasis on management and policy. I also am a Six Sigma Green Belt for process improvement.

(*continued*)

Name: MEGAN MELVIN (*continued*)

4. What is the most challenging part of your job?

The challenge is to continuously manage resources efficiently and appropriately to enable healthcare teams to deliver care and service. Implementing effective, empowered functional work groups and working within a complex labor management partnership environment necessitates being knowledgeable about several labor contracts, and requires comfort and effectiveness working with ambiguous decision-making processes.

5. What do you consider to be the best part of your job?

Daily interactions with our Kaiser Permanente members—giving me a real-time pulse on what is going on in the clinic and the community. I thoroughly enjoy helping our members with their healthcare needs and making a difference in their lives.

6. What path did you take to get to the job you are in today?

I started my career in management consulting. This position led me to a position working in the Los Angeles Medical Center Emergency Department in Administration. After leaving Kaiser Permanente, I worked for Regence Blue Cross Blue Shield in marketing leading a cross-functional team for Benefit Management and Product Design; 4 years later, I found myself back at Kaiser Permanente working in Primary Care Administration managing an outpatient clinic.

Career path—consulting (project management) frontline operations (represented labor and exempt staff management).

7. What advice do you have for someone who is interested in a job such as yours?

I personally feel as though it was beneficial to start my career managing projects and learning organizations from the ground up prior to managing staff, as it has given me the opportunity to prove my management skills in small incremental steps. I have

Name: MEGAN MELVIN

also found that hiring managers are hesitant to take on a new manager who has not managed direct reports—which makes it difficult to break through and get that first direct report managing position. It is vital to get as much management experience possible and continue to be assertive in pursuing any opportunities to manage a project or staff. I would also recommend informational interviews with individuals to learn more about specific organizations and positions. Networking is key and will make a difference during the hiring process.

48. DIRECTOR OF FINANCE

JOB DESCRIPTION

The Director of Finance provides leadership and management of the organization's financial, business planning, and administrative activities. The Director of Finance is accountable for financial operating polices and internal controls, financial reporting, and budget preparation. In collaboration with the CEO/Administrator and department staff, the Director of Finance develops plans and objectives regarding short- and long-range requirements in specific areas such as budgeting, capital equipment, space, profit and loss analysis, accounting systems, reporting, internal auditing, and corporate tax filing.

EDUCATION AND EXPERIENCE

Directors of Finance typically hold a bachelor's degree in accounting, business administration, or a related field. Ideally, this person will be master's prepared. More than 6 years of professional experience in accounting and finance as a supervisor including 3 years in a medical practice group is required.

CORE COMPETENCIES AND SKILLS

- Outstanding interpersonal skills including the ability to effectively communicate with persons throughout the organization
- Excellent verbal and written communication skills

- Demonstrated track record of developing and maintaining collaborative relationships among diverse groups, including board members, medical staff, as well as key external stakeholders
- Ability to build and maintain appropriate peer relationships to facilitate organizational objectives
- Skill in interpreting governmental regulations as required for billing and financial reporting
- Skill in analyzing financial, volume, and market data
- Working with clinic leadership, to develops financial statements, including balance sheets, profit/loss statements, and analysis of budget variances
- Experience in presenting financial reports and other information to clinic physicians, administrative leaders, and board members
- Leads the development and implementation of annual capital and operating budgets
- Directs special projects in forecasting, performance to budget and financial analyses, and service line expansion.
- Ability to utilize standard computer-related applications

COMPENSATION

The Director of Finance can expect to earn between $50,000 and $90,000 per year. This salary will vary depending on the size, location, and medical specialty of the practice. Small practices will typically outsource their accounting and bookkeeping functions to an external group. Only mid-to large-size physician practices can afford to have their own Director of Finance.

EMPLOYMENT OUTLOOK

The U.S. Department of Labor projects strong growth of Directors of Finance with faster than average growth. A significant part of this growth is due to changes projected to occur as a result of healthcare reform that will shift the focus of care from the hospital to the physician clinic.

FOR FURTHER INFORMATION

- MGMA (http://www.mgma.com)
- Healthcare Financial Management Association (http://www.hfma.org)

49. HUMAN RESOURCES SPECIALIST

JOB DESCRIPTION

The Human Resources (HR) Specialist manages and conducts the employee relations functions within the practice. Responsibilities include advising managers on relationships, performance improvement, disciplinary procedures, and employee complaint procedures. The HR Specialist counsels employees on issues, including relationships, complaint procedure, and policy interpretation. The HR Specialist maintains an advanced understanding of the clinic's pay program, consults on appropriate pay decisions, including employment-based salary changes. Works effectively with other HR staff to resolve issues and complete projects. The HR Specialist advises on performance, market, and internal equity. This person coordinates the recruiting function within assigned areas, consults on ad placement and development, identifies effective recruiting sources, and coordinates and attends job fairs. The HR Specialist ensures compliance with federal and state regulations, administers the internal documentation process, works effectively with the other HR staff to recruit and retain employees in the difficult to recruit areas. The HR Specialist maintains an advanced understanding of the system benefit programs and supports assigned departments through organizational development and training efforts.

EDUCATION AND EXPERIENCE

An undergraduate degree in business or health administration is required. Larger physician clinics typically ask for at least 3 years of experience in HR with specific experience in physician practices preferred.

CORE COMPETENCIES AND SKILLS

- Outstanding interpersonal skills including the ability to effectively communicate with persons throughout the organization
- Excellent verbal and written communication skills
- Demonstrated skill to make decisions independently through the use of analytical and critical thinking, as well as the ability to conduct research; utilizes available data and negotiating skills
- Demonstrated ability to effectively conduct and complete individual and group projects

- Proven ability to coach and mentor managers and employees. Must be an effective team member, as well as an individual contributor
- Demonstrated ability to conduct training and presentations to groups of people at various organizational levels and sizes
- Ability to identify opportunities for improvement and change
- Ability to utilize standard computer-related applications

COMPENSATION

HR Specialists compensation falls under a wide range of salaries. Entry-level HR specialists can expect an annual salary of between $40,000 and $60,000, while more experienced HR specialists can earn as much as $100,000. As is the case in all physician practices, small practices of fewer than five physicians usually cannot justify supporting a separate HR department so most, if not all, of the HR duties will fall on the practice administrator. Larger practices will typically have fully staffed HR departments.

EMPLOYMENT OUTLOOK

There exists an ongoing demand for persons skilled in HR management. The HR Specialist is an excellent entry-level position for persons interested in healthcare management, and new positions open frequently as persons are either promoted up within HR management or move to other parts of the organization.

FOR FURTHER INFORMATION

- MGMA (http://www.mgma.com)
- American Medical Group Association (http://www.amga.org)
- Society for Human Resource Management (http://www.shrm.org)

Name:
RYAN OSTER
Title: Compliance Coordinator
Organization: Kaiser Permanente

1. **Briefly describe your job responsibilities.**
   Communicate changes in Center for Medicare and Medicaid Services (CMS) Conditions of Participation and state law. Facilitate the development of policies, procedures', and practice changes that reflect changes in CMS, Joint Commission standards, and state law. Lead auditing and monitoring efforts for compliance-related issues. Provide assistance to departments in follow-up on internal and external audits. Create and maintain RAC (Recovery Audit Contractor) database. Conduct investigations into compliance complaints. Develop and provide education regarding compliance issues. Lead multidepartment teams to solve complex compliance-related issues.

2. **Please give an example of what you would consider to be a "typical" day for you.**
   A typical day involves following up on audits and corrective action plans. Assisting managers, staff, and physicians with interpreting laws, CMS regulations, and Joint Commission standards. Conducting interviews related to investigations. Developing policies and/or education related to compliance.

3. **What education or training do you have? Is it typical for your job?**
   I have a BS in Health Management and Policy from Oregon State University and an MBA with a healthcare focus from Marylhurst

(*continued*)

Name: RYAN OSTER *(continued)*

University. I also have a certification in Health Care Compliance from the Health Care Compliance Association.

Compliance professionals come from many backgrounds. Some are nurses, others are from business backgrounds, and yet others are lawyers. Obtaining a certification has become an industry standard for those in compliance.

4. What is the most challenging part of your job?

The most challenging part of my job is building relationships with my business partners in the organization. Compliance is often seen as a roadblock or obstacle to getting things done. I work every day to help my business partners understand that involving compliance early in the process of making changes makes things move faster. The reality of compliance is that we cannot be everywhere at once and need our business partners to be our eyes and ears.

5. What do you consider to be the best part of your job?

The best part of my job is that I get to work with every part of the business. This has allowed me to understand how every department that is in the hospital or supports the hospital operates.

6. What path did you take to get to the job you are in today?

My path to this position was not a traditional one. I started my career in healthcare as a Certified Nursing Assistant (CNA). I work as a CNA, Psychiatric Technician, and as an Emergency Department Technician for 9 years. After obtaining my BS, I became the Accreditation Coordinator of a small hospital. In this role, I learned about the operations side of healthcare and got a taste of the regulations that we are burdened with. After gaining knowledge and experience there, I moved on to my current position.

Name: RYAN OSTER

7. What advice do you have for someone who is interested in a job such as yours?

The best advice I can give someone interested in compliance is to learn as much about the field as you can. Find out who the Compliance Officer is at your hospital and ask them about what they do and what you might do to get a job working for them. Check the Health Care Compliance Association website for lots of good information about compliance. You will also find information about regional conferences in your area. Go to one. It is a good place to meet local compliance professionals and to learn about the pressing issues facing compliance professionals today.

50. INSURANCE COORDINATOR

JOB DESCRIPTION

The primary responsibilities of an Insurance Coordinator consist of effective billing and claims management. Insurance Coordinators are tasked with sending out patient statements and running balance control reports to monitor outstanding payments. They are also responsible for all functions that involve reimbursement for assigned payers, such as managing payment of claims, tracking aging accounts receivable, and communicating with payers. Additionally, Insurance Coordinators must be knowledgeable and able to assist patients with any billing-related inquiries. Insurance Coordinators serve as the liaison between payers and providers to ensure that patients receive the care they need and are covered for it and that providers collect adequate payment.

EDUCATION AND EXPERIENCE

A bachelor's degree is a minimum expectation for most Insurance Coordinator positions. Educational background should be in business administration, finance, accounting, healthcare administration, or another related field. Prior experience in medical office insurance claims submission and follow-up, coding, billing, payment posting, and collections is often preferred.

CORE COMPETENCIES AND SKILLS

- Strong computer skills
- Good listener
- Excellent customer service skills
- Knowledge of medical terminology
- Knowledge of third-party payer fee schedules and reimbursement requirements
- Problem identification and resolution skills

COMPENSATION

The majority of Insurance Coordinators make between $35,000 and $50,000 annually. This number fluctuates primarily based on experience and the location and size of the practice.

EMPLOYMENT OUTLOOK

The demand for Insurance Coordinators is typically high. Because of continued changes to the U.S. healthcare system, knowledge of insurance and reimbursement procedures is incredibly valuable. Physician practices are continually employing individuals who are skilled in these areas to ensure effective operations.

FOR FURTHER INFORMATION

- America's Health Insurance Plans (http://www.ahip.org)
- MGMA (http://www.mgma.com)

Name:
GREG RHODES
Title: Associate Director, Professional Billing
Organization: NYU Langone Medical Center

1. Briefly describe your job responsibilities.

I am responsible for overseeing the revenue operations for approximately 900 physicians in 85 practices. My many roles include the following:

Managing all coding and billing functions in our Central Billing Office and offsite locations

Monitoring and improving cash flow through revenue initiatives

Working with operational managers to improve performance

Initiating process improvement projects

Developing and enforcing policies and procedures

Implementing system improvements and patient-friendly billing changes

Responding to payer and regulatory changes

2. Please give an example of what you would consider to be a "typical" day for you.

The interesting part of my job is that every day is different.

My role is more metric-driven than most management positions, which means that I can see the results of our initiatives very easily.

Everything we do is quantifiable. Throughout the month, my team and I look at different indicators and identify potential problems and areas for improvement.

I also spend a lot of time meeting with physicians, administrators, and staff to go over results and to implement operational changes that can improve cash flow.

(*continued*)

Name: GREG RHODES *(continued)*

3. What education or training do you have? Is it typical for your job?

I have an undergraduate degree in biology and a Master of Public Administration from NYU Wagner. My specialization was in healthcare policy and management. While I gained knowledge of the healthcare system from lab bench, clinical research, and policy-related activities, the degree was my first exposure to healthcare management. When I enrolled, my intention was to study policy. Shortly thereafter, my interest in management increased. I was intrigued by our ability as managers to positively improve critical measures like patient satisfaction and performance. I had not had as much exposure to the operations side of the industry and quickly learned that it is exciting.

My management team, and colleagues at other organizations, have similar educational backgrounds. It is typical for managers to have some level of management training but the bulk of the education comes from on-the-job experience. What I do day-to-day is not often taught in a classroom.

4. What is the most challenging part of your job?

Perhaps the most challenging part of my job is the administrative inefficiency in the healthcare system. We are implementing state-of-the-art technology in my organization. Despite that, we have many staff dedicated to manual processes that the insurance carriers require, who could otherwise be dedicated to more productive activities. Payers also make errors that result in patient dissatisfaction and impact our cash flow.

5. What do you consider to be the best part of your job?

The most exciting part of my job is implementing change and seeing our metrics improve. We are doing it through the centralization of many of our core processes and by implementing a new fully integrated medical information and revenue cycle system.

Name: GREG RHODES

I also recently formed a team solely dedicated to process improvement and finding opportunities that impact on our revenue. The model we have developed has quickly led to significant, measurable successes.

6. What path did you take to get to the job you are in today?

My professional career includes working at Health Plus, one of NYC's largest HMO plans. While there, I did a lot of work with the executive team, which spanned preparations for state audits, participation in performance improvement projects, and development of a dashboard for the Board of Directors. Following my work at Health Plus, I accepted a position as the Rheumatology Practice Administrator at NYU Hospital for Joint Diseases (HJD). I was later hired as an Administrative Practice Manager at NYU School of Medicine in the Faculty Group Practice corporate office where I worked with the Radiation Oncology, OBGYN, Psychiatry, Pulmonary and Critical Care Medicine, Physical Medicine and Rehabilitation, Dermatology, Ophthalmology, and Otolaryngology practices, and the Dermatology hospital outpatient unit. I was responsible for their revenue cycle, finances, and operations.

7. What advice do you have for someone who is interested in a job such as yours?

The single most important skill for a position such mine is the ability to think critically—to ask and be prepared to answer critical questions—about the performance of the business. This requires gaining knowledge of the industry and also a keen understanding of the key performance indicators. As with any management position, it is also important to have strong interpersonal skills to be able to build relationships with colleagues and to be able to communicate formally and informally.

51. LABORATORY SERVICES DIRECTOR

JOB DESCRIPTION

The Laboratory Services Director is responsible for the overall administration and operation of the laboratory. The Director is responsible for ensuring the laboratory is in compliance with regulations and guidelines. If the Director is qualified, he/she may perform the duties of the technical consultant, clinical consultant, and testing personnel.

EDUCATION AND EXPERIENCE

A Laboratory Services Director needs to have a substantial amount of education. A doctorate in laboratory science, clinical studies, or a related field is required. If the laboratory performs medical studies, the Director must possess a medical degree and be board certified within his or her specialty. Additionally, they will have at least 10 years of progressive administrative management experience combined with at least 15 years of clinical experience.

CORE COMPETENCIES AND SKILLS

- Outstanding interpersonal skills including the ability to effectively communicate with persons throughout the organization
- Excellent verbal and written communication skills
- Understanding of the regulations and guidelines associated with laboratory operations
- Promotes excellent customer service with all staff members and works to ensure that customer service measures are achieved
- Ability to identify opportunities for improvement and change
- Ability to utilize standard computer-related applications

COMPENSATION

Laboratory Services Directors can expect to earn between $80,000 and $110,000 per year. This salary will vary depending on the size, location, and medical specialty of the practice. Not all practices have the need for this position.

EMPLOYMENT OUTLOOK

As a result of an increased demand for medical and pharmaceutical services, employment of individuals within the field of scientific research and development services is anticipated to grow by 9% through 2016 according to the U.S. Bureau of Labor Statistics (BLS).

FOR FURTHER INFORMATION

- MGMA (http://www.mgma.com)
- American Medical Group Association (http://www.amga.org)
- American Academy of Family Physicians (http://www.aafp.org/online/en/home.html)

52. MEDICAL RECORDS DIRECTOR

JOB DESCRIPTION

The Medical Records Director is responsible for maintaining all patient medical records in compliance with federal and state regulations. Depending on the practice, medical records may be in paper or electronic form. The Director must ensure their staff is compiling complete and organized medical records.

EDUCATION AND EXPERIENCE

A bachelor's degree in a related field is the minimum requirement. A master's degree in a medical discipline or business-related field is recommended. Experience working with medical records is required.

CORE COMPETENCIES AND SKILLS

- Outstanding interpersonal skills including the ability to effectively communicate with persons throughout the organization
- Excellent verbal and written communication skills
- Understanding of the regulations and guidelines associated with laboratory operations
- Promotes excellent customer service with all staff members and works to ensure customer service measures are achieved
- Ability to identify opportunities for improvement and change
- Ability to utilize standard computer-related applications

COMPENSATION

Medical Records Directors can expect to earn between $80,000 and $110,000 per year. This salary will vary depending on the size, location, and medical specialty of the practice. Not all practices have the need for this position.

EMPLOYMENT OUTLOOK

The job outlook is positive and increasing for individuals with experience working with electronic health records. As physician practices continue to implement health IT systems, there will be an increased demand for directors that are familiar with the operation and management of this technology.

FOR FURTHER INFORMATION

- MGMA (http://www.mgma.com)
- American Medical Group Association (http://www.amga.org)
- American Academy of Family Physicians (http://www.aafp.org/online/en/home.html)

Name:
HICKORY TERMINE
Title: Operations Manager, Blaustein Pain Treatment Center
Organization: The Johns Hopkins Hospital, Outpatient Center

1. **Briefly describe your job responsibilities.**
   As Operations Manager, I am the direct supervisor of a five-person scheduling team and five-person nursing team in conjunction with 11 physicians. I am responsible for all scheduling, the revenue cycle of two cost centers, all IT systems, continual process improvement, customer satisfaction, and anything else happening in clinic that day.

2. **Please give an example of what you would consider to be a "typical" day for you.**
   On a "typical" day, I check three daily reports generated every morning that outline all appointments, financial insurance clearance, and clinic details for the upcoming 2 days. I submit hospital billing for the facility fee. A good portion of my day involves dealing with patient issues: insurance denials, complex scheduling, formal letters, or billing inquiries. When possible, I focus on larger implementation projects such as the latest IT project, process improvement or policy development, customer satisfaction tactics, or other daily troubleshooting.

3. **What education or training do you have? Is it typical for your job?**
   I received my Bachelor of Arts from Tulane University in Anthropology. Adding to that, I received my Master's of Health Services Administration from the George Washington University. Prior to my current position, I had a 1-year administrative residency

(*continued*)

Name: HICKORY TERMINE *(continued)*

at LifeBridgeHealth, 1-year healthcare strategic planning experience, as well as 1-year acute care pharmacy operations experience.

I believe my current position is a typical entry-level management position with responsibility for one clinical area and frontline employees.

4. What is the most challenging part of your job?

The most challenging part of my job is the human resource aspect. Prior to this position, I had not had direct management of employees. I am reminded every day that we are all human. Each employee has a family, problems, expectations, motivations, successes, and occasional failures. I am involved in all of those aspects for about 20 people on a daily basis.

5. What do you consider to be the best part of your job?

The most rewarding part of my job is being able to implement changes and make a difference, and to reflect on the improvements seen over my tenure during the last year. Through data and a monthly dashboard, I can monitor as customer satisfaction improves, volume and revenue increase, wait times decrease, and so on.

I met a particularly challenging patient in January of 2011, when he lodged a formal complaint with the Patient Relations Department for his extended wait and incorrect prescription, among other problems. In September of 2011, he wrote a formal letter to my manager expressing his appreciation and admiration for how hard the Pain Treatment Center had "far surpassed any previous standards under my leadership." I have never been so flattered, as this man went out of his way to note my efforts in a nonbiased and sincere way.

6. What path did you take to get to the job you are in today?

My path began with my undergraduate degree followed by 1 year of acute pharmacy operations in a major medical center. I then began

Name: HICKORY TERMINE

my graduate degree, including 1-year strategic planning experience, while attending classes, and a 1-year administrative residency.

7. **What advice do you have for someone who is interested in a job such as yours?**
I would strongly recommend gaining all work experience possible, especially before or during graduate school. During each interview for both residency and my current position, I used those stories of experience to demonstrate my strongest qualities. With that, I highly suggest doing a 1-year administrative residency or fellowship. The application process can be strenuous, but the effort will be well worth your time.

When applying for jobs, I suggest setting simple parameters in which help include or exclude openings. For example, during my most recent search, I required my next position to be (1) in operations, (2) have management responsibility for frontline staff, and (3) a boss who encourages growth. Be careful not to exclude jobs on aspects like a less-than-sexy title or department, because the manager of housekeeping is learning the exact same managerial and operations experience I am.

Lastly, I cannot say enough for emotional intelligence. While I may not know all the logistics and answers to every operational question, I usually know who to go for help and how best to communicate with that person. To anyone entering a new career, read as much as possible about emotional intelligence. At the very least, take a variety of personality tests to learn about yourself, how you communicate, how you learn best, or how you handle confrontation. Getting results is often about how effectively you motivate and communicate, not how many tactics are listed in your project plan.

53. NURSING SUPERVISOR

JOB DESCRIPTION

In addition to providing care, Nursing Supervisors also oversee the entire nursing staff. Nursing Supervisors direct and supervise all aspects of patient care. This includes making sure that there is enough staffing in units, interacting with patients and families, and managing issues that arise during a particular shift. The Nursing Supervisor is also responsible for training staff. The Supervisor usually plans and organizes orientation for newly hired nurses, and in-service training for existing nurses as well. To improve nursing care and customer service within a healthcare facility, the Supervisor generally conducts studies and gathers information from medical staff and hospital administrators on nursing problems within the facility. The Nursing Supervisor develops strategies for dealing with these nursing problems and makes sure that patient needs are met. They may also be involved in assisting with the budgeting process as well.

EDUCATION AND EXPERIENCE

A Nursing Supervisor usually has a master's degree in nursing. However, some healthcare organizations will accept a 4-year Bachelor of Science in Nursing, if one has requisite work and clinical experience. As a RN, the Supervisor must have already passed the National Counsel Licensure Examination (NCLEX-RN) to be a licensed nurse.

CORE COMPETENCIES AND SKILLS

- Knowledge of healthcare and medical procedures and terminology
- Excellent interpersonal/human relations skills
- Attention to detail
- Ability to respond to emergency situations
- Ability to delegate responsibility and to prioritize duties
- Proficiency in accounting and budgeting
- Strong supervisory skills

COMPENSATION

Nursing Supervisors can work in hospitals, clinics, or long-term care facilities, which play a factor in their earnings. Nursing Supervisor salaries in hospitals range between $63,289 and $84,860, while those working in acute care facilities earn between $74,714 and $101,447. Experience also plays a role in Supervisor salaries as those with 20 years or more of experience earn between $60,677 and $84,721. Supervisors with 1 to 4 years of experience earn between $48,348 and $67,731.

EMPLOYMENT OUTLOOK

Opportunities for Nursing Supervisors are expected to increase in the coming years. Nurses with the highest level of training and experience will be in higher demand. Nursing Supervisors will have job security in clinics, research facilities, and hospitals.

FOR FURTHER INFORMATION

- American Nurses Association (www.nursingworld.org)

54. PATIENT ACCOUNTS MANAGER

JOB DESCRIPTION

Similar to an Insurance Coordinator, a Patient Accounts Manager's primary responsibility is ensuring effective financial performance of patient accounting services. Specifically, Patient Accounts Managers work with insurance companies and patients to collect payments in a timely manner. The Patient Accounts Manger oversees the accounts receivable process for the physician practice and makes changes as necessary to improve profits and liquidity. The individual in this position is also responsible to track claim submissions, third-party follow-ups, denials, and to create healthy customer service and vendor relationships for the practice. Managers are also expected to set various performance goals and be experts in the reimbursement process.

EDUCATION AND EXPERIENCE

A bachelor's degree in accounting, finance, or a related field is required. An increasing number of Patient Accounts Managers now possess master's degrees. Employers prefer candidates with proper accounting accreditation and typically 7 years of experience in a related field.

CORE COMPETENCIES AND SKILLS

- Must have vast knowledge of Medicare, Medicaid, and health insurance regulations
- High level of analytical and financial skills
- Understanding of billing procedures
- Demonstrates professional approach in dealing with others
- Outstanding leadership and supervisory skills to effectively manage staff

- Excellent verbal presentation and written communication skills
- Proficient in technology
- Excellent customer service skills

COMPENSATION

The majority of Patient Accounts Managers make between $99,000 and $130,000 annually. This number fluctuates greatly based on practice size, experience, and geographic location.

EMPLOYMENT OUTLOOK

The demand for Patient Accounts Managers is strong. Healthcare-related organizations are always looking for individuals who have strong financial skills and extensive reimbursement knowledge. Because of increasing costs and tighter budgets, organizations need people to eliminate unnecessary waste and improve financial standing.

FOR FURTHER INFORMATION

- Health Financial Management Association (www.hfma.org)
- MGMA (http://www.mgma.com)

55. PAYROLL MANAGER

JOB DESCRIPTION

A Payroll Manager makes sure that the payment of salaries to employees is accurate. They make sure the appropriate deductions have been taken out from employees' gross salaries to satisfy local and federal regulations. As managers, they are responsible for supervising payroll support personnel as well. A Payroll Manager may work in either a large or small company. When a current employee is transferred, promoted, or terminated, they are in charge of issuing final checks and adjusting their pay rates. If a company offers benefits packages, they are in charge of them. These benefits include stock options, retirement funds, and the awarding of bonuses. If employees have questions about their benefits, the Payroll Manager is the one who would answer their questions. The Payroll Manager usually is in communication with accounting and HR managers in order to ensure efficiency throughout a corporation's financial operations. They prepare and submit reports to upper-level management to detail how much the company is paying for taxes, benefits, and vacation accruals.

EDUCATION AND EXPERIENCE

The job of a Payroll Manager normally requires a bachelor's degree in finance and accounting, though some corporations prefer a master's degree in the same concentrations. However, if a person has more than 5 years of experience in payroll management and administration, the educational requirements may be reduced or even waived.

CORE COMPETENCIES AND SKILLS

- Excellent quantitative and analytical skills
- Superior interpersonal and communicative skills
- Strong organizational skills
- Ability to manage a team of employees
- Proficient at MS Office
- Must be a team player
- Experience of payroll tax at the federal, state, and local level

COMPENSATION

Payroll Managers with 1 year of experience or less make $31,444 to $39,067. Managers with 20 years of experience or more make an average of $49,573 to $73,802. Hospital-paid managers earn $44,439 to $67,909. Managers who work in New Jersey received the highest average salaries at $48,615 to $74,688. Other high-paying states include California, Illinois, and New York.

EMPLOYMENT OUTLOOK

The U.S. Bureau of Labor Statistics projects favorable opportunities for payroll administrators. Those who have bachelor's degree in finance and accounting and have earned industry certification in demonstrating their proficiency in complex payroll issues will have an advantage in this competitive job market.

FOR FURTHER INFORMATION

- American Payroll Association (http://www.americanpayroll.org)

Name:
DANA WOLF
Title: Administrator
Organization: Park Avenue ENT

1. Briefly describe your job responsibilities.

When casually asked, I usually respond: "I'm a firefighter, a plumber, an electrician, a counselor/mediator, a mother, a painter, a designer, IT technician, and a director." Everyday has its different challenges, and everyday I have different responsibilities and I have to be ready to accommodate those responsibility changes, but in general and more formally:

Bookkeeping/accounting

Employee oversight

Employee scheduling of 10FTE and 5PTE

Management of Electronic Medical Record (EMR) implementation

Project management

Practice analysis and trending

Compliance

Equipment purchasing

2. Please give an example of what you would consider to be a "typical" day for you.

On a typical day, I work about 10 to 11 hours and am usually at the office by 7 a.m. Normal routine in the morning includes checking and responding to e-mails and voice mails, and returning messages. We have four office locations and, periodically, I stop in to take a look and see what changes need to be implemented in

Name: DANA WOLF

that particular facility. At my main office, I get my hands dirty and really make sure every day that even the basic equipment on the floor is running and take notes on what needs to be fixed, replaced, reordered, and so on. Once everyone arrives for their shift, I am back at my desk analyzing the previous day's revenue and the next few days schedule, pay bills, review additional reports, and so on. Once a week, I run through the accounts outstanding and sit down with my billing staff to review and update. Generally, around lunchtime, I call a huddle of the staff to go over quick fixes of patient issues and practice concerns, and get feedback from the staff.

A mentor told me once to take 15 minutes every day and be silent. These 15 minutes allow my mind to relax and be open.

After lunch, usually sitting at my desk, I check in with the providers to see how their day is going and find out what are their needs. I also try to stay a few hours on the floor every week to get new ideas of how to increase patient flow, decrease waste time, and really try to integrate myself into the frontlines and get a different perspective.

Toward the end of the day, I finish up any necessary paperwork, reports, purchasing, and staff scheduling. Every day presents new challenges and new responsibilities, and I should have time throughout the day to manage surprises.

Side note—One position I held in the beginning of my career, years ago, had my desk in the basement and my boss wanted me to be on floor for most of the day. I initially didn't like this idea because it was going to be impossible to do my job if I wasn't at my desk and I didn't want to have to babysit the staff. What I didn't realize at the time was that I wasn't babysitting the staff, but I was getting a different perspective that would help me be able to restructure the practice to be more efficient, productive, and profitable. This was an eye-opening experience and I find it very important to know each and every role of your practice to be able to manage the practice effectively.

(*continued*)

Name: DANA WOLF *(continued)*

3. What education or training do you have? Is it typical for your job?

I received my undergraduate degree in healthcare administration from Oregon State University and am currently working on my prenursing pathway. However, as valuable as my formal education was, it is extremely important to continue learning through education seminars and group associations, such as Medical Group Management Association (MGMA), Healthcare Leaders of New York (HLNY), and American College of Healthcare Executives (ACHE). In addition, I also work in a specialty field and am a member of the Association of Otolaryngology Administrators (AOA). In today's society, having a graduate degree or additional formal education is becoming more important to succeeding in this industry.

Personally, I am working on my prenursing pathway to obtain an accelerated BSN, and then possibly my MSN and work as a consultant or in nursing administration.

4. What is the most challenging part of your job?

There are three main challenges:

Keeping up with compliance changes in the healthcare industry

Delegating tasks and responsibilities (more of a personal challenge)

Knowing when to be a leader and when to be a manager

5. What do you consider to be the best part of your job?

Being an administrator requires a lot of quick and accurate thinking on your feet. I like surprises and find it fun and rewarding when I encounter a new challenge that requires quick thinking.

I also like when I hear feedback, both positive and negative, from patients. It helps me to determine the strengths and weaknesses of the practice.

Name: DANA WOLF

6. What path did you take to get to the job you are in today?

Basic path: college → internship → first job in supervisory position → few more administrator jobs → current administrator position.

More specific: Oregon State University, BS in Health Care Administration, internship at Park 56 Dental Group, first job as Patient Care Coordinator at Park 56 Dental Group, second job as Practice Administrator for Vein Treatment Center and eventually a consultant, third job as Administrator at Hospital for Special Surgery, and fourth job as Administrator for Park Avenue ENT.

7. What advice do you have for someone who is interested in a job such as yours?

It would be advisable to have some form of formal education in the healthcare industry, but if not, they should have experience in management, human resources, and be involved in an organization such as MGMA. The networking opportunities and the experience you gain from the associations are invaluable as an administrator.

56. PHYSICIAN COMPLIANCE DIRECTOR

JOB DESCRIPTION

The Physician Compliance Director will be responsible for planning, design, implementation, and maintenance of system-wide physician compliance programs, and associated policies and procedures. This individual will serve as the expert for compliance matters relating to employed, independent, and contracted physicians, as well as allied health providers, and will serve as a compliance resource for quality-of-care compliance matters. The Director is responsible for monitoring and disseminating pertinent new laws and regulations and/or revisions to current laws and regulations, as they pertain to physician compliance. Examples of these include, but are not limited to, the Federal Sentencing Guidelines and the Affordable Care Act.

EDUCATION AND EXPERIENCE

A graduate degree in health, law, or business administration is the required educational preparation. Typically, 5 years experience in a medical care delivery organization is required. Most organizations hiring Physician Compliance Directors require a minimum of 5 years of experience in healthcare operations, regulatory compliance, risk management, audit, law, or a similar field.

CORE COMPETENCIES AND SKILLS

- Outstanding interpersonal skills including the ability to effectively communicate with persons throughout the organization
- Excellent verbal and written communication skills
- Demonstrated knowledge of the Federal Sentencing Guidelines, healthcare laws/regulations, and fraud and abuse laws
- Serves as the compliance expert for the practice on matters involving physician compliance
- Provides leadership for the development, implementation, maintenance, and evaluation of policies, procedures, tools, and templates to address changes in current laws and regulations and/or revisions to current laws and regulations related to physician compliance
- Identifies key areas for training and required policies and procedures related to physician compliance objectives
- Analyzes reports, data, and trends to keep management and governance informed of the current regulatory environment and the potential impact to the practice. Works with multiple stakeholder groups to develop and assess physician and clinical outlier risks through analysis of billing and quality data
- Experience in monitoring governmental recovery efforts for trends or patterns of noncompliance with billing, medical necessity, and coding issues affecting physician services
- Provides consultation services, guidance, and ongoing education to various entities on new laws and regulations and/or revisions to current laws and regulations impacting physician relationships
- Ability to identify opportunities for improvement and change
- Ability to utilize standard computer-related applications

COMPENSATION

Physician Compliance Directors can expect to earn between $60,000 and $90,000 per year. Those Physician Compliance Directors with law degrees can expect to earn approximately $150,000 annually. This salary will vary depending on the size, location, and medical specialty of the practice. Small practices will typically use the CEO/Administrator to fill this role. Only mid-to large-size physician practices can afford to have their own Physician Compliance Director.

EMPLOYMENT OUTLOOK

There exists an ongoing demand for persons skilled in physician compliance. There are a multitude of new and existing laws for which physician practices are responsible for adhering to, and it is unlikely that individual physicians have the time to keep up with these laws and regulations.

FOR FURTHER INFORMATION

- MGMA (http://www.mgma.com)
- American Medical Group Association (http://www.amga.org)

57. PRACTICE OPERATIONS DIRECTOR

JOB DESCRIPTION

The Practice Operations Director generally works for large, multispecialty physician group practices and directs, administers, and controls the day-to-day operations and activities of the group's medical locations. The Practice Operations Director serves as a member of the senior leadership team of the practice.

EDUCATION AND EXPERIENCE

Practice Operations Directors require a bachelor's degree with master's preferred, such as MBA, MPH, or Master's of Health Administration (MHA). Minimum of 10 years experience in a healthcare organization is required. Knowledge or experience with managed care is required. Successful candidates will possess a minimum of 5 years experience with progressive advancement in leadership positions in physician practice operations. Multispecialty experience is strongly preferred. Experience in data management and clinical applications, such as EMR, would also greatly benefit the candidate.

CORE COMPETENCIES AND SKILLS

- Outstanding interpersonal skills including the ability to effectively communicate with current and potential customers, along with persons throughout the organization

- Excellent verbal and written communication skills
- Ability to resolve medical–administrative problems and keep lines of communication open with staff to ensure high employee morale and a professional atmosphere
- Ensure clinic compliance with all regulatory agencies governing healthcare delivery and the rules of accrediting bodies
- Collaborate with other departments to direct compliance issues to appropriate channels for investigation and resolution
- Develops and formulates budget requests for coming fiscal year and multiple years
- Effectively supervise and manage a multidisciplinary team of employees
- Ability to work in an environment where changing priorities are the norm and flexibility is a must; demonstrated skills in managing multiple tasks
- Maintain professional affiliations and enhance professional development to keep current in the latest healthcare trends and developments
- Ability to use standard computer office software
- Working knowledge and awareness of state and federal requirements and codes governing treatment

COMPENSATION

Practice Operations Directors earn $100,000 to $189,000 per year, exclusive of performance and other incentive compensation. This salary is a function of the size of the practice and the part of the country in which it is located.

EMPLOYMENT OUTLOOK

The employment outlook for Practice Operations Directors is good. Ever-growing numbers of physicians are choosing to move into larger group practices and these complex businesses require skilled administrative staff to keep them running at peek effectiveness, particularly with the challenges faced by reduced levels of reimbursement.

FOR FURTHER INFORMATION

- MGMA (http://www.mgma.com)

Name:
JOE YODER
Title: Manager, Foot and Ankle and Reconstructive Surgery
Organization: Legacy Health

1. Briefly describe your job responsibilities.

Manage the business and clinical operations (inpatient and outpatient) of Foot and Ankle and Reconstructive Surgery services.

2. Please give an example of what you would consider to be a "typical" day for you.

Most days are filled with meetings. In between meeting times, I try to be present in the clinics where I can interact with staff and address issues/concerns. Each day I will be sure to find time to be at my desk and catch up on e-mails and analyze reports.

3. What education or training do you have? Is it typical for your job?

BS in Health Management and Policy (Oregon State University)

MS in Health Administration (University of Alabama, Birmingham)

My education level is typical for my position in this part of the country. I have noticed through speaking with colleagues that qualifications for certain jobs are quite variable and are not consistent by region.

4. What is the most challenging part of your job?

Managing change—the only thing constant is change. Maintaining employee/physician satisfaction in an environment that lacks consistency in process is difficult.

(*continued*)

Name: JOE YODER *(continued)*

5. What do you consider to be the best part of your job?
Ensuring positive patient care—when a patient card or compliment comes into the office, it is very uplifting and a joy to share with the teams.

6. What path did you take to get to the job you are in today?
Started out in undergrad thinking that PT (physical therapy) would be the route for me. I heard a presentation from Dr. Friedman on the challenges and rewards of healthcare administration. I knew that my strengths were better aligned with the leadership side of healthcare, as opposed to delivery. It wasn't until further discussing my aspirations with Dr. Friedman that I realized that pursuing a graduate degree was the path for me. Upon finishing grad school, I was given the opportunity to be an Administrative Fellow with Legacy Health. The Administrative Fellow experience has been the most valuable in my career and has shaped the leader I am/strive to be today.

7. What advice do you have for someone who is interested in a job such as yours?
Be sure you are getting into it for the right reasons. Know that you have a desire to improve the health of others. Be patient.

58. QUALITY/RISK MANAGEMENT DIRECTOR

JOB DESCRIPTION

The Quality/Risk Management Director works closely with the Medical Legal Consultant, Practice Operations Director, Medical Director, and CEO to ensure comprehensive program delivery and quality patient care. The Quality/Risk Management Director coordinates with all physicians, program and department directors monitoring programs to ensure high levels of quality performance. The Director develops goals and objectives for the risk management and quality management programs of the clinic and explains quality, risk, and compliance management policies, procedures, systems, and objectives to all personnel employed by the clinic.

EDUCATION AND EXPERIENCE

A bachelor's degree in health or business administration is required, with a master's degree in one of these disciplines as the preferred educational preparation. Typically, 5 years experience in a medical care delivery organization is required. Four years of experience in peer review with quality management responsibility is also required. Five years of nursing or patient care experience is preferred. Some clinics prefer nationally recognized certification as a Risk/Compliance Officer.

CORE COMPETENCIES AND SKILLS

- Outstanding interpersonal skills including the ability to effectively communicate with persons throughout the organization
- Excellent verbal and written communication skills
- Regularly communicates with physicians and providers regarding quality and risk management problems, issues, and potential resolutions
- Ability to assist supervisors, managers, and directors in the development, review, and revision of clinical policies and procedures
- Responds to requests for quality management intervention, provides troubleshooting assistance. Maintains strict confidentiality related to medical records and other data generated by departmental functions
- Monitors patient complaints by overseeing concerns and complaints reported through clinical staff. Addresses, resolves, and follows up as needed
- Address and follow up on alleged violations of rules, regulations, policies, procedures, and standards of conduct. Develops a program for such violations
- Experience in conducting risk assessments on potential and actual litigations and assisting insurers and counsel with defense issues
- Ability to identify trends and motivate workforce toward changes needed to adopt and remain competitive
- Promotes excellent customer service with all staff members and works to ensure customer service measures are achieved
- Ability to identify opportunities for improvement and change
- Ability to utilize standard computer-related applications

COMPENSATION

Quality/Risk Management Directors can expect to earn between $65,000 and $115,000 per year. This salary will vary depending on the size, location, and medical specialty of the practice. Small practices will typically use the CEO/Administrator to fill this role. Only mid-to large-size physician practices can afford to have their own Quality/Risk Management Director.

EMPLOYMENT OUTLOOK

The U.S. Department of Labor projects strong growth of Quality/Risk Management Directors with faster than average growth. A significant part of this growth is due to changes projected to occur as a result of healthcare reform that will shift the focus of care from the hospital to the physician clinic.

FOR FURTHER INFORMATION

- MGMA (http://www.mgma.com)
- American Medical Group Association (http://www.amga.org)

6 ■ CAREERS IN LONG-TERM CARE

59. ADMINISTRATOR

JOB DESCRIPTION

Long-term care Administrators can work in a variety of service organizations, such as nursing homes, assisted-living or continuing care retirement communities, and home and hospice care. Administrators manage facilities that provide these types of personal care to elderly or incapacitated patients who can no longer care for themselves. Long-term care administrators oversee all of the various departments within the healthcare organization. Their primary job is to ensure effective operations through careful oversight of offered services and financial management. Administrators serve as the primary leadership position within a long-term care facility.

EDUCATION AND EXPERIENCE

In order to become an Administrator, most organizations require a master's degree in long-term care administration. While some facilities may only require an appropriate bachelor's degree, increased responsibility has led to a preference for those with advanced educational degrees. A large majority of organizations require considerable years of experience (10 years or more) in order to qualify. In order to direct the operations of a nursing home, Administrators need to complete a 6-month administrator-in-training program and successfully pass federal and state licensure examinations.

CORE COMPETENCIES AND SKILLS

- Business management skills
- Extensive financial management knowledge
- Excellent written and verbal communication skills
- Analytical skills
- Thorough knowledge of healthcare industry

- Excellent intrapersonal skills
- Demonstrated ability to teach, mentor, and manage staff

COMPENSATION

The majority of long-term care Administrators make between $80,000 and $100,000 annually; however, this number has increased significantly in recent years and trends indicate that salaries will continue to increase. This number is also dependent on the size and geographic location of the organization and an individual's level of experience.

EMPLOYMENT OUTLOOK

There is a great need for long-term care Administrators. Given the vast amount of aging baby boomers, there will be a significant need for individuals with the appropriate skills to lead a long-term care organization. If anyone is considering a career in administration, long-term care would be an excellent choice.

FOR FURTHER INFORMATION

- American College of Healthcare Administrators (http://www.achca.org)
- American Health Care Association (http://www.ahcancal.org)

Name:
PETER KAROW
Title: Administrator
Organization: Incarnation Children's Center

1. Briefly describe your job responsibilities.

I am the Administrator of a small pediatric skilled nursing facility for children with HIV/AIDS. My job responsibilities include oversight of day-to-day operations of the facility, regulatory compliance, budget development and implementation, management of staff and maintenance of a safe physical environment, strategic planning, participation in fundraising activities, and completing grant applications.

2. Please give an example of what you would consider to be a "typical" day for you.

A typical day is very atypical. Every once in a while there is a quiet orderly day with scheduled meetings and tasks taking place according to a predetermined plan; more routinely, there are a variety of unscheduled interruptions and "mini" emergencies that require attending to. Ultimately, this means I need to be very flexible and organized to get anything done. Work is accomplished in short concentrated periods of time sandwiched between meetings and putting out fires. Interruptions are routine. An example would be the pending arrival of Hurricane Irene: When the hurricane was announced and the Mayor declared an emergency, all other work was dropped to implement the facility's disaster plan and prepare the facility, staff, and residents for the storm and to be sure we were ready to accept residents from other facilities should there have been a need to. So, each day is unique and, like life itself, frequently full of surprises.

(*continued*)

Name: PETER KAROW *(continued)*

3. What education or training do you have? Is it typical for your job?

I have a BS in Physical Therapy, and an MPA and PhD in Public Administration. Additionally, I am a licensed Nursing Home Administrator.

My education and training are both typical and atypical for my job. In health administration, it is not unusual for people with clinical degrees (Doctors of Medicine [MDs], registered nurses [RNs], physical therapists, occupational therapists, etc.) to go on and get a master's degree in business or public administration and then move into administrative roles. It is a bit more unusual for people to continue on to the doctoral level, if they are not working in an academic or research setting. From the perspective of my PhD, I am academically overqualified for my administrative job.

4. What is the most challenging part of your job?

The most challenging part of my job is providing high-quality care within the budgeting and regulatory restraints of today's ever-shifting healthcare environment. There is a constant ratcheting down of reimbursement, making it imperative that organizations do more with less. There never seems to be enough resources to provide high-quality care without a struggle. Reimbursement rules are extremely complex and always changing in the direction of there being fewer funds. This makes providing good care an ongoing battle. Similarly, from a regulatory perspective, there are constant changes. As my facility is a bit unusual being a pediatric skilled nursing facility (SNF), we are always trying to fit into a regulatory schema designed for a different population—this challenge is compounded by the ever-changing nature of today's regulatory environment.

5. What do you consider to be the best part of your job?

The best part of my job is when I feel I have done something positive for one of our residents or their families: when I feel I have

Name: PETER KAROW

helped them or made their life better in some way. It is great if I implement a new program or initiative, but it can be just as satisfying to do something that is small. I try to have contact with the residents every day and do something tangible for a resident as a way of reminding myself why I am in this line of work. This contact and sense of service is inspiring and keeps me going.

6. What path did you take to get to the job you are in today?

The path to my job was fairly long and circuitous. I started my career as a physical therapist, got a master's degree in public administration, and then went on to work in a home healthcare agency and hospital administration. Eventually, I acquired a nursing home administrator's license. I then worked as a nursing home administrator and then went into a pediatric setting. I also went on to complete a PhD in Public Administration.

I have moved around and worked in several different settings and jobs in my career. This mobility has allowed me to develop a broad set of skills that are applicable to a wide array of jobs and settings. I like the diversity of my career and the experience of having worked in a variety of sectors and positions. My present job is in a small facility where I have great deal of autonomy; I value this independence greatly.

7. What advice do you have for someone who is interested in a job such as yours?

First of all, get a good education, which these days probably involves having a degree at the master's level. I would also encourage master's students to participate in internships, residency programs, or other experiential training programs to gain as much working experience as possible. This type of experience is invaluable, particularly in a situation where a mentor shares his or her knowledge with the student. This leads to a second recommendation which would be to seek out a professional mentor who can serve as a guide. When starting to work, I would recommend getting as broad

(*continued*)

Name: PETER KAROW *(continued)*

a base of experience as possible. If students know the specific career path they want, it is great and they can focus on that path, but if they are not sure, it is good to just get as much experience as possible in different types of jobs so that they can see what they like and at the same time develop a variety of skills. Having a broad set of marketable skills is a great asset, especially in the current time of economic austerity. Finally, to be a nursing home administrator, one must get licensed; so it is good to learn the requirements for licensure and start fulfilling them as early as possible, as they can take a fair amount of time to complete.

60. DIRECTOR OF NURSING

JOB DESCRIPTION

Directors of Nursing oversee and are responsible for the performance of an entire nursing staff in a hospital or other healthcare facility. They may also be responsible for helping to develop and implement patient care services. In addition to overseeing the nursing staff, Directors also perform administrative duties. This includes developing and implementing a budget for the nursing department and preparing reports for higher levels of management within the organization. As Director, they are responsible for the recruitment, retention, and training of nurses. They make sure that the work standards, legal procedures, and nursing laws are met in the healthcare facility. Directors will also inform nurses of any new nursing policies and procedures.

EDUCATION AND EXPERIENCE

The person in this position is a RN who is required to have a bachelor's degree in nursing, though most prefer a master's degree. In addition, the Director must have 4 to 8 years of nursing experience, with at least 2 of those years in a supervising or leadership role, such as a nurse supervisor or nurse manager. Depending on the state and nursing work environment, other certifications may also be needed.

CORE COMPETENCIES AND SKILLS

- Strong motivational skills
- Excellent interpersonal/human relations skills
- Attention to detail
- Ability to respond to emergency situations
- Ability to delegate responsibility and to prioritize duties
- Proficiency in accounting and budgeting
- Strong management skills

COMPENSATION

A Director of Nursing with less than 1 year of experience will make between $52,072 and $75,354. An experience of 2 to 5 years will increase that number to $54,953 to $85,000. An experience of 20 or more years will earn a median salary between $66,559 and $99,421.

EMPLOYMENT OUTLOOK

The employment outcome is positive for Directors of Nursing. Jobs for healthcare managers such as Directors of Nursing are expected to increase by 16% between 2006 and 2016 according to the Bureau of Labor Statistics.

FOR FURTHER INFORMATION

- American Nurses Association (www.nursingworld.org)
- National Association of Directors of Nursing Administration in Long Term Care (http://www.nadona.org)

61. HOME HEALTHCARE AGENCY DIRECTOR

JOB DESCRIPTION

A Home Healthcare Agency Director administers day-to-day operations and activities of a homecare agency, nursing home, assisted-living facility, home healthcare, or other long-term care organizations. In some cases, the position is appointed by the Board of Directors. The position requires following the organization's mission, objectives, and values to ensure economical and efficient performance. Directors are responsible for creating and maintaining an operating budget and for overseeing the development of methods to measure agency activities. A Home Healthcare Agency Director must follow ethical and legal guidelines and compliance. Another responsibility is to employ qualified personnel and give continuous staff education and evaluations.

EDUCATION AND EXPERIENCE

The minimum education requirement is a bachelor's degree in management or a related field. Prior experience in finance, healthcare management, or business administration is critical. Home Healthcare Agency Director positions require at least 5 years experience in home health or a related field. The organization might require a current RN license.

CORE COMPETENCIES AND SKILLS

- Advocate for patients and employees
- Strong experience in finance
- Solve financial and quality-related problems
- Independent thinker, who works unsupervised
- Maintain numerous projects at one time
- Process working knowledge of federal and state regulations
- Strong written and verbal communication skills
- Creativity is expected
- Excellent work ethic and work under stressful situations

COMPENSATION

Home Healthcare Agency Directors median annual salary is $104,000. The salary range is wide, from $80,000 to $130,000 per year. Those working in an urban area stand to make more than those living in a rural area.

EMPLOYMENT OUTLOOK

The position of Home Healthcare Agency Director is an ongoing learning experience. With an aging population, home healthcare agencies will continue to expand and grow. The shortage of Home Healthcare Agency Directors allow for continuous growth of those already in the field.

FOR FURTHER INFORMATION

- National Association for Home Care and Hospice (http://www.nahc.org)

Name:
BEN Y. YOUNG
Title: Administrator
Organization: ManorCare Health Services–Salmon Creek, Vancouver, Washington

1. Briefly describe your job responsibilities.

In a nutshell, I manage all areas of business operations for the 120-bed skilled nursing and rehabilitation center through the coordination and direction of my departmental supervisors. As the licensed administrator for the center, I am ultimately accountable for all financial and quality activities within the program and report to my Regional Director of Operations above me.

2. Please give an example of what you would consider to be a "typical" day for you.

This can be the trickiest question asked of a skilled nursing facility (SNF) administrator. Our days are rarely alike due to how they can each be dictated by the immediate needs of our patients and their families. Also, we're a brand-new building in start-up, so we're not quite yet at typical, or routine, operations. However, I will always make the first effort of my day to go around my facility; greeting staff and anyone that I meet on the floor, checking the appearance of the place and our clients to ensure we're meeting our commitments to our high standards for quality. This also helps me be visible to staff and patients.

I'll go back to my office to begin reviewing any e-mails, census, and labor activity since the previous day. At 9 a.m., my interdisciplinary team and I meet to review the previous 24 hours of facility activities, including new orders, admissions, discharges, and changes in patients' conditions. I have routine meetings scheduled

(*continued*)

Name: BEN Y. YOUNG (*continued*)

throughout the day, each focused on a specific function of the operation. These can range from reviewing minimum data set assessments to staffing and recruitment. Throughout the day, department supervisors and other staff will access me for authorizations or to give me updates.

At 3 p.m., the clinical team and I reconvene to follow-up issues identified at the 9 a.m. meeting. This ensures that we don't leave items unresolved.

3. What education or training do you have? Is it typical for your job?

I received my BS in Healthcare Administration from Oregon State University (OSU), with a minor in business administration and certificate in gerontology.

My state and federal licensing required a 6- to 12-month Administrator-in-Training (AIT) course, where I participated first-hand in each discipline of the SNF operation. I believe that this was the most valuable training available because it offered hands-on education with each department, giving a true appreciation for the work being done in an SNF.

4. What is the most challenging part of your job?

The state and federal regulations for SNFs are many. In fact, it is said that we're the most highly regulated industry in the United States. Although I truly believe that the rules and codes are designed to advocate for patients' rights and ensure high-quality healthcare, they can also be restrictive in allowing us to operate in the interest of the patient. The state/federal auditing, or "survey" practices, can be very punitive to SNF operators, so you have to make sure that your attention to compliance is closely "wed" to how you deliver great care and services to your patients. It can be easy to focus too strongly on the interpretation of the rule. The true point of it all is that you need to first focus on what the patient, the person, needs and wants.

Name: BEN Y. YOUNG

5. What do you consider to be the best part of your job?

The staff who choose to work in skilled nursing. It is a difficult business. I believe it is more of a calling than a career. They return each day to help sick and inured people live with as much dignity and satisfaction as they can. Seeing patients improve, or live a better life, rewards us.

6. What path did you take to get to the job you are in today?

The path to this career was natural for me. I pursued studies in general/acute care at the same time that I studied long-term care at OSU. While at school, I volunteered at a local SNF and was president of the American College of Healthcare Executives and American College of Health Care Administrators in the same year, all of which allowed me to experience operations firsthand. I found the people in long-term care to be uniquely sincere and purpose driven. I also loved the proximity to the patients.

I completed my AIT in the summer following graduation and was licensed in the fall. I took an Assistant Administrator position in southern Oregon and followed a career track through a few different facilities as administrator. The opportunity to help build a program from the ground up is rare and my current position with this start-up has been incredible in my personal and professional growth.

7. What advice do you have for someone who is interested in a job such as yours?

Spend time either working or volunteering in skilled nursing before pursuing a career in administration. Our responsibilities to the delivery of care will always match or exceed the business components. You need to empathize with the patient and your staff and really have a feel for what kind of care needs to be given in order to be successful.

62. MARKETING/BUSINESS DEVELOPMENT DIRECTOR

JOB DESCRIPTION

Marketing/Business Development Directors are responsible for pursuing new business opportunities for the healthcare organization. They develop, coordinate, and implement marketing initiatives that are designed to maintain existing business, but at the same time capture new opportunities to increase business. The Director is often involved in operations planning and strategic marketing with top executives. They set the objectives and methods to achieve organizational growth initiatives in the regional market and target customer segments, and the potential to satisfy customer needs with a new service or product. They also develop the training plans to educate and motivate employees in order for them to perform at their most optimum level for the healthcare facility. Additional duties include delivering presentations; participating in meetings with clients, external vendors, and advisors; and conducting workshops.

EDUCATION AND EXPERIENCE

A bachelor's degree is required, preferably with an emphasis in marketing or business. Many top employers show a preference to individuals who possess a master's in business administration. In addition, a minimum of 3 to 5 years of sales or marketing experience is required before promotion to Director.

CORE COMPETENCIES AND SKILLS

- Excellent interpersonal/human relations skills
- Attention to detail
- Ability to delegate responsibility and to prioritize duties
- Strong management skills
- Excellent negotiation skills
- Excellent oral and written communication skills
- Strong presentation skills
- Advanced computer skills

COMPENSATION

National salary data show that Marketing/Business Development Directors have a median total income of about $126,540, with those in the 25th to 75th percentile earning between $88,912 and $164,172.

EMPLOYMENT OUTLOOK

Employment of top business managers, such as Marketing/Business Development Directors, will grow rapidly in the coming years as businesses become more complex. This demand is likely to be driven by the requirement for diversification of long-term care housing and medical care options.

FOR FURTHER INFORMATION

- American College of Health Care Administrators (http://www.achca.org)

7 ■ CAREERS IN COMMERCIAL HEALTH INSURANCE

Name:
ROB BAUER
Title: Director of Quality Assurance
Organization: ATRIO Health Plans, Inc.

1. Briefly describe your job responsibilities.

- Oversee the operations of internal staff and outsourced vendors involved in the company's Medicare and Medicaid health plan products to ensure ongoing program effectiveness
- Develop and implement new business growth/expansion products and manage the renewal and enhancement of current Medicare Advantage products
- Oversee the annual bid submissions to the Centers for Medicare and Medicaid Services (CMS)
- Manage relationships with government entities such as CMS (Medicare) and State of Oregon (Medicaid)
- Direct supervision of the marketing, sales, and pre-enrollment customer service staff
- Reporting, reconciliation, and analysis responsibilities via multiple data sources to ensure operations are within budget and industry benchmarks
- Manage CMS and State of Oregon routine contract-focused audits

(*continued*)

Name: ROB BAUER *(continued)*

- Create and manage the technical writing of all of the company's Medicare plan materials
- Create the benefit design and marketing plan for the company's Medicare Advantage products

2. Please give an example of what you would consider to be a "typical" day for you.

As I talk with my friends and peers in the health plan management field, I believe that I have a typical high-paced, multitasking, e-mail responding, report creating, meeting attending, memo reading kind of day. My day starts out at the office in the morning where I would poor a cup of coffee, read e-mail, and organize my inbox for about half an hour. From there, if I didn't have a meeting that morning, I would start working my task list that is always full. This would consume the better part of my day outside of lunch and would always include any combination of developing a report, creating a presentation, updating multiple project plans for the day, troubleshooting an enrollment-related issue, and having an ad hoc meeting with a department head related to some contract or memo. I would always finish my day at the office by clearing out the e-mails that had piled up throughout the day, reviewing my calendar for and creating a new task list for the next day. I finally get to the gym or home in between 5:30 p.m. and 7 p.m.

3. What education or training do you have? Is it typical for your job?

- **MBA**: George Fox University, Portland, Oregon, December 2005
- **BS**: Oregon State University (OSU), Corvallis, Oregon, June 1999
    - **Major**: healthcare administration; **Minor**: business administration

4. What is the most challenging part of your job?

It would have to be the unrelenting cycle of project after project all through the year and through every single moving part of company's operations.

Name: ROB BAUER

5. What do you consider to be the best part of your job?

Getting to be involved at a decision-making level in every part of the health plans' operations.

6. What path did you take to get to the job you are in today?

My path began with my sophomore year at OSU when I decided to enroll in the Healthcare Administration program for my undergraduate major. During an internship with a large provider clinic in my senior year, Dr. Friedman suggested that I have an informational interview with Jan Buffa, the Chief Executive Officer (CEO) of Mid-Valley Independent Practice Association (IPA). A few weeks later, I had a great informational interview with Jan over lunch and left my resume. After 2 years of working as a data analyst at a Medicaid health plan, I had the opportunity to call Jan one day for a reference. Jan remembered me, still had my resume, and said that the IPA had an analyst position open that I would be perfect for.

I began working for Mid-Valley IPA in November 2001 as a financial analyst. In 2003, I enrolled in the part-time MBA program at George Fox University. As I was nearing graduation from the MBA program in 2005, Jan gave me the opportunity to project manage two very large proposals that would expand the company's health plan lines of business. We were successfully awarded a contract to be a Medicare Advantage organization, and I was promoted to Project Manager. I managed several projects until 2007, when it had become clear that the Medicare line of business needed a full-time program manager. Because I had project managed the launch for our first Medicare health plan, I was promoted to Health Plan Operations Manager. Recently in 2011, via a merger, I became the new Director of Quality Assurance with another Medicare Advantage organization, ATRIO Health Plans.

7. What advice do you have for someone who is interested in a job such as yours?

I would say first of all make sure you are happy. Not just with your job but in the many areas of your life. Next, I would stress

(*continued*)

Name: ROB BAUER *(continued)*

the importance of knowing how to work with data through spreadsheets and databases, and reading and writing effective reports. This provides a strong knowledge base and shows vital association and multitasking skill sets. From here, I would focus on project management. Strong analytical skills paired with the ability to manage projects shows leadership and the ability to see the bigger picture across other projects and departments.

63. CLAIMS ANALYST

JOB DESCRIPTION

A Claims Analyst working for commercial health insurance reviews claims submitted to the company to determine whether or not the claims meet eligibility standards. The person in this position must have a clear understanding of the insurance company's coverage, policies, and procedures, as well as Medicare and Medicaid. If a claim is incomplete or unclear in any way, this person must know what information to collect to make a proper determination on the claim. The Claims Analyst is then responsible for sending payment or a denial letter in a timely manner, dependent upon the result of the claim.

EDUCATION AND EXPERIENCE

A bachelor's degree in a quantitative field, such as business administration, finance, accounting, or mathematics, is strongly preferred. Experience working in claims processing, however, can be used to substitute for an undergraduate degree. Typically employers look for 2 to 5 years experience with a health insurance background. Knowledge of International Classification of Diseases-9th modification (ICD-9) and Current Procedural Terminology (CPT) coding are also highly desirable.

CORE COMPETENCIES AND SKILLS

- Excellent quantitative and analytical ability
- Demonstrated knowledge of Medicare and Medicaid policies, as well as previous experience working with health insurance coverage

- Superior interpersonal and communication skills
- Previous customer service experience
- Experience with ICD-9 and CPT coding
- Knowledge of medical terminology
- Ability to work in a fast-paced environment, as this individual will be handling numerous claims daily

COMPENSATION

Claims Analysts often make between $30,000 and $42,000. They can stand to make as much as $55,000; however, this is dependent upon education and experience. Other factors that affect salary include geographical area, position responsibilities, and the individual insurance company.

EMPLOYMENT OUTLOOK

Coding and documentation will continue to account for a large percentage of the healthcare industry. Furthermore, coding systems will experience major updates over the next year, such as the mandated implementation of ICD-10 by October 1, 2013. As this system develops, knowledgeable Claims Analysts will continue to be in high demand. New analysts, with less experience, may find it easier to enter this field with a new coding system.

FOR FURTHER INFORMATION

- America's Health Insurance Plans (http://www.ahip.org)
- American Health Care Association (http://www.ahcancal.org)

Name:
KELLEY C. KAISER
Title: Chief Executive Officer
Organization: Samaritan Health Plans

1. Briefly describe your job responsibilities.

The CEO of Samaritan Health Plans is responsible for the organization as it accomplishes its mission and goals. The CEO will report directly to the CEO of Samaritan Health Services (SHS) and the Board of Directors of Samaritan Health Plans. The CEO will have responsibility for the company's overall performance and for ensuring the company's financial integrity and membership growth. The CEO will be in charge of the company's ability to provide superior customer value and service, while constantly seeking to manage the costs and improve the quality of the services provided to its members. The CEO will have the responsibility for creating a strategic direction for the company, determining the appropriateness and timing of strategic partnerships, and/or acquisitions/mergers and appropriately expanding the products and services of the company in partnership with the Board of Directors of Samaritan Health Plans. The CEO must be able to help the company adapt for any event that may come in the future.

2. Please give an example of what you would consider to be a "typical" day for you.

Given that my role within SHS is broader than just the health plans, my day can vary greatly. Right now I am doing a lot of reform work as I also act as the vice president (VP) of government affairs for our delivery system. As a system, we are also in the middle of a core system selection and implementation in order to meet

Name: KELLEY C. KAISER

meaningful use, and I am a member of our Executive Transformation Team that is leading this task for the system. A typical day:

Five-mile run to maintain physical and mental health

Returning e-mails and voice mails

Site meeting for the facility I am responsible for

One-on-one with a direct report

Community meeting on planning a town hall about reform

Information Systems transformation meeting

Off to Salem to meet with the Oregon Health Authority about our Medicaid plan

Home for dinner with my family

3. What education or training do you have? Is it typical for your job?

I have a bachelor's degree in Health Care Administration and a master's degree in Public Health with a focus on Health Policy and Management. Yes, in my job a master's degree or higher is required, usually an MPH, MBA, or an MPA is the area of focus.

4. What is the most challenging part of your job?

The most challenging part of my job is the balance between all the pieces. I report up through the system so I do a lot at the system-level, with integration with our hospitals and physicians in how we deliver care. I tend to get tasked with taking the lead in terms of federal and state reform, as it relates to Accountable Care Organization (ACO) and Chief Compliance Officer (CCO) (Oregon's reform) development. I am responsible for a facility with over 500 employees, and I need to make sure the health plans are functioning as they should. Life balance is very important in a job like mine.

(continued)

Name: KELLEY C. KAISER *(continued)*

There are many early morning and/or late night meetings and making sure that this is balanced with my home life is important.

5. What do you consider to be the best part of your job?
Although I outlined the challenges above, the variety is also the best part of my job. I have the opportunity to be involved in many areas and therefore help shape our health systems as it grows. This is a very exciting opportunity that I am honored to have.

6. What path did you take to get to the job you are in today?
I have been around healthcare my whole life and always knew I did not want to be a clinician. I started working in physicians' offices and then moved to the hospital side, which led to the Integrated Delivery/Health Plan side. I took my time and made sure I learned from every job I had. No matter what you are doing, there is always a learning opportunity.

7. What advice do you have for someone who is interested in a job such as yours?
If you are interested in a job like mine, it is important to be able to see all sides of healthcare to be successful. Having been on the hospital, physician, and health plan side allows me to see the big picture in a more realistic way. I truly believe in the Integrated Delivery System model as being the key to healthcare in the future.

Being able to hear all sides of an issue and balance the system perspective and the community perspective are crucial. We are a community-based system and therefore need to make sure we are good partners in the communities we serve.

64. CLAIMS MANAGER

JOB DESCRIPTION

Similar to a Claims Analyst working for commercial health insurance, a Claims Manager must be an expert with regard to the insurance company's claims policies. This person reviews claims to determine whether they are complete and accurate. State and federal regulatory requirements must also be met to approve a claim for reimbursement. Those claims that follow these standards will facilitate reimbursement, while those that are not will be denied. The Claims Manager is responsible for overseeing all or part of the claims division of an insurance company. This person will train and mentor Claims Analysts on a daily basis. This role also serves as the intermediary between the claims department and other top management positions at insurance companies.

EDUCATION AND EXPERIENCE

A bachelor's degree is a minimum expectation for most Claims Manager positions. Educational background should be in business administration, finance, accounting, healthcare administration, or another related field. Prior experience in health insurance claims management is crucial. Many employers expect Claims Managers to have at least 5 to 7 years of relevant prior experience.

CORE COMPETENCIES AND SKILLS

- Superior knowledge of ICD-9 and CPT coding
- Ability to work in a fast-paced environment and maintain a steady number of daily claims files
- Excellent quantitative and analytical ability
- Outstanding interpersonal and communicative skills, as the person in this position will be responsible for working with top management and numerous Claims Analysts
- Demonstrated ability to teach, mentor, and manage a team of employees
- Understanding of medical terminology
- Strong written ability
- Proven ability to make accurate determinations on claims

COMPENSATION

The majority of Claims Managers make between $75,000 and $100,000 annually. They can make as little as $60,000 or as much as $115,000. Managers with broader responsibilities at larger firms will likely earn a higher salary. Similarly, those working in a busier, urban area stand to make more than someone living in a rural setting.

EMPLOYMENT OUTLOOK

Just like a Claims Analyst, this position will continue to be in high demand as providers switch from ICD-9 to ICD-10. Whereas new analyst can be trained new systems, Claims Managers' knowledge and experience will be indispensable in aiding the transition to ICD-10.

FOR FURTHER INFORMATION

- America's Health Insurance Plans (http://www.ahip.org)
- American Health Care Association (http://www.ahcancal.org)

65. CLAIMS REPRESENTATIVE

JOB DESCRIPTION

A Claims Representative serves as the insurance company's first line of contact to providers or individuals submitting claims. It is the responsibility of the person in this position to be knowledgeable about the insurance company's claims policies and procedures in order to answer any potential customer questions. The Claims Representative is often one of the first people to make initial assessments on a claim. This person will usually check for processing errors and missing information before moving the claim to a supervisor. If the Claims Representative deems a file incomplete or inaccurate, the Representative will reach out to the client to resolve the matter.

EDUCATION AND EXPERIENCE

The Claims Representative position is an entry-level position within the claims department of an insurance company. Having an associate's degree or a bachelor's degree in a related field is strongly preferred. Any previous experience working with insurance claims is a bonus. As this position involves heavy customer interaction, previous customer service experience is often required.

CORE COMPETENCIES AND SKILLS

- Demonstrated quantitative and analytical ability in order to resolve daily claims problems in a swift, efficient manner
- Superior customer service experience and demonstrated ability to resolve customer issues
- Ability to work in a fast-paced work environment

- Excellent time management skills
- Demonstrated ability to learn new information, such as medical terminology and ICD-9 coding systems
- Must be able to work within a team

COMPENSATION

Claims Representatives receive a fairly wide-ranging salary. Dependent upon geographical location, the insurance company, and experience, Claims Representatives should expect to earn between $35,000 and $65,000, with $45,000 being the approximate median.

EMPLOYMENT OUTLOOK

Claims Representatives are the entry-level positions in claims divisions at insurance companies. There will continue to be positions available as long as coding and documentation systems remain as prevalent as they are today. While these are entry-level positions, struggling insurance companies, however, may be more inclined to lay these positions off first.

FOR FURTHER INFORMATION

- America's Health Insurance Plans (http://www.ahip.org)
- American Health Care Association (http://www.ahcancal.org)

66. HEALTHCARE RISK MANAGER

JOB DESCRIPTION

Healthcare Risk Managers are in charge of anticipating and reducing the number of accidental incidents at hospitals. The person in this position is responsible for implementing a risk management system that incorporates policies, procedures, and guidelines that hospitals use to avoid accident claims. Education is a key component of a risk management system because hospital employees must learn new, safer, more efficient procedures. The Healthcare Risk Manager often supervises risk management teams to spearhead these educational programs. It is not uncommon for the Healthcare Risk Manager to work closely with a hospital's legal staff when dealing with accidents that lead to lawsuits.

EDUCATION AND EXPERIENCE

Individuals interested in healthcare risk management should have a bachelor's degree in business, mathematics, nursing, or another health-related field. An associate's degree in risk management (ARM) or a master's degree would also be beneficial. Providers hiring Healthcare Risk Managers typically expect to see 3 to 7 years of previous experience in business or healthcare.

CORE COMPETENCIES AND SKILLS

- Demonstrated quantitative skills required for departmental data analysis
- Superior management ability to lead a team in developing and implementing a risk management system throughout the provider
- Ability to communicate with a wide range of healthcare workers, such as doctors, nurses, case managers, and other administrative managers
- Strong time-management skills, as this position requires the individual to balance numerous tasks at once
- Excellent problem-solving skills
- Proven ability to work with a team to achieve a task under general direction
- Superior organizational skills

COMPENSATION

A Healthcare Risk Manager's salary is dependent upon the position's responsibilities. The person in this position stands to make anywhere from $50,000 to $100,000. Managers should expect to earn $60,000 to $75,000, while Directors of Risk Management often make well over $80,000. Other contributing factors to a Healthcare Risk Manager's salary include the institution's geographic location and the individual's previous experience.

EMPLOYMENT OUTLOOK

While risk management does not experience the level of growth that other healthcare departments receive, this department is critical to providers' success. Hospitals will continue to utilize Healthcare Risk

Managers in the future to ensure that they are providing the safest and highest quality care available.

FOR FURTHER INFORMATION

- American Health Information Management Association (http://www.ahima.org)
- Healthcare Compliance Association (http://www.hcca-info.org)
- American Society for Healthcare Risk Management (http://www.ashrm.org)

8 ■ CAREERS IN PUBLIC HEALTH ORGANIZATIONS

67. COMMUNITY HEALTH CENTER DIRECTOR

JOB DESCRIPTION

The Community Health Center Director is responsible for planning, directing, and analyzing community health programs in a community. The person in this position is responsible for evaluating community health problems and establishing programs that address these issues. Some of these programs offer medical services to children, provide nursing care to the elderly, or educating families about disease prevention. This individual confers with other county departments and agencies to implement these programs. Additionally, the Community Health Center Director speaks for the community during legislative hearings and works with local, state, and federal representatives on community health matters.

EDUCATION AND EXPERIENCE

A master's degree in public health or another related field is generally the anticipated level of education for a Community Health Center Director. When applying for this position, candidates are expected to have at least 5 years of experience working in public health. An additional 1 to 2 years of supervisory experience is desirable. Many candidates also come from a nursing background before moving to public health.

CORE COMPETENCIES AND SKILLS

- Excellent management skills and a proven ability to lead a team toward achieving community health goals
- Ability to hire, train, and integrate the right staff into various programs
- Superior communication skills, as this position will require working with staff, program participants, and families, as local, state, and federal officials

- Working knowledge of community health legislation that will affect the standards of health delivery agencies
- Superior understanding of how to assess community health needs and how to implement the right programs to address these issues
- Demonstrated quantitative skills and ability to collect and analyze data
- Exceptional writing skills

COMPENSATION

Community Health Center Directors should expect to earn between $75,000 and $100,000 a year. The discrepancy in salary range is largely attributable to the individual's education and experience, the size and geography of the community health center, and the position's level of responsibility.

EMPLOYMENT OUTLOOK

The economic recession of 2008 made it difficult for community health centers to expand services and hire new employees. Director positions will continue to exist as long as these programs function. Fortunately, community health center funding has slowly gained momentum over the last year or two.

FOR FURTHER INFORMATION

- National Association of Community Health Centers (NACHC; http://www.nachc.com)
- For more information on local programs, research the state's association for community health centers

68. COUNTY HEALTH DEPARTMENT ADMINISTRATOR

JOB DESCRIPTION

The County Health Department Administrator directs operations of the Health Department through the development of policies; setting and developing goals; managing resources; obtaining funding through various state and federal grants, and not-for-profit foundations; and selection of key personnel. Directs and provides the basic "core public health functions" and the essential services of public health, including community health assessments and evaluations to determine the public's health needs of the county and public health preparedness requirements for public health departments. The Administrator obtains and utilizes resources to meet programs and services through developing policies and procedures, establishing budgets, hiring qualified employees, evaluating programs and employees, overseeing revenues and expenditures, maintaining facility and equipment, and ensuring staff remain current in their public health training, educational requirements, and required continuing education programs.

EDUCATION AND EXPERIENCE

Depending on the size of the county health department, a bachelor's degree in nursing, social work, or other clinical area is typically required. Many county health departments give preference to persons with a master's degree in health administration. Most County Health Department Administrator positions require a minimum of 3 years of experience in public health administration.

CORE COMPETENCIES AND SKILLS

- Outstanding interpersonal skills including the ability to effectively communicate with persons throughout the organization
- Excellent verbal and written communication skills
- Demonstrated track record of developing and maintaining collaborative relationships among diverse groups, including elected officials, medical staff, as well as key external stakeholders
- Experience in facilitating the prioritization of community health needs and identification and initiation of responsible solutions
- Skill in coordinating department services with various other healthcare providers and community agencies
- Ability to direct operations according to regulatory agencies and county commission requirements
- Thorough knowledge of the principles, practices, and objectives of public health administration
- Demonstrated understanding and practice of ethical and legal issues associated with public health administration
- Experience with the principles and practices of financial and managerial accounting, including budgets and/or grants
- Ability to utilize standard computer-related applications

COMPENSATION

County Health Department Administrators can earn between $37,000 and $160,000 per year. This wide variation is due to the size and overall budget of the particular county. The vast majority of these positions report to an elected group of local officials (usually county commissioners or supervisors) and, hence, the compensation is frequently a function of competing budget priorities within the county.

EMPLOYMENT OUTLOOK

The employment outlook for County Health Department Administrators is expected to be stable. There is a growing need for persons in this role with training in management given the complexity of managing personnel and budget, and planning and meeting the diverse needs of communities in an era of shrinking budgets for county health departments.

FOR FURTHER INFORMATION

- American Public Health Association (http://www.apha.org)
- National Association of County and City Health Officials (http://www.naccho.org)

Name:
NICK MACCHIONE, MS
Title: Director
Organization: County of San Diego, Health and Human Services Agency

1. Briefly describe your job responsibilities.

Implement policy directives of an elected Board of Supervisors relating to issues involving public health, medical care, and social services.

Lead one of the nation's largest government-run health and social service delivery networks at the local level, serving a population of 3.2 million residents with direct client services to over 500,000 children, adults, and seniors annually.

Manage an annual operating budget of over $2 billion with a diverse professional workforce of 5,200 employees and hundreds of volunteers.

Manage the day-to-day operations of the County of San Diego, Health and Human Services Agency (HHSA), the major departments of which include the following: Public Health, Behavioral Health, Inpatient Medical Care (109-licensed bed acute care Psychiatric Hospital and 192-licensed bed subacute care Edgemoor Hospital), Public Assistance Services, Child Welfare Services, Aging and Independence Services, Public Guardian and Public Administrator, Early Childhood Development Services, and the Executive Office (finance, operations, human resources, compliance, strategy, information technology, legislative affairs, media, and contracts). Specific client services include the following: public health for the entire county, behavioral health for 70,000 clients, inpatient medical care for over 225 patients, an extensive Medicaid managed care network for 353,000 beneficiaries, employment assistance and other key public assistance programs for 85,000 individuals in subsidized employment training and 225,000 in food assistance, child welfare

(*continued*)

Name: NICK MACCHIONE, MS *(continued)*

services for 6,000 children, adult protective services for hundreds of seniors, and numerous early childhood development programs.

Manage a diverse portfolio of over 500 for-profit and not-for-profit contracted agencies.

2. Please give an example of what you would consider to be a "typical" day for you.

I run a "5–10" routine most of the time: up at 5 a.m. for a brisk jog, followed by responding to new e-mails, then breakfast with my wife and two kids, where as a family we are discussing their goals for the school day. Then, it is off to the shower; dress for success and in the car listening to radio news while en route to the office. I arrive by 7 a.m.; respond to more e-mails for the first 30 or so minutes, with the next 30 minutes dedicated to reviewing paperwork for signature and reading mail and online news service alerts for various search topics related to health, medical care, and human services. I hold a briefing at 8 a.m. with my executive team (Chief Operations Officer, Chief Financial Officer, Human Resources Director, and Director for the Office of Strategic Innovations) to discuss the week's objectives, with an emphasis on mitigating major risks (financial, operational, legal, and political). Then, I meet with my executive assistant to map out the schedule for the day and week. Next, I participate in meetings (ranging from in-person to WebEx and conference calls) that run on average from 15 to 30 minutes in length with various stakeholders: executive team members, executive committees, elected officials and/or their staff, community members, service contractors and IT vendors, funders (including federal and/or state administrators), and media. Meetings run through noon, before I break for a 30-minute lunch (which is often at my desk, while I am responding to e-mails... although, on occasion, I enjoy having lunch with my wife). In the afternoon, I participate in meetings from 1 to 5 p.m. (which occasionally includes traveling to offsite meetings at community events or Agency sites), before ending the day responding to more e-mails and paperwork for the last hour or so.

Name: NICK MACCHIONE, MS

In the evening, I head out to the fitness center for a quick workout and arrive home in time for dinner with the family to discuss how everyone's goals were met or unmet. Also, I discuss current events taking place locally and throughout the world, assist with my kids' homework, and spend time with my wife before the end of the evening.

3. What education or training do you have? Is it typical for your job?

I completed two master's degrees that helped round out my interests and needs in public policy and healthcare management.

First, I completed my Bachelor of Arts (BA) degree in biology, with minor in Psychology from Rutgers State University in New Jersey. As part of my Senior Honor's Program, I completed my thesis by conducting basic science research and publishing the results in a peer-reviewed journal in the field of neurobiology. Overall, my undergraduate education served as a solid foundation in understanding the basic science of medicine and public health.

Next, I sought a better understanding of managing organizations, specifically in the healthcare field. I completed a master's degree in management from New York University's Robert F. Wagner's Graduate School of Public Service. Under Dr. Tony Kovner's mentorship, my degree had specific emphasis on strategic healthcare management.

Over the next few years, I felt I still needed a further understanding of how public policy influences healthcare organizations in the delivery of medical care and public health. I completed a master's degree at Columbia University in New York City. Specifically, I completed the executive master's program in public health (EMPH) that prepares mid- to senior-level executives to understand the relationship between health policy, heath services management, and population health.

And finally, lifelong learning is a must for positions in leading large integrated health and human services agencies. While employed

(*continued*)

Name: NICK MACCHIONE, MS *(continued)*

at HHSA, I completed three different professional fellowships over the course of a decade. First, I completed the Public Health Leadership Scholar program sponsored by the Public Health Leadership Institute and federal Centers for Disease Control and Prevention. Next, I completed the Creating Healthier Communities Fellowship with the Health Forum/American Hospital Association. Lastly, I became a Fellow of the American College of Healthcare Executives (ACHE), and served a 3-year term as the elected ACHE Regent for San Diego and Imperial Counties.

Although everyone's individual journey to a career as a health and human services director will vary, having an understanding of how policy, management, and public health interact is crucial. A high-quality graduate education from accredited programs in health, psychology, social service, public policy, and/or management is essential. It is also important to supplement graduate education with professional fellowships that expand one's knowledge of healthcare policy and practice. Lastly, networking with other professionals in the health and social service fields is a key aspect to one's success.

4. What is the most challenging part of your job?

Constantly balancing budgets against public service demands in open theater where media pundits and advocates criticize your decisions is always challenging. It is like being Don Quixote, Robin Hood, and Niccolo Machiavelli, all wrapped in one. The daily action of the job requires balancing three major roles. First, you need a high level of idealism of what impact the Agency is trying to make per your Board's direction; then, it comes down to knowing what is right to do and not get caught up in doing it right. Second, in this line of work, new revenue maximization is often not enough of a solution to meet your client needs, so you are confronted with cost-shifting from one program to another. Third, the business of public health and human services is political. Knowing how to navigate within large and complex political bureaucracies is not for the faint of heart, but the strong in political acumen. In sum, the most challenging part of this job is having a solid

Name: NICK MACCHIONE, MS

working connection between a strong mind, big heart, tough gut with lots of intestinal fortitude, and Teflon-like thick skin.

5. What do you consider to be the best part of your job?

The best part of my job is the personal gratification I receive in fulfilling the organizational purpose in building better health, safety, and well-being for 3.2 million people living in the fifth largest county in the nation (equivalent to the size of the State of Connecticut). It is absolutely fulfilling to me in knowing that the 5,200 professionals who work for my Agency are helping to make a positive difference in the lives of 500,000 San Diegans who are among the most vulnerable and needy of our community.

6. What path did you take to get to the job you are in today?

Other than choosing the HHSA career path, the Directorship opportunity presented itself to me after working over 10 years as the Agency's Deputy Director. For over a decade, I directed over 1,000 dedicated HHSA employees. Through many innovative public–private partnerships involving hundreds of community-based stakeholders, we completed remarkable community transformations in the improvement of health, safety, and well-being. Successful transformations in improving the health and safety status of children and adults, including the economic well-being of disadvantaged families, were my admission to my current position.

7. What advice do you have for someone who is interested in a job such as yours?

I would offer the following pieces of advice:

Learn as much as you can from your faculty members and invited guest speakers while going through your undergraduate and graduate school education. While you are at it, ask questions and gain knowledge—don't simply memorize the answers to the questions. Also, pursue the more challenging (but rewarding) progressive curvilinear

(*continued*)

Name: NICK MACCHIONE, MS *(continued)*

learning path, and not just point-to-point progression. For example, learn the intersection between social welfare policy and childhood obesity, and not just the biologic determinants that contribute to type II diabetes. See the big picture as much as you can while going through your education: that you are practicing what you will be doing as a future director leading an institution that influences the social determinants of health and well-being.

Do an undergraduate/graduate internship (or even volunteer) in a public health department, child welfare office, mental health outpatient clinic, or public assistance eligibility office. Experiencing firsthand what the health and human services professionals do each and every day will provide you the best insight into the mission of public institutions to protect the public's health, safety, and well-being.

Search for your nearest professional chapter affiliated with the ACHE, American Public Health Association, or any other related public health and human services associations. Attend some of their educational programs. These seminars provide great insight into current events in the health and human services field. Oftentimes, the speakers are a mixture of practitioners and academicians. In addition, it is a great way to network with fellow colleagues and future prospective academic advisors and/or employers.

Strong body, strong mind, strong spirit! Healthy, happy people with spiritual beliefs and meaningful social interactions live the longest (and are the healthiest, too). Start now by serving as a role model for your future profession. Take care of your physical well-being; your education will be sure to stimulate lots of intellectual challenges along the way and having your physical faculties in good working order will help you tackle those challenges.

Find your inner true calling in whatever you do, but especially in this profession, public service involving public health, medical care, and social services. You will need to answer to your purpose-driven career objectives each and every day. A deep conviction of your purpose in making a positive difference for population health, safety, and well-being will not only help guide you in your ethical decision making in dealing with the complex challenges of the profession, but also, most importantly, it will result in a thriving and highly satisfying career.

69. DEPUTY HEALTH SYSTEM ADMINISTRATOR—INDIAN HEALTH SERVICE

JOB DESCRIPTION

The Deputy Health System Administrator serves as the primary assistant to the Chief Executive Officer (CEO) of the designated health system within the Indian Health Service (IHS). Deputy Health System Administrators have day-to-day operational authority and responsibility for the activities of their health system. In consultation and coordination with the CEO, the Deputy recommends and initiates program improvements and modifications to meet the changing needs of the beneficiary population in order to achieve IHS goals and objectives, while making the best possible use of all available resources. The Deputy plans and assigns work to be accomplished, either directly or in general terms to supervisors, and reviews work product/evaluations made by supervisors of work accomplishments. The person in this position will have direct responsibility and supervision over the procurement/property and supply, information technology, compliance program, facilities management, and housekeeping departments.

EDUCATION AND EXPERIENCE

The minimum education required for this position is a Master of Health Administration degree from a program accredited by the Commission for Accreditation of Healthcare Management Education (CAHME). The position requires that the candidate possess at least 1 year of specialized management experience equivalent to at least the General Schedule (GS)-13 level.

CORE COMPETENCIES AND SKILLS

- Outstanding interpersonal skills including the ability to effectively communicate with persons throughout the organization
- Excellent verbal and written communication skills
- Demonstrated experience in overall management duties with planning, organizing, directing, and evaluating clinical and environmental support services

- Experience in evaluating and adjusting organizational structure to ensure the most effective and efficient delivery of healthcare and healthcare programs
- Significant experience in leading quality improvement teams
- Experience in facilitating the prioritization of community health needs, and identification and initiation of responsible solutions
- Skill in ensuring customer service to Tribal Health Programs, urban health programs, alcohol treatment programs, behavioral health programs, and federal service units
- Knowledge of planning, coordination, and execution of business functions, resource allocation, and production
- Ability to influence, motivate, and challenge others; adapts leadership styles to a variety of situations
- Demonstrated ability to make sound, well-informed, and objective decisions; perceives the impact and implications of decisions; commits to action, even in uncertain situations, to accomplish organizational goals; and causes change
- Demonstrated understanding and practice of ethical and legal issues associated with health administration
- Experience with the principles and practices of financial and managerial accounting, including budgets and/or grants
- Ability to utilize standard computer-related applications

COMPENSATION

Deputy Health Services Administrators in IHS can earn between $97,000 and $126,000 per year. These are positions funded by the U.S. government and persons in these roles receive all the benefits available to federal employees.

EMPLOYMENT OUTLOOK

The employment outlook for health services administration in IHS will be strong in the foreseeable future. Preference for these jobs is given to veterans and members of the U.S. Public Health Service (USPHS) Commissioned Corps.

FOR FURTHER INFORMATION

- American Public Health Association (http://www.apha.org)
- IHS (http://www.ihs.gov)

70. EMERGENCY MANAGEMENT COORDINATOR

JOB DESCRIPTION

The Emergency Management Coordinator will work as part of the leadership team in city, county, or state government agencies. The Coordinator's role is to plan and coordinate comprehensive emergency management program activities. The person in this position will be responsible for developing, implementing, and maintaining emergency management programs, plans, policies, and procedures with the goal of reducing injury and loss of life, property, or environment in the city/county/state as a result of an emergency or disaster. This person will work in all aspects of emergency management programs, including mitigation, preparedness, response, and recovery. In addition, this person will perform a role during Emergency Operations Center (EOC) activations.

EDUCATION AND EXPERIENCE

Emergency Management Coordinators generally possess a bachelor's degree in communication, business administration, education, emergency management, healthcare management, or public administration along with a minimum of 2 years of experience in emergency management. In addition, Emergency Management Coordinators must have completed a series of courses (either in person or online) in the areas of incident command and National Incident Management System (NIMS). Finally, experience in emergency and disaster plans development is highly desirable.

CORE COMPETENCIES AND SKILLS

- Outstanding interpersonal skills including the ability to effectively communicate with current and potential customers along with persons throughout the organization
- Excellent verbal and written communication skills
- Knowledge of natural hazards and hazards caused by humans, with particular attention paid to those common to the area in which the person will work
- Knowledge of the functions of emergency management, including mitigation, preparedness, response, and recovery
- Knowledge of incident command systems and emergency/recovery support functions

- Knowledge of federal and state emergency management planning requirements
- Facilitation skills in working with multidisciplinary and multi-agency groups
- Ability to work in an environment where changing priorities are the norm and flexibility is a must; demonstrated skills in managing multiple tasks
- Ability to conduct research and present recommendations, both orally and in writing
- Ability to use standard computer office software
- Experience conducting risk analysis using software such as HAZUS or other loss estimation tools is preferred

COMPENSATION

Emergency Management Coordinators typically earn $60,000 to $120,000 per year depending upon the level of experience and the size of the government entity.

EMPLOYMENT OUTLOOK

The employment outlook for Emergency Management Coordinators is generally good. City, county, and state governments are required to actively work at being prepared for emergencies and disasters, so there is a continuing need for skilled persons in these roles.

FOR FURTHER INFORMATION

- National Emergency Management Association (http://www.nemaweb.org)

Name:
MIA A. PRICE
Title: Former Chief Operations Officer
Organization: Milwaukee Health Services, Inc. (MHSI)

1. Briefly describe your job responsibilities.

When I worked for MHSI, I had an abundance of responsibilities. I provided direction for all health center programs and services, with an emphasis on general administrative and day-to-day operations; maintained and oversaw all health center operations in conjunction with executive management team; assumed responsibility for MHSI in the absence of the CEO; trained staff, demonstrating ability to speak publicly and engage audience; produced, maintained, and disseminated statistical reports descriptive of health center performance and productivity.

In addition to the aforementioned, I also conducted corporate presentation sessions both onsite and offsite; ensured organization and all subsystems, processes, departments, teams, and employees worked together to achieve desired outcome through performance management; conducted ongoing community needs assessments to advise corporate leadership on programming direction; produced corporate correspondence; addressing local, state, and national issues; and coordinated completion of corporation's grant application, development, and implementation. I reported directly to the CEO.

2. Please give an example of what you would consider to be a "typical" day for you.

Every day I went to work, I had to answer questions: What do I do now, why do we have to do this, which budget line item will cover this cost, is this item needed, what is the return of investment for this item, and so on.

(*continued*)

Name: MIA A. PRICE *(continued)*

So a typical day involved tremendous communication (whether written or verbal), making sound judgment calls, and exercising restraint when navigating through challenges with patients, staff, providers, and so on with varying demands.

3. What education or training do you have? Is it typical for your job?
I have a BS in Psychology (Central State University) and an MSA in Health Services Administration (Central Michigan University). I am currently working on acceptance into the Urban Studies PhD program (University of Wisconsin–Milwaukee).

4. What is the most challenging part of your job?
The most challenging was dealing with changes daily. Working in community health, or in operations for that matter, is multifaceted; there is rarely a day when one mirrors the next, so being able to effectively manage through a sea of change is vital to your professional growth and development as a leader.

5. What do you consider to be the best part of your job?
The best part of any job for me is being allowed the chance to coach and train staff. When you are able to make change as part of the solution, there is nothing better.

6. What path did you take to get to the job you are in today?
I took a huge risk and moved to places where I had no family, no friends, and built a community of support.

Sometimes one must move out of an element of comfort in order to succeed: That is exactly what I did. I wish I could say that all my decisions were easy, but they were not; it was all about accomplishing a goal that I set for myself. I stuck to it: I did exactly what I said I was going to do.

Name: MIA A. PRICE

7. What advice do you have for someone who is interested in a job such as yours?

Go for it! Document what you want (I mean clearly define your next position), go to the people that can make it happen for you (human resource Directors, CEOs, Chief Operating Officer [COOs]), and ask for what you want without hesitation.

Further, it has been my experience that a good leader is someone who invests in other potential leaders. One must look for those leaders and seek mentorship; this is how one learns (both personally and professionally).

Being a student of life will take you wherever you want to go. Case in point, my leadership development came through associations in which I sought development with: National Association of Health Services (NAHSE), Great Plains Public Health Institute (GPPHI), ACHE, and NACHC. To date, I continue to seek development with those I am affiliated with through these vehicles and always willing to listen to sage advice from the experts.

71. ADMINISTRATIVE OFFICER—INDIAN HEALTH SERVICE

JOB DESCRIPTION

An Administrative Officer within IHS oversees the management and administrative duties of multiple departments within a facility. The person in this position may oversee departments that include, but are not limited to, Human Resources, Finance, Facilities, and Supplies. The Administrative Officer is responsible for staffing an administrative team that will evaluate designated departments of the facility. This team will review departments' policies and procedures, identify inefficient practices, and make recommendations for future program improvements.

EDUCATION AND EXPERIENCE

Applicants for Administrative Officer positions will be expected to have at least a bachelor's degree in hospital administration, healthcare administration, business administration, finance, or other related field. A master's degree in one of these fields is strongly encouraged. Additionally, a PhD or 3 years of relevant postgraduate experience is beneficial. One year of GS-09 grade level experience can be used to substitute for a PhD or an equivalent doctoral degree.

CORE COMPETENCIES AND SKILLS

- Previous experience and familiarity working with the Native American population
- Strong ability to manage a team toward achieving departmental goals
- Demonstrated ability to evaluate department procedures, collect and analyze data, and implement plans to eliminate inefficiencies
- Strong written and communication skills
- Superior ability to educate the departments about new policies and procedures
- Must be self-directed and able to carry out self-made plans
- Ability to hire, train, and integrate the right staff into various programs

COMPENSATION

Administrative Officers at IHS facilities should expect to earn between $55,000 and $75,000 each year. The individual's background experience and the position's level of responsibility will largely determine the exact salary.

EMPLOYMENT OUTLOOK

IHS positions are required by law to give preference when hiring to qualified Indian applicants and employees. When hiring, IHS committees look to hire applicants that will serve in the institution for an extended period of time. The IHS is constantly looking for young, qualified candidates to place in organizations around the country.

FOR FURTHER INFORMATION

- IHS: The Federal Health Program for American Indians and Alaska Natives (http://www.ihs.gov)
- National Indian Health Board (http://www.nihb.org)

72. PUBLIC HEALTH PROGRAM MANAGER

JOB DESCRIPTION

A Public Health Program Manager works on the daily operations of preparing, building, coordinating, and maintaining a community health program. Whereas a Community Health Center Director would be involved in numerous community programs, the Program Manager would focus on just one. This individual creates and evaluates how the program's services affect the respective community. The Public Health Program Manager works within a budget to coordinate a small community health team. This team will speak with families in the community and evaluate data to instill program tactics that benefit community behavior. The Program Manager coordinates the budget by writing grant proposals and receiving donations.

EDUCATION AND EXPERIENCE

A bachelor's degree in public health, nursing, or other related field is often the minimum expected level of education. Candidates applying for a Public Health Program Manager position should have 2 to 4 years of experience coordinating public health services and community health programs. A master's degree in a relevant field can often be used as a substitute for experience in the field.

CORE COMPETENCIES AND SKILLS

- Demonstrated ability to analyze community health needs and coordinate a program to address those needs
- Prior experience writing grant proposals for community health programs
- Excellent communication skills, as this positions requires speaking with participants' families, coworkers, and community representatives
- Superior management and writing skills
- Working knowledge of community health legislation that will affect the standards of health delivery agencies
- Exceptional problem-solving ability and comfort evaluating data
- Ability to educate participants about preventive services

COMPENSATION

A Public Health Program Manager should expect to make between $45,000 and $70,000. This salary range is largely attributable to the individual's previous experience, the size of the community health program this position is responsible for, and the program's geographical area.

EMPLOYMENT OUTLOOK

Community Health Center Director and Public Health Program Manager positions have largely not been affected by the struggling U.S. economy. While these positions still remain, they have had to learn to achieve more results with fewer resources. Community health centers are beginning to see more, as hospitals team with centers to combat chronic community diseases. This indicates that more Program Manager positions may be available in the future.

FOR FURTHER INFORMATION

- NACHC (http://www.nachc.com)
- APHA (www.apha.org)

Name:
SAMUEL SCHAFFZIN

Title: Lieutenant Commander (LCDR); Senior Health Insurance Specialist/Medicaid Health IT Coordinator
Organization: U.S. Public Health Service Commissioned Corps
Current Assignment: Centers for Medicare and Medicaid Services

1. Briefly describe your job responsibilities.

I am a Lieutenant Commander in the USPHS Commissioned Corps, which is made up of more than 6,500 public health professionals of many disciplines who are dedicated to public health promotion and disease prevention programs, and advancing public health science. As one of America's seven uniformed services, the Commissioned Corps fills essential public health leadership roles within federal government agencies and programs. USPHS Commissioned Corps officers have opportunities for mobility among multiple government agencies throughout their careers, and we are encouraged to expand our knowledge base and expertise. We are trained and equipped to respond to public health crises and national emergencies, such as natural disasters, disease outbreaks, or terrorist attacks, and belong to multidisciplinary teams that are capable of responding to domestic and international humanitarian missions.

As part of my duties to the Commissioned Corps and the nation, I am a member of a Regional Incident Support Team that provides rapid assessments and initial incident coordination and assistance to state, tribal, and local health authorities in times of large scale disaster. There are specific training and deployment responsibilities that come with this response team and I am "on call" 24/7 to respond to disasters and events that have public health emergency implications and require resources and support from the federal government. I also participate in special security events that may have health and medical support needs.

(*continued*)

Name: SAMUEL SCHAFFZIN *(continued)*

Most recently, I was activated to support the 2011 State of the Union Address, the Independence Day Celebration, and the President's Address to the Joint Session of Congress. During these events, I am typically assigned as a liaison to state and local government-led emergency operation centers on behalf of the U.S. Department of Health and Human Services (DHHS). In addition to interfacing with multiple agencies and stakeholders responsible for overseeing and carrying out a successful response or activity, I serve as a direct line of communications between the lead response entity (state or locality) and DHHS. Over the course of the event, I am constantly analyzing the emergency situation, providing updates to both sides, fielding requests, identifying key resources, and offering guidance.

My current job assignment is in the Centers for Medicare and Medicaid Services (CMS), where I serve as a Senior Health Insurance Specialist and Medicaid Health IT Coordinator within the Center for Medicaid and CHIP Services (CMCS). In this role, I help develop, implement, and evaluate the Medicaid Electronic Health Record (EHR) Incentive Program that supports the DHHS's goal of adoption of EHR for most Americans. I also serve as a liaison to Center for Medicare and Medicaid Services (CMS) regional office staff and other federal partner agencies on Health IT matters. I am currently leading a regulation writing team tasked with drafting future policy for the EHR Incentive Program. Finally, I am a project officer for two contracts: one that evaluates how states are implementing Medicaid EHR Incentive Programs and another that focuses on providing technical assistance to states that are implementing the program.

2. Please give an example of what you would consider to be a "typical" day for you.

A typical day is full of conference calls, meetings, and policy review and development. My job is highly collaborative and I spend a great deal of time each day corresponding with team

Name: SAMUEL SCHAFFZIN

members, program partners, and stakeholders. My day may begin with a coordination meeting with a team of federal partners who are exploring the topic of mobile health and how to implement health resources nationwide. It may follow with a status update meeting with a contractor who is supporting our efforts to evaluate how individual states are implementing the program. I often participate in "Communities of Practice" calls, which bring together state Medicaid officials to share promising practices and address hot button issues as they relate to the developing program. Because I have been at my position for only 6 months, I often try to set aside time in the day to review and develop program-related resources in order to build on my knowledge base and become a subject matter expert on Medicaid, the EHR Incentive Program, and the field of Health IT. I frequently attend national-level conferences to either present or participate in training sessions. Communication is key in this position, so I am frequently monitoring and responding to e-mail.

In addition, as an officer, I have ongoing responsibilities to the USPHS Commissioned Corps and the nation. I serve on several professional committees including the Junior Officer Advisory Group that advises the Surgeon General on policy matters and the Health Administration Professional Advisory Subcommittee that convenes a team of officers to explore health policy and management issues as they relate to the Corps. I also serve on a Corps-wide work group that looks at ways to engage youth in public health and prevention activities. As I mentioned earlier, I am assigned to a deployment team that provides incident coordination and assistance to state, tribal, and local health authorities in times of disaster. There are specific training and deployment responsibilities that come with this response team and I am "on call" 24/7 to respond to disasters and events that have public health emergency implications and require resources and support from the federal government.

(*continued*)

Name: SAMUEL SCHAFFZIN *(continued)*

3. What education or training do you have? Is it typical for your job?

I have a BA in Sociology with a minor in Public Health (Rutgers University) and a MPA in Health Policy and Management (New York University, Wagner School of Public Service).

The USPHS Commissioned Corps is comprised of officers in different categories based on their training and education. With my background, I was able to take a commission in the Health Service Officer category at the rank of Lieutenant and based on my previous training and work experience in the public health field, I was promoted to Lieutenant Commander after 1 year. As you move up in your career, the promotion process becomes more and more competitive. I will be eligible to compete for the rank of Commander in the next few years.

My USPHS Commissioned Corps colleagues have a variety of backgrounds and may be part of the following categories: Physician, Pharmacist, Dentist, Veterinarian, Nurse, Dietitian, Scientist, Engineer, Therapist, Environmental Health, and Health Services (which consists of health administrators and related specialties, psychologists, podiatrists, optometrists, social workers, physician assistants, dental hygienists, and medical technologists). My CMS colleagues have a variety of educational backgrounds as well, including degrees in law, public health, public affairs, public policy and administration, and business, along with a variety of clinical degrees, including medicine, nursing, pharmacy, physical therapy, psychology, and social work. My team is specifically designed to bring together a wide variety of backgrounds in order to successfully implement the EHR Incentive Program.

4. What is the most challenging part of your job?

As with many careers, identifying and juggling priorities and managing time effectively are among the challenges I face each day. This can be somewhat heightened by my dual responsibilities to CMS and USPHS Commissioned Corps. However, the greatest

Name: SAMUEL SCHAFFZIN

challenge is navigating government bureaucracy. Each agency has its own hurdles and red tape and determining how to get contracts, documents, and funding channeled to the correct parties, reviewed, and approved, can be daunting and frustrating.

5. What do you consider to be the best part of your job?

The best part of my current position is knowing that I have the potential to impact and shape the U.S. public health and healthcare system. I work with many bright, motivated, and passionate people and I feel we are achieving our goals and improving the healthcare system in a very tangible way.

In a broader sense, I feel fortunate to be a member of the Commissioned Corps because it affords me the opportunity to work in different areas of public health, healthcare, and across the federal government and gives me freedom to pursue my professional interests and the opportunity to grow as a leader. I am glad to serve the country in return for the combination of flexibility and job security.

6. What path did you take to get the job you are in today?

After completing my bachelor's degree, I worked at Memorial Sloan-Kettering Cancer Center in New York City as a Clinical Session Assistant, which was an entry-level position in the field of health administration. For 2 years I served as liaison between the patient, family, and clinical team during ambulatory visits, while rotating through outpatient surgery, medical oncology, and chemotherapy clinics, and learning the day-to-day fundamentals of hospital operations. Knowing that I wanted to pursue a career in health administration, I decided to return to school to pursue a Master's of Public Administration, with an emphasis on health policy and management. I chose this degree because I felt it would provide me with the fundamentals that I needed to launch a career in the broad field of public health and healthcare, and across the

(*continued*)

Name: SAMUEL SCHAFFZIN *(continued)*

government, nonprofit, and private sectors. Upon completion of my master's degree in 2003, I worked at the American Red Cross in Philadelphia as a Disaster Health and Mental Health Services Coordinator. In this role, I had the opportunity to manage a team of 300 health professional volunteers who provided specialized services to those impacted by fires, floods, ice storms, and other disasters. I also gained firsthand experience in managing shelters, mass care operations, and the logistics, as part of a Red Cross disaster response.

The experience at the Red Cross piqued my interest in the field of disaster preparedness and response. After attending a State Public Health Association conference, I learned about a developing public health preparedness program called the Medical Reserve Corps (MRC). Soon after, I left the Red Cross to accept a position as a consultant to the federal government to serve as a Regional Coordinator to the MRC Program. Based in Philadelphia, in this position, I provided management and outreach support to the Regional Health Administrator in recruiting, establishing, supporting, and sustaining local MRC volunteer units within the DHHS Region III (Pennsylvania, Delaware, Maryland, District of Columbia, Virginia, and West Virginia). I also offered technical assistance and guidance to established and emerging MRC units about resources available to aid in developing, implementing, maintaining, and raising awareness of the MRC program throughout the region.

After 6 months in this position, I was promoted to serve as the National Technical Assistance Coordinator for the MRC program. In this role, I worked directly in the Office of the Surgeon General in Rockville, Maryland, and provided technical assistance and guidance to national-level program partners, state- and local-level officials, and others on public health, preparedness, and volunteer management issues. I also managed ten Regional Coordinators who were positioned in regional HHS offices. The Surgeon General, who is the spokesperson for the MRC program, also oversees the operational command of the USPHS Commissioned Corps and

Name: SAMUEL SCHAFFZIN

through my work in the Office of the Surgeon General, I met many Commissioned Corps officers who were assigned to different DHHS agencies. After serving as the National TA Coordinator for 4 years, I had the opportunity to switch roles within the MRC program and move into a federal position as a program officer responsible for national-level outreach. In April 2009, I took a commission, became a USPHS Commissioned Corps Officer, and joined the Office of the Surgeon General as a federal staff member. This was my first assignment in the USPHS Commissioned Corps. After 2 years in this role, I moved to my current assignment at CMS in Baltimore. The Commissioned Corps is unique from other uniformed services in that officers are responsible for finding their "next position." Since I was interested in working in the area of Health IT Policy and Healthcare Reform, I thought CMS, which is both a high-profile federal agency and is at the center of the Recovery and Affordable Care Acts, would be a good fit. I was able to secure a job as a Senior Health Insurance Specialist and Medicaid Health IT Coordinator within the Center for Medicaid and CHIP Services and started my new assignment in May 2011.

7. What advice do you have for someone who is interested in a job such as yours?

It can be difficult to break into the federal government and the USPHS Commissioned Corps is no exception. The Corps recruits professionals with a wide array of backgrounds, but looks for unique individuals who are committed to protecting, promoting, and advancing the health and safety of our nation. So it is important to stand out within your field of training and expertise. I would generally advise someone interested in the USPHS Commissioned Corps to gain exposure to as many real-life training and professional experiences as possible that relate to the broad fields of public health and healthcare.

Some general guidance: Do not be shy, seek out mentors and mentorship opportunities, and do not be afraid to "ask." People

(*continued*)

Name: SAMUEL SCHAFFZIN *(continued)*

are more willing to help than you think and are also open to sharing their knowledge and experience. Take risks and get outside of your comfort zone. Finally, learn a lot about different topics and disciplines so that you are considered a mini subject matter expert. Once you've landed in a job, stay focused on your organization's mission. If you are interested in my CMS job assignment or my position within the USPHS Commissioned Corps, for example, I encourage you to research everything there is to know about these organizations. Consider setting up informational interviews and shadowing opportunities with professionals who may be in the field of public health and healthcare and have knowledge and expertise to share with you as you launch a career in this important field.

73. VETERANS HEALTH ADMINISTRATION—HEALTH SYSTEMS SPECIALIST

JOB DESCRIPTION

The Health Systems Specialist provides a wide variety of specialized management services, including healthcare management and statistical analysis, financial management, program analysis, long-range policy and planning, and general administrative support to the Clinical Director/Director of the various health service lines within the Veterans Health Administration (VHA).

EDUCATION AND EXPERIENCE

As a federal agency, the VA Health System employs the GS developed by the Office of Personnel Management to determine the education and experience required for each job as classified by where it is placed in the GS rating system. Program Analysts are ranked as either a GS 12 or 13. This position requires a master's degree preferably in business administration or health administration. Necessary experience includes at least 1 year at a GS 11 for appointment as a GS 12 and 1 year of experience at a GS 12 for appointment as a GS 13.

CORE COMPETENCIES AND SKILLS

- Outstanding interpersonal skills including the ability to effectively communicate with current and potential customers along with persons throughout the organization
- Excellent verbal and written communication skills
- Product planning to include documenting and maintaining product strategies and roadmaps
- Recommends changes for improvement, implements/initiates approved processes, and monitors the improvements
- Responsible for the tactical, business, and strategic plans within the service line
- Develops and formulates budget requests for coming fiscal year and multiple years
- Establishes guidelines and performance expectations for subordinates that are clearly communicated through the formal employee performance management system
- Ability to work in an environment where changing priorities are the norm and flexibility is a must; demonstrated skills in managing multiple tasks
- Ability to conduct research and present recommendations, both orally and in writing
- Ability to use standard computer office software
- Develops performance standards and writes position description and observes performance. Resolves informal complaints and grievances

COMPENSATION

VA Health Systems Specialists earn $68,800 to $105,900 per year.

EMPLOYMENT OUTLOOK

The employment outlook for VA Health Systems Specialists is generally good. The VA Health System is growing to respond to the need created by veterans who served in Korea and Vietnam, but most recently for those who served in the Iraq and Afghanistan conflicts. The large number of injured young veterans will require health services over multiple decades and the VA must be able to respond in kind.

FOR FURTHER INFORMATION

- VA Careers (http://www.vacareers.va.gov)

74. VETERANS HEALTH ADMINISTRATION—PROGRAM ANALYST

JOB DESCRIPTION

The Program Analyst works within the VA Point of Service (VPS) Office in the Chief Business Office (CBO). The Program Analyst is responsible for assisting the Deputy Program Director with product planning, communication, and execution throughout the product lifecycle. The Program Analyst works to determine product needs and customer requirements, and collaborates closely with internal teams and external contractors to ensure development according to project vision and agency strategy and goals. In this position, the Program Analyst will implement business plans and maintain project schedules and budget.

EDUCATION AND EXPERIENCE

As a federal agency, the VA Health System employs the GS developed by the Office of Personnel Management to determine the education and experience required for each job as classified by where it is placed in the GS rating system. Program Analysts are ranked as either a GS 12 or 13. This position requires a master's degree preferably in business administration or health administration. Necessary experience includes at least 1 year at a GS 11.

CORE COMPETENCIES AND SKILLS

- Outstanding interpersonal skills including the ability to effectively communicate with current and potential customers along with persons throughout the organization
- Excellent verbal and written communication skills
- Product planning to include documenting and maintaining product strategies and roadmaps
- Manage activities associated with systems engineering and modeling systems
- Testing and implementing healthcare software in medical centers at a nation-wide level
- Provide guidance on patient and clinical processes in a medical center to support healthcare program development and healthcare tracking software improvement
- Facilitation skills in working with multidisciplinary and multi-agency groups

- Ability to work in an environment where changing priorities are the norm and flexibility is a must; demonstrated skills in managing multiple tasks
- Ability to conduct research and present recommendations, both orally and in writing
- Ability to use standard computer office software
- Veterans Health Information Systems and Technology Architecture (VistA) program knowledge in a healthcare setting

COMPENSATION

VA Program Analysts earn $68,800 to $105,900 per year.

EMPLOYMENT OUTLOOK

The employment outlook for VA Program Analysts is generally good. The VA Health System is growing to respond to the need created by veterans who served in Korea and Vietnam, but most recently for those who served in the Iraq and Afghanistan conflicts. The large number of injured young veterans will require health services over multiple decades and the VA must be able to respond in kind.

FOR FURTHER INFORMATION

- VA Careers (http://www.vacareers.va.gov)

9 ■ CAREERS IN CONSULTING FIRMS

Name:
ALICE LAM
Title: Senior Manager
Organization: Manatt Health Solutions

1. **Briefly describe your job responsibilities.**
   Manatt Health Solutions (MHS) is an interdisciplinary policy and business advisory division of Manatt, Phelps and Phillips, LLP, one of the nation's premier law and consulting firms. I provide policy analysis, project implementation support, and strategic and regulatory advice to healthcare, human services, and advocacy organizations.

2. **Please give an example of what you would consider to be a "typical" day for you.**
   Like many jobs, there really isn't a typical day. The combination and types of activities vary from a day-to-day basis—another reason I like my job—but could include the following: reviewing federal and state policies, drafting memoranda and policy briefs, providing strategic advice and counsel to clients based on my understanding and analysis of the healthcare environment, and organizing and managing planning and implementation projects for clients.

(*continued*)

Name: ALICE LAM *(continued)*

3. What education or training do you have? Is it typical for your job?

I completed a Master's in Public Administration, with a focus on health policy and management. Holding a graduate degree in public administration, public policy, public health, or law is typical for my job.

4. What is the most challenging part of your job?

The two most challenging parts of my job are juggling different demands under aggressive timelines and navigating political complexities, which are usually outside of my control.

5. What do you consider to be the best part of your job?

I enjoy being able to work on issues relevant to shaping health policy, and how such policy is implemented on the federal, state, and local levels. It has given me a true appreciation of the need for practical policymaking.

6. What path did you take to get to the job you are in today?

I pursued higher education in the health policy field immediately after completing an undergraduate degree. Acknowledging that I had limited work experience, I pursued internships while completing my studies, including an administrative residency at an academic medical center. While the residency was not directly health policy-focused, it started to imbue in me the importance of understanding operational considerations in policymaking.

After graduate school, I completed the Presidential Management Fellows (PMF) program in Washington, DC. While I was based at an Executive Branch healthcare agency, the fellowship also provided the opportunity for me to complete several rotational assignments working in Congress and at two health policy think tanks. All of these experiences allowed me to sharpen my focus on the types of career opportunities I enjoyed and intended to pursue.

Name: ALICE LAM

7. What advice do you have for someone who is interested in a job such as yours?

For someone interested in pursuing a career in health policy, I think it is critical to gain an understanding of content, process, and dynamics. Become familiar with current policy issues and choose an area of focus. Gain knowledge of the process and dynamics by working for, or with, governmental entities. In addition, pursue experiences that give you a variety of perspectives, which will give you a more well-rounded understanding and make you a better analyst.

75. BUSINESS SOLUTIONS ADVISOR

JOB DESCRIPTION

Business Solutions Advisors work closely on projects with physician groups, hospitals, health systems, and other customers to drive system changes. Business Solutions Advisors are experts in their respective project's field, which includes health information technology (IT), supply chain management, operations, and finance. The person in this position analyzes the customer's needs and develops strategic metrics for measuring improvement. The Business Solutions Advisor serves as a project expert throughout the project's transition period, coaching key institutional employees.

EDUCATION AND EXPERIENCE

Whereas the Business Solutions Advisor is considered an expert on each project, significant relatable experience and education is required. A master's degree in a field that associates with the projects the individual will work on is often expected. A minimum of 5 to 7 years of demonstrated experience working in healthcare or business is required.

CORE COMPETENCIES AND SKILLS

- Demonstrated success working with operational projects during previous employment

- Ability to analyze system inefficiencies and develop strategic metrics
- Superior quantitative skills and comfort working with data reports
- Proven ability to communicate with a broad range of people, including physicians, nurses, and administrative staff
- Outstanding leadership skills, as this position requires mentoring customers during project implementation

COMPENSATION

Salaries for Business Solutions Advisors vary due to a range of issues, such as the position's field of expertise, the individual's background experience, and the position's level of responsibility. Business Solution Advisors should expect to make anywhere from $75,000 to $140,000.

EMPLOYMENT OUTLOOK

Consulting in general is a stable field that health systems and individual providers will continue to utilize. External expert opinions will continue to be a primary source of improving healthcare systems. Significant experience is required to become a Business Solutions Advisor because such expertise is highly regarded by hospitals around the country.

FOR FURTHER INFORMATION

- National Society of Certified Healthcare Business Consultants (http://www.nschbc.org)
- Health Financial Management Association (www.hfma.org)

76. RESEARCH ANALYST

JOB DESCRIPTION

Research Analysts are responsible for coordinating, designing, and implementing research for healthcare clients. They collect and analyze data on market trends and business opportunities using a variety of methods such as literature reviews, focus groups, site visits, and surveys. The Research Analyst needs to be skilled in writing for various types of audiences. Often, they publish their research and present it at conferences. They are experts in the healthcare industry and as such help to provide status reports and create business strategies for their clients. Research A analysts also seek to create and maintain relationships with healthcare organizations.

EDUCATION AND EXPERIENCE

A bachelor's degree is the minimum educational requirement for most Research Analyst positions; most positions prefer applicants to have a graduate degree with a focus in business administration, healthcare administration, or public health. Prior research experience is critical as is experience in the use of statistical programming. Most organizations require 2 years of work experience as a Research Analyst.

CORE COMPETENCIES AND SKILLS

- Knowledge of statistical databases, such as SPSS, SAS, STATA, NVivo, Excel
- Excellent quantitative, analytical, and critical thinking abilities
- Strong writing ability
- Ability to work in a team environment
- Experience with communication and presentation of concepts and results
- Ability to work in high-intensity environment

COMPENSATION

The mean wage of Research Analysts is around $55,000. They can make as little as $35,000 or as much as $80,000. Research Analysts with more experience or those working at larger firms will likely earn a higher salary. Similarly, those working in a busier, urban area stand to make more than someone living in a rural setting.

EMPLOYMENT OUTLOOK

This position will be in high demand as healthcare providers try to navigate through healthcare reform and the changing characteristics of the population. As healthcare providers seek strategies to gain market share and maximize reimbursements, they will need to use the expertise of consulting firms and their healthcare Research Analysts.

FOR FURTHER INFORMATION

- American Association of Healthcare Consultants (www.aahc.net)
- American College of Healthcare Executives (www.ache.org)

77. REVENUE CYCLE/OPERATIONS CONSULTANT

JOB DESCRIPTION

The Revenue Cycle/Operations Consultant is responsible for assessing customer provider's revenue cycle efficiency. This individual works with the customer to implement projects that will assist with revenue cycle turnaround. The Revenue Cycle/Operations Consultant must develop metrics that strengthen the functions of revenue cycle management. This individual strategizes plans that will implement policies and procedures within providers to ensure they receive reimbursements for all services rendered in a timely manner. During project implementation, the Revenue Cycle/Operations Consultant coaches his or her customer's employees to smoothen the transition period.

EDUCATION AND EXPERIENCE

A master's degree in finance, accounting, business administration, or a healthcare-related field is often expected. Demonstrated success in a relevant field for a period of 5 to 10 years is also required, as this position is regarded to be an expert with regard to the revenue cycle. Generally, this experience is expected to come in a healthcare setting.

CORE COMPETENCIES AND SKILLS

- Considerable experience working in finance and providers' revenue cycle
- Working knowledge of International Classification of Disease-9th Revision (ICD-9), International Classification of Disease-10th Revision (ICD-10), Health Insurance Portability and Accountability Act (HIPAA) 5010, and clearinghouses
- Demonstrated success working with data analysis and implementing strategic metrics to improve the customer's revenue cycle
- Superior communication skills and the ability to present solutions to executives and other staff
- Excellent problem-solving abilities, as this position is required to identify solutions to potential revenue cycle process inefficiencies
- Successful leadership skills and the ability to coach teams during transitional projects
- Ability to be self-motivated, as this is an unstructured position

COMPENSATION

The importance of Revenue Cycle/Operations Consultants is well reflected in their average salaries. These consultants receive anywhere from $70,000 to $115,000, dependent upon the individual's experience, the organization's financial standing, and the geographic location.

EMPLOYMENT OUTLOOK

Similar to many consulting positions, this line of work is highly competitive, making it difficult to break into. Providers can lose millions of dollars each year on revenue cycle inefficiencies. For this reason, successful Revenue Cycle/Operations Consultants will continue to be highly coveted by providers and health systems around the country.

FOR FURTHER INFORMATION

- Health Financial Management Association (www.hfma.org)
- National Society of Certified Healthcare Business Consultants (http://www.nschbc.org)

10 ■ CAREERS IN HEALTH INFORMATION TECHNOLOGY

78. DIRECTOR OF HEALTH INFORMATION TECHNOLOGY PLANNING AND OPERATIONS

JOB DESCRIPTION

The Director of Health Information Technology (IT) Planning and Operations is accountable for IT strategic planning, IT governance, portfolio operations, and ensuring all IT priorities are aligned with the organization's strategic priorities and goals. The Director must have extensive understanding of healthcare, future trends in the areas of technology portfolio management, and the role of IT in advancing the organization's capabilities. The Director maintains a strong understanding of IT technologies and the technologies to deliver services to the organization and works closely with all other IT management personnel in identifying, evaluating, and selecting specific IT that support the business plans and IT strategic direction.

EDUCATION AND EXPERIENCE

A bachelor's degree in business administration or IT is the minimum academic qualification, although a master's degree in either business or IT is becoming the standard level of education for IT Directors. Most hospitals require a minimum of 7 to 10 years of senior IT experience within healthcare organizations.

CORE COMPETENCIES AND SKILLS

- Outstanding interpersonal skills including the ability to effectively communicate with persons throughout the organization
- Excellent verbal and written communication skills
- Deep understanding and proven track record over several years in IT strategy delivery, and excellent awareness of the strategic goals and ability to define and influence those goals

- Exhibit strong process improvement orientation, with experience in establishing portfolio management and IT governance frameworks
- Ability to lead effectively and utilize social influence to achieve organizational objectives
- Ability to coach and mentor a wide variety of staff
- Strong analytic skills
- Substantial knowledge of technology solutions in a healthcare provider environment

COMPENSATION

Directors of Health IT Planning and Operations earn in the range of $120,000 to $180,000, although the total salary will vary depending on the size and location of the healthcare organization.

EMPLOYMENT OUTLOOK

The employment outlook for Directors of Health IT Planning and Operations is particularly strong. Each and every hospital in the nation is working to develop their IT infrastructure in response to demands by the federal government and the need to provide ever-higher levels of quality care. Possessing an IT background is an important requirement, but the applicant must also be familiar with the unique requirements of healthcare delivery.

FOR FURTHER INFORMATION

- Health Information Management Systems Society (http://www.himss.org)

79. EDUCATION AND TRAINING DIRECTOR

JOB DESCRIPTION

The Education and Training Director functions under the direction of the Senior Director of Information Systems and provides direct supervision of the Corporate Training Development Team who are responsible for developing training materials necessary for Health Information Systems (HIS) and technology education and support. The Director is responsible for building and providing direction to the overall IT training program. The training materials and delivery media are designed to facilitate the train-the-trainer sessions and facilitate independent interactive learning for IT system implementations and enhancements. The person in this position oversees the collaboration with content and IT system experts in developing the materials in cooperation with the care site training and support personnel. The Director may oversee contract fulfillment and service levels of an outsourced training function, assigns personnel to the various training tasks and directs their activities, and reviews and evaluates work and prepares performance reports related to training programs. The person in this position will be responsible for directing multiple concurrent projects and will provide guidance to multiple teams on issues that range from prioritizing, operational issues, and conflict management that may be associated with multiple projects.

EDUCATION AND EXPERIENCE

The Education and Training Director requires a minimum of a bachelor's degree in computer science or a related area. Preferred education includes a master's degree in business administration or health administration. Experience in instructional design is highly preferred. A minimum of 2 years of database development and design, web design, and technical assistance is required.

CORE COMPETENCIES AND SKILLS

- Outstanding interpersonal skills including the ability to effectively communicate with persons throughout the organization
- Excellent verbal and written communication skills
- Advanced-level computer skills, including MS Word, Excel, PowerPoint, Access, Visio, and Web design
- Familiarity working in a data warehouse environment
- Outstanding customer service skills
- Experience with negotiations and contract development
- Demonstrated ability to develop creative solutions to complex problems
- Ability to utilize creative and analytical problem-solving techniques to extremely varied situations
- Substantial knowledge of technology solutions in a healthcare provider environment

COMPENSATION

Education and Training Directors earn in the range of $60,000 to $90,000, although the total salary will vary depending on the size and location of the healthcare organization.

EMPLOYMENT OUTLOOK

The employment outlook for Education and Training Directors is particularly strong. Each and every hospital in the nation is working to develop their IT infrastructure in response to demands by the federal government and the need to provide ever-higher levels of quality care. Possessing an IT background is an important requirement, but the applicant must also be familiar with the unique requirements of healthcare delivery.

FOR FURTHER INFORMATION

- Health Information Management Systems Society (http://www.himss.org)

80. ELECTRONIC MEDICAL RECORDS DIRECTOR

JOB DESCRIPTION

The Electronic Medical Records (EMR) Director directs and oversees the EMR information system that supports the integration of the organization's business entities. Works with senior and middle management to develop strategic plans and priorities for the EMR system and ensures implementation of agreed upon objectives. The Director will utilize creative and analytical skills to solve new and complex problems. The EMR Director directs a staff of information systems and training professionals consulting with and assisting all levels of management and staff throughout the organization. Technical currency is maintained by on going education tempered and supplemented by applicable work experience.

The EMR Director recommends goals and objectives for the EMR automated information system to senior management. The EMR Director establishes plans and recommends policies and procedures for the EMR System within Information Systems Department to meet the organization's mission.

The EMR Director oversees large-scale development efforts, implementations of commercial software package, and modifications to the EMR System. The EMR Director maintains quality of Information Systems, implement corrective action, and identify needs for new or improved information services. The EMR Director directs activities of Information Systems relative to the EMR System for the entire organization.

EDUCATION AND EXPERIENCE

EMR Directors typically possess a master's degree in computer science, business administration, or health administration along with 5 years of increasingly responsible information system management experience, preferably in a healthcare computer environment.

CORE COMPETENCIES AND SKILLS

- Outstanding interpersonal skills including the ability to effectively communicate with persons throughout the organization
- Excellent verbal and written communication skills
- Ability to work independently and in a complex team environment
- Ability to make decisions consistent with overall corporate and departmental objectives
- Maintains confidentiality and integrity of data, materials, and user information within the program
- Ability to utilize creative and analytical problem-solving techniques in extremely varied situations
- Substantial knowledge of technology solutions in a healthcare provider environment
- Ability to effectively manage activities and personnel

COMPENSATION

EMR Directors earn in the range of $50,000 to $180,000 although the total salary will vary depending on the size and location of the healthcare organization.

EMPLOYMENT OUTLOOK

The employment outlook for EMR Directors is particularly strong. Each and every hospital in the nation is working to develop their IT infrastructure in response to demands by the federal government and the need to provide ever-higher levels of quality care. Possessing an IT background is an important requirement, but the applicant must also be familiar with the unique requirements of healthcare delivery.

FOR FURTHER INFORMATION

- Health Information Management Systems Society (http://www.himss.org)

Name:
MICHAEL BANYAS
Title: Public Health Analyst and Communications Lead, Health Resources and Services Administration, U.S. Department of Health and Human Services
Organization: Office of Health Information Technology and Quality

1. Briefly describe your job responsibilities.

Currently, I work for the Health Resources and Service Administration's (HRSA) Office of Health IT and Quality. HRSA is an agency within the U.S. Department of Health and Human Services (DHHS) and is the primary federal agency for improving access to healthcare services for people who are uninsured, isolated, or medically vulnerable. In my position, I am a Public Health Analyst and the Communications Lead. My responsibilities as Communications Lead include developing communications strategies and managing outreach projects regarding health IT and quality issues within HRSA. In addition, I direct HRSA's Health IT and Quality Improvement websites, produce HRSA's monthly Health IT and Quality newsletter, write press releases, and plan technical assistance articles highlighting HRSA grantee work. I also work with other HHS agencies in developing technical assistance materials relevant to HRSA's grantees based on federal healthcare initiatives. Furthermore, I am the liaison to HRSA's Office of Rural Health Policy and coordinate with their staff on health IT and quality issues affecting rural providers such as critical access hospitals and rural health clinics.

2. Please give an example of what you would consider to be a "typical" day for you.

My day is a mix of both big and small meetings, leading projects, and writing. Among these items, writing consumes 85% of my day. For the most part, I am writing or drafting e-mails, web pages, press releases, memos, or project plans, as well as working on drafts of these products with colleagues.

Name: MICHAEL BANYAS

3. What education or training do you have? Is it typical for your job?

I have an undergraduate degree in Political Science and English, as well as a Master's in Public Administration (MPA). MPAs are common for management positions in my field. The MPA provides an understanding of how to manage people and projects, and to implement policy, all within a nonprofit or government environment. These two degrees provide me with a solid foundation for my career and current position. Nonetheless, continued training in such areas as health informatics, project management, writing, and leadership skills are important for my work.

4. What is the most challenging part of your job?

Writing is the most challenging aspect of my job. Since college, I have known the importance of strong writing skills and continuously developed this skill throughout my professional career. When writing memos, e-mails, web pages, grantee articles, and press releases, each piece of writing requires a different writing style depending on the audience. These reasons make writing one of the most valuable and frustrating aspects of my job and career. The constant shift in writing styles coupled with the volume of writing required for my job often causes fatigue and frustration. Typically, fatigue arises when a document's final product is not satisfactory to yourself and your leadership. However, drafts and colleague comments are necessary to not only improve my writing skills, but also deliver a high-quality product.

5. What do you consider to be the best part of your job?

Developing relationships and working with smart and dedicated people is the best part of my job. My job requires working with people across HHS and HRSA on a variety of problems and solutions. Without the input and collaboration of my colleagues, I would not grow professionally or produce high-quality work helpful to HRSA's grantees.

(*continued*)

Name: MICHAEL BANYAS (*continued*)

6. What path did you take to get to the job you are in today?
After I was accepted in to the U.S. Public Health Service, I applied for a position in HRSA's former office of Health IT and was hired. I obtained this position not only because of my professional work in the U.S. Senate, hospitals, and DHHS, but also the skills I developed in these positions. Skills such as project management, policy analysis, writing, and understanding of both health IT and the healthcare delivery systems all matched the qualifications of the person my supervisors were seeking for my position.

7. What advice do you have for someone who is interested in a job such as yours?
Aside from good writing skills, it is important that one does not become isolated by e-mail in communicating with your colleagues. E-mail limits a person in building interpersonal relationships with colleagues and can impede your development as a professional. Whether it's leading a work group, receiving feedback on a document, or trying to get an understanding of a problem, I feel it is helpful to have a phone or face-to-face conversation with a person. While some conversations need to be documented in an e-mail, for example, when discussing a contract with a vendor or dispersing a set of tasks to a project team, I believe it is critical that a professional develops interpersonal relationships with their colleagues as an important way to produce high-quality work and develop professionally.

81. HEALTH INFORMATION EXCHANGE INTEGRATION ANALYST

JOB DESCRIPTION

The Health Information Exchange (HIE) Integration Analyst manages and implements the complex integration projects of the HIE initiative, analyzes client systems to ensure compatibility, ensures problem resolution, and provides system support to users. The HIE Integration Analyst writes project plans and implements and manages projects with complex Health Level

(HL) 7 interfaces between multiple clinical systems. The Analyst creates work estimates for interface development and programming for clients in the healthcare sector. The HIE Integration Analyst conducts project planning and scheduling, status reporting, resource allocation, as well as issue and risk management, while cultivating the relationship with the customer.

EDUCATION AND EXPERIENCE

A bachelor's degree in a healthcare-related field, computer sciences, IT, clinical informatics, or similar field, or 10 additional years of equivalent experience in healthcare IT and integration is required. Preferred training includes a master's degree in computer science, IT, clinical informatics, or similar field. Certification in project management is frequently required.

CORE COMPETENCIES AND SKILLS

- Outstanding interpersonal skills including the ability to effectively communicate with persons throughout the organization
- Excellent verbal and written communication skills
- Deep knowledge of Health IT techniques and procedures; HL7 and interoperability standards (including IHE, CCD, and Direct standards); networking and operating systems; and knowledge of interface engines
- Possesses proven ability to successfully design and implement complicated interface projects and develop interfaces and requirements to implementation. Understands (or learns) enough about the sending and receiving systems to validate how data are being stored, used, and presented
- Ability to work independently and in a complex team environment
- Maintains a close working relationship with the local medical community
- Maintains confidentiality and integrity of data, materials, and user information within the program
- Strong analytical skills
- Substantial knowledge of technology solutions in a healthcare provider environment

COMPENSATION

HIE Integration Analysts earn in the range of $70,000 to $120,000, although the total salary will vary depending on the size and location of the healthcare organization.

EMPLOYMENT OUTLOOK

The employment outlook for HIE Integration Analysts is particularly strong. Each and every hospital in the nation is working to develop their IT infrastructure in response to demands by the federal government and the need to provide ever-higher levels of quality care. Possessing an IT background is an important requirement, but the applicant must also be familiar with the unique requirements of healthcare delivery.

FOR FURTHER INFORMATION

- Health Information Management Systems Society (http://www.himss.org)

82. HEALTH INFORMATION MANAGEMENT EXCHANGE SPECIALIST

JOB DESCRIPTION

A Health Information Management Exchange Specialist manages HIE, planning, and implementation of projects. The person in this position collaborates with vendors to ensure success of technological implementations. The Exchange Specialist must assist in the review and evaluation process of proposals. It is the responsibility of the Health Information Management Exchange Specialist to monitor the health exchange project for timeliness and accuracy to achieve compliance and project goals. The position requires directing and delegating staff members by overseeing execution and problem solving. Finally, it is critical that the Exchange Specialist keeps projects under budget.

EDUCATION AND EXPERIENCE

Health Information Management Exchange Specialists require a bachelor's degree in business, health administration, economics, IT, or a related field. A master's degree is preferred. The position requires at least 5 years of experience in implementation and management of IT projects.

CORE COMPETENCIES AND SKILLS

- Strong background working with HIE operations
- Strong familiarity with healthcare environment and HIE services and products

- Ability to follow federal and state guidelines and regulations
- Experience in managing numerous projects effectively
- Ability to communicate across industries and political lines for the good of the organization
- Excellent listening skills
- Excellent verbal and written communication and presentation skills

COMPENSATION

The salary range for Health Information Management Exchange Specialists is $64,000 to $90,000. Organizations that require broad responsibilities will pay higher than those with narrow responsibilities. Those in urban, fast-paced areas will stand to make a higher salary than those in rural areas.

EMPLOYMENT OUTLOOK

Over the next 5 years, the Health Information Management Exchange Specialist will experience a shortfall of 50,000. Health information exchange is the way of the future in healthcare information. Organizations nationwide will require individuals knowledgeable in information exchange.

FOR FURTHER INFORMATION

- Healthcare Information and Management Systems Society (www.himss.org)

83. INFORMATION MANAGEMENT SPECIALIST

JOB DESCRIPTION

The main responsibility of an Information Management Specialist is to process, maintain, compile, and report patient information for purposes defined by the organization. Patient medical records must be compiled, processed, and maintained following medical, administrative, ethical, and legal requirements. An Information Management Specialist retrieves patient information for physicians and other medical personnel while protecting the security of the medical records. Another responsibility is to release information to agencies or other organizations, according to regulation. Information Management Specialists review patient medical records for accuracy, completeness, and compliance with regulations. This position requires the development and maintenance of data storage and retrieval systems to organize and classify information.

EDUCATION AND EXPERIENCE

A bachelor's degree is a minimum education requirement for most Information Management Specialist positions. The expectation is for at least 3 years of experience within the healthcare sector where the job occurs, that is, insurance or consulting. Employers expect applicants to have high verbal and written communication skills.

CORE COMPETENCIES AND SKILLS

- Expert knowledge of various research methods
- Excellent written and oral communication skills
- Expert in use of office productivity applications
- Ability to predict the organization's data collection
- Provide innovative solutions
- Excellent time management and experience in time scheduling
- Excellent organizational skills
- Proficient with Microsoft Word applications

COMPENSATION

The average annual salary for an Information Management Specialist is roughly $75,000. The salary range is quite large, between $47,000 and $120,000. The more seniority in the position will result in higher compensation.

EMPLOYMENT OUTLOOK

In most organizations, the Information Management Specialist position is considered middle level. However, there is significant growth available within the position. With added knowledge, individuals can be promoted within the position. Specialists with technical training generally have better opportunities for advancement.

FOR FURTHER INFORMATION

- Healthcare Information and Management Systems Society (http://www.himss.org)

84. INFORMATION TECHNOLOGY AUDITOR

JOB DESCRIPTION

In many organizations, the IT Auditor position is a third-level position. The job title can end with I, II, or III, depending on the experience and knowledge of the individual. IT Auditor I is considered an entry-level position, while IT Auditor III is the most advanced position. All levels have the same job description; however, salary, independence, and responsibility are greater as the levels increase. The position requires the audit of information systems and procedures to be in accordance with the organization's guidelines for efficiency, accuracy, and security. The IT Auditor evaluates the IT infrastructure to determine risk to the organization, while providing improvements for current risk issues.

EDUCATION AND EXPERIENCE

All IT Auditor levels require a bachelor's degree in IT or a related field. IT Auditor I is an entry-level position that requires at least 1 year of experience in the field. IT Auditor II and III are more advanced and require 2 to 5 years of experience in the field.

CORE COMPETENCIES AND SKILLS

- Knowledge of concepts, practices, and procedures within the field
- Conducting audit interviews to identify key control activities
- Preparing vulnerability assessments of technology and supporting business and IT processes
- Identifying control issues and assessing the adequacy of controls
- Completing all audit program steps
- Communicating and validating findings
- Participating in special projects and performing other duties as assigned
- Excellent written and verbal communication

COMPENSATION

The median salary range for an IT auditor is $45,000 to $90,000. Depending on the level of auditor, the individual's position determines the salary range of the position. On average, Auditor I earns $50,000, Auditor II earns $65,000, and Auditor III earns $80,000.

EMPLOYMENT OUTLOOK

The growing use of IT in healthcare requires individuals to maintain systems within organizations. Promotion within IT is endless, even within one organization. IT systems need such positions to validate security and make crucial improvements.

FOR FURTHER INFORMATION

- Healthcare Information and Management Systems Society (www.himss.org)

85. KNOWLEDGE MANAGEMENT SPECIALIST

JOB DESCRIPTION

The Knowledge Management Specialist supports the healthcare organization's vision; mission; strategic initiatives; clinical, business, and program priorities; and organizational goals by using clinical and business systems and technical expertise; and by designing, creating, and developing automated business intelligence solutions and providing internal consultation and project management. This person provides knowledge in business/clinical processes and analytical expertise, knowledge, and strong leadership skills to work with key stakeholders, end users, and project team members. Identifies and resolves issues throughout the project phases of assessment, design build, testing, training, and implementation. Accountable for identifying opportunities for continuous improvement in workflow processes in the implementation of technology solutions. The Knowledge Management Specialist is responsible for frequently taking a formal or an informal lead on project tasks.

EDUCATION AND EXPERIENCE

Knowledge Management Specialists typically possess a bachelor's degree in health science, computer science, math, business, or a related field, or equivalent technical training/certification. Work experience that demonstrates technical competency may be substituted for formal education along with at least 8 years of experience in progressively more responsible work as a data analyst and consultant or equivalent.

CORE COMPETENCIES AND SKILLS

- Outstanding interpersonal skills including the ability to effectively communicate with persons throughout the organization

- Excellent verbal and written communication skills
- Ability to create, read, understand, and interpret data models
- Familiarity working in a data warehouse environment
- Ability to work independently and in a complex team environment
- Strong experience with MPP (Massively Parallel Processing), specifically Netezza
- Strong SQL skills
- Ability to utilize creative and analytical problem-solving techniques to extremely varied situations
- Substantial knowledge of technology solutions in a healthcare provider environment

COMPENSATION

Knowledge Management Specialists earn in the range of $50,000 to $80,000, although the total salary will vary depending on the size and location of the healthcare organization.

EMPLOYMENT OUTLOOK

The employment outlook for Knowledge Management Specialists is particularly strong. Each and every hospital in the nation is working to develop their IT infrastructure in response to demands by the federal government and the need to provide ever-higher levels of quality care. Possessing an IT background is an important requirement, but the applicant must also be familiar with the unique requirements of healthcare delivery.

FOR FURTHER INFORMATION

- Health Information Management Systems Society (http://www.himss.org)

86. PROJECT MANAGER

JOB DESCRIPTION

The Project Manager manages the clinical informatics project process, including requests, reviews, approvals, scoping, feasibility studies, and project delivery. Leads multidisciplinary teams of stakeholders to ensure projects are evaluated, triaged, initiated, and completed in a timely manner, within projected scope and budget. The Project Manager consults with clinical and administrative IT initiatives in the organization requiring project management expertise, leads business process analyses, needs assessments, and cost/benefit analyses in an effort to align informatics solutions with business initiatives. Organizes, directs, and develops project team resources in order to effectively meet project commitments and business objectives.

EDUCATION AND EXPERIENCE

The Project Manager requires a minimum of bachelor's degree in computer science, business administration, or health administration. Preferred education includes a master's degree in business administration or health administration. Experience in instructional design is highly preferred. A minimum of 2 years of database development and design, web design, and technical assistance is required.

CORE COMPETENCIES AND SKILLS

- Outstanding interpersonal skills including the ability to effectively communicate with persons throughout the organization
- Excellent verbal and written communication skills
- Advanced-level computer skills, including MS Word, Excel, PowerPoint, Access, Visio, and project management software
- Outstanding customer service skills
- Experience with conflict resolution
- Demonstrated ability to work effectively in team-oriented environments
- Ability in utilize creative and analytical problem-solving techniques in extremely varied situations
- Substantial knowledge of technology solutions in a healthcare provider environment

COMPENSATION

Project Managers earn in the range of $50,000 to $95,000, although the total salary will vary depending on the size and location of the hospital, and the scope of responsibility.

EMPLOYMENT OUTLOOK

The employment outlook for Project Managers is particularly strong. Each and every hospital in the nation is working to develop their IT infrastructure in response to demands by the federal government and the need to provide ever-higher levels of quality care. Possessing an IT background is an important requirement, but the applicant must also be familiar with the unique requirements of healthcare delivery.

FOR FURTHER INFORMATION

- Health Information Management Systems Society (http://www.himss.org)

11 ■ CAREERS IN DURABLE MEDICAL EQUIPMENT

87. ACCOUNT MANAGER

JOB DESCRIPTION

The job of the Account Manager is to lead and manage the sales and support of the given medical device in a particular geographic region or to a given sector of the healthcare industry (e.g., hospitals or physician offices). The Account Manager is responsible for supervising the activities of the sales representatives in his/her particular area. The Account Manager plans and executes sales activities, including development of key account strategies, their implementation, and the required coordination of resources. The Account Manager develops proposals and price quotations for a variety of healthcare professionals, including physicians, nurses, biomedical engineers, and administrators. Finally, the Account Manager completes quarterly business reviews, detailing all account activity and strategies employed for ensuring the attainment of sales goals.

EDUCATION AND EXPERIENCE

The Account Manager requires a minimum of bachelor's degree in health administration, business administration, or science. Account Managers typically possess at least 5 to 7 years of medical device sales experience.

CORE COMPETENCIES AND SKILLS

- Outstanding interpersonal skills including the ability to effectively communicate with current and potential customers along with persons throughout their organization
- Excellent verbal and written communication skills
- Direct selling experience of medical devices in a competitive, strategy-intensive market

- Experience in negotiations with executive administration levels; that is, Chief Financial Officer (CFO), Chief Information Officer (CIO), Chief Executive Officer (CEO), and Chief Medical Officer (CMO)
- Strong data analysis, evaluation, and problem-solving skills
- Demonstrated creative coaching for field personnel recognizing different styles and types of motivation
- Demonstrated ability to achieve sales plans
- Ability to provide evaluation of performance after sales calls, presentations, and so on, in order to improve technical and selling skills of sales people
- Relationship management, strategy development, problem solving, and change management skills
- Demonstrated ability to use standard computer software programs, including Word, Excel, Access, and PowerPoint

COMPENSATION

Account Managers generally earn a base salary and then a commission based on the total sales of the team. A base salary of $50,000 is typical for medical device Account Managers with additional commission pushing the total package as high as $120,000, depending on the geographic area and type of device sold. The nature of the work requires significant travel and, in most cases, Account Managers receive compensation for the use of their personal vehicle.

EMPLOYMENT OUTLOOK

The employment outlook for Account Managers is good. This represents the first supervisory managerial position available in the domain of medical device sales. There is regular turnover in these positions, particularly for well-known medical device manufacturers. Medical devices represent an important technology for every healthcare organization, and there are a number of start-up firms every year that require experienced Account Managers.

FOR FURTHER INFORMATION

- Medical Device Manufacturers Association (http://www.medicaldevices.org)

88. REGIONAL MANAGER

JOB DESCRIPTION

The job of the Regional Manager is to lead and manage a large geographic region in the sales of one or several medical device products. The Regional Manager will lead a group of Corporate and National Account Managers, and achieve and exceed sales plans within specified budget. The Regional Manager will also recruit, hire, develop, and retain Regional Sales Personnel. The Regional Manager provides input to the National Director of Sales regarding sales and negotiation strategies and plans. The Regional Manager develops sales goals and objectives for each territory on a fiscal and quarterly basis in order to achieve the organizational sales annual operating plan. The Regional Manager ensures that all field personnel are meeting or exceeding all objectives set, including both revenue-/cost saving-based objectives and market development objectives.

EDUCATION AND EXPERIENCE

The Regional Manager requires a minimum of a bachelor's degree in health administration, business administration, or science. Regional Managers typically possess at least 7 to 10 years of medical device sales experience.

CORE COMPETENCIES AND SKILLS

- Outstanding interpersonal skills including the ability to effectively communicate with current and potential customers along with persons throughout their organization
- Excellent verbal and written communication skills
- Experience and success in negotiating contracts, selling to medical directors of health plans, and working collaboratively with field sales personnel to achieve goals
- Demonstrated skills in business planning, consulting, and territory financial analysis
- Strong data analysis, evaluation, and problem-solving skills
- Demonstrated creative coaching for field personnel recognizing different styles and types of motivation
- Ability to interpret and explain business/marketing policies and programs to employees in order to maintain consistency and

responsiveness to customer needs, ensuring that market and territory strategies are fully executed
- Ability to provide evaluation of performance after sales calls, presentations, and so on, in order to improve technical and selling skills of sales people

COMPENSATION

Regional Managers generally earn a base salary and then a commission based on the total sales of the team. A base salary of $75,000 is typical for medical device Regional Managers with additional commission pushing the total package as high as $200,000, depending on the geographic area and type of device sold. The nature of the work requires significant travel and, in most cases, Regional Managers receive compensation for the use of their personal vehicle.

EMPLOYMENT OUTLOOK

The employment outlook for Regional Managers is stable. This is one of the highest level positions available in the domain of medical device sales. There is limited turnover in these positions, particularly for well-known medical device manufacturers. That said, medical devices represent an important technology for every healthcare organization, and there are a number of start-up firms every year.

FOR FURTHER INFORMATION

- Medical Device Manufacturers Association (http://www.medicaldevices.org)

89. SALES REPRESENTATIVES

JOB DESCRIPTION

The job of the Sales Representative is to conduct sales calls to physicians and hospitals to promote, sell, and service the particular products manufactured and sold by the firm. The Sales Representative will make regular calls on clients to assist in all aspects of product training and evaluation. It is expected that the Sales Representative will possess a high level of technical expertise about the particular products being sold.

EDUCATION AND EXPERIENCE

The Sales Representative requires a minimum of a bachelor's degree in health administration, business administration, or science. Experience in a high-pressure sales environment is strongly desired along with experience selling medical devices.

CORE COMPETENCIES AND SKILLS

- Outstanding interpersonal skills including the ability to effectively communicate with current and potential customers
- Excellent verbal and written communication skills
- Experience in making multiple referral calls on a daily basis
- Outstanding selling and negotiation skills
- Ability to successfully plan and manage accounts
- Demonstrated ability to work effectively in team-oriented environments
- Ability to develop and successfully follow through with a strategic plan
- Substantial knowledge of technology solutions in a healthcare provider environment

COMPENSATION

Sales Representatives earn in the range of $50,000 to $95,000, although the total salary will vary depending on the type of product being sold and the number of years of experience in the field. In many cases, Sales Representatives are compensated based on the number of sales made in a given time period. The nature of the work requires significant travel and, in most cases, Sales Representatives receive compensation for the use of their personal vehicle.

EMPLOYMENT OUTLOOK

The employment outlook for Sales Representatives is robust. This is frequently used as the entry-level position for persons interested in medical devices and durable medical equipment; therefore, there is a great deal of turnover as persons are either promoted to supervisory roles or leave the field entirely.

FOR FURTHER INFORMATION

- Medical Device Manufacturers Association (http://www.medicaldevices.org)

90. MARKETING ASSOCIATE

JOB DESCRIPTION

A Marketing Associate works on a range of projects and must therefore carry out a range of job functions. This position requires selling products, from a piece of medical equipment to marketing solutions, by demonstrating the product's added benefit to healthcare providers. A Marketing Associate must constantly create new contacts at providers, assess the respective provider's needs, and develop strategies for selling a product that will address the needs. This individual must demonstrate outstanding communication abilities, as he or she will sell products and services through presentations to potential customers.

EDUCATION AND EXPERIENCE

The amount of experience required for this position entirely depends on the level of responsibility that the respective position will hold. Senior Marketing Associates, for example, are expected to have at least 10 years of experience in marketing, business, or a healthcare-related field. Entry-level Marketing Associate positions look for at least 5 years of experience. Marketing Associates will generally have at least a master's degree in a relatable field, such as health information technology (IT), finance, marketing, or healthcare.

CORE COMPETENCIES AND SKILLS

- Profound communication skills, as this position's success lies ultimately on the individual's ability to promote a product's benefits
- Must be a self-starter because this position can be unstructured, requiring the individual to create new contacts for potential business
- Familiarity with the healthcare industry, and how a respective product would impact a customer practices and procedures
- Must be available to travel to potential customers in a given region
- Demonstrated success selling products and comfortable communicating with executive management
- Ability to analyze data and communicate the data's implications

COMPENSATION

Marketing Associate compensation is largely dependent upon the position's level of responsibility. An individual heading up a larger project at a prestigious institution should expect to make just over $100,000, while entry-level Marketing Associates could earn closer to $65,000.

EMPLOYMENT OUTLOOK

This field is incredibly competitive, especially at the entry-level status. It may take an individual several years to develop a network of potential customers, as well as an expert understanding of the industry. Those individuals who are successful will be well received by providers who look for ways to continuously improve the quality of care.

FOR FURTHER INFORMATION

- Healthcare Marketing Association (http://healthcaremarketingassociation.com)
- Society for Healthcare Strategy and Market Development (http://www.shsmd.org)
- National Society of Certified Healthcare Business Consultants (http://www.nschbc.org)

12 ■ CAREERS IN PHARMACEUTICAL FIRMS

91. ACCOUNT MANAGER

JOB DESCRIPTION

A pharmaceutical company Account Manager is in charge of the budgets, performance evaluations, and development of sales accounts. The area of responsibility could represent a small or large sales area with a varying number of sales teams being managed. The Account Manager stays in contact with customers, acts as a liaison between the pharmacy and the buyers, and implements programs that will increase sales and service activities. Account Managers are professionals, problem solvers, and data analyzers. They interact with clients and work within their organizational structure to build new relationships for sale opportunities. They are the face of the company.

EDUCATION AND EXPERIENCE

A bachelor's degree is a minimum expectation for most Account Manager positions. Many qualification listings desire a background in medicine of some sort: pharmacy, nursing, or health education. Work experience in a leadership role is a benefit.

CORE COMPETENCIES AND SKILLS

- Outstanding presentation skills for internal and external customers
- Exceptional verbal and written communication skills
- Ability to work with standard computer software programs
- Proven analytical skills and ability to solve complex customer problems
- Ability to interact with a wide range of diverse groups
- Demonstrated ability to manage the work of sales representatives

- Demonstrated organizational goals and ability to deal effectively with multiple demands
- Knowledge of pharmaceuticals for which the Account Manager is responsible and the healthcare industry as a whole

COMPENSATION

The majority of Account Managers make between $50,000 and $90,000 annually. They can make as little as $40,000 or as much as $150,000. Account Managers at larger firms with a greater client base and more bonuses will likely earn a higher salary. Similarly, those traveling more and having the ability to reach out to larger users of pharmaceuticals will have a greater chance at increasing their income.

EMPLOYMENT OUTLOOK

With the ever-changing healthcare environment, it is hard to tell what the future holds for care. In the pharmaceutical area, there has historically been gap coverage for prescription medication. Changes in this pay scale along with healthcare reform will allow more people access to healthcare and medications that they need. Skilled Account Managers who can deal with large healthcare firms along with smaller offices to gain a client base will have a great opportunity in the future of our healthcare market. An increasing elderly population and the possibility of "universal" coverage mean more demand for pharmaceuticals. People have also started to become more active in their purchasing of pharmaceuticals and marketing to individuals is becoming more important to pharmaceutical companies.

FOR FURTHER INFORMATION

- National Association of Pharmaceutical Representatives (http://www.napsronline.org)

92. SALES REPRESENTATIVE

JOB DESCRIPTION

A pharmaceutical company Sales Representative is a salesman. They directly market to the customer and follow the plan set forth by the Account Manager on their areas and sales goals. The market for Sales Representatives is competitive and they must continually build their client base and gain new customers for the company. It is their job to interact and establish new connections for the company.

EDUCATION AND EXPERIENCE

A bachelor's degree is a minimum expectation for most Sales Representative jobs. Most have a business or healthcare-focused background or education. Sales experience or other healthcare/pharmacy experience can sometimes be substituted for educational experience.

CORE COMPETENCIES AND SKILLS

- Outstanding presentation skills for internal and external customers
- Exceptional verbal and written communication skills
- Ability to work with standard computer software programs
- Proven analytical skills and ability to solve complex customer problems
- Ability to interact with a wide range of diverse groups
- Demonstrated organizational abilities and ability to deal effectively with multiple demands
- Knowledge of pharmaceuticals for which the Account Manager is responsible and the healthcare industry as a whole

COMPENSATION

The majority of Sales Representatives make between $40,000 and $80,000 annually. There are different levels of Sales Representatives, such as Sales Specialist and Manager. These increased titles also come with increasing salaries and can earn upward of $120,000 when managing sales of large areas and receiving bonuses.

EMPLOYMENT OUTLOOK

Pharmaceuticals are a growing business. With a possible increase in coverage for Americans with the Health Reform Laws, there will be more people with the ability to access doctors and needed pharmaceuticals. The Sales Representative is a key player in making sure that the doctors and hospitals have the required drugs in their pharmacies that their patients desire. The Sales Representative will also network to help doctors better understand the specific brand of drug that is prescribed in order to increase use and get it added to the formulary.

FOR FURTHER INFORMATION

- National Association of Pharmaceutical Representatives (http://www.napsronline.org)

13 ■ CAREERS IN OVERSEAS ORGANIZATIONS

93. PROGRAM MANAGER

JOB DESCRIPTION

A global Program Manager is like a department manager who can work anywhere in the world. They manage teams and build programs. They normally work in a hospital setting and have oversight of a specific department or program area. They can also develop plans for large systems on how to best "roll out" new programs in other countries. They utilize change management theory and have oversight of large amounts of resources and project members.

EDUCATION AND EXPERIENCE

Education and experience varies in the global market. Most desire a minimum of a bachelor's degree, with most wanting some sort of further education, such as a master's, or significant work experience. Educational focus should be project management theory, business, or healthcare related. Many desire long track records of working in the field, around 8 years for many job requirements.

CORE COMPETENCIES AND SKILLS

- Knowledge of global marketplace and regulations
- Exceptional verbal and written communication skill
- Outstanding analytical ability and skill at solving complex problems
- Exceptional interpersonal skills with diverse groups of customers
- Skill and demonstrated experience in change management
- Proven ability to work independently in rapidly changing environments
- Significant experience working overseas with many different cultures
- Knowledge of global marketplace and regulations

- The ability to speak, write, and understand languages other than English
- Presentation ability and able to speak with diverse groups

COMPENSATION

The compensation for Program Managers varies greatly. Depending on the location of the project and the size of the organization, salaries can be larger or smaller. The size of the project and scope of responsibility also play a role. This career has a starting salary of what appears to be about $40,000 and increases greatly when doing large-scale work.

EMPLOYMENT OUTLOOK

Increased need in other countries for people who are trained in management will continue. Healthcare is a growing market worldwide and being able to borrow competencies from other countries is an emerging competitive advantage that other countries, as well as the United States, are trying to capitalize upon.

FOR FURTHER INFORMATION

- Medical Tourism Association (http://www.medicaltourismassociation.com/en/index.html)

94. GLOBAL SERVICES QUALITY MANAGER

JOB DESCRIPTION

Global Services Quality Managers have many different titles. They can work all over the globe or in the United States and oversee large projects abroad. They apply quality improvement principles, such as Six Sigma, Lean Management, and other continuous quality improvement methodologies to hospitals and healthcare systems across the globe. Quality Managers must also adhere to legal guidelines and regulations in the country and understand social norms and values. Monitoring and process review are part of their job and they analyze data, such as customer feedback, financial information, and demographic health needs, to better use change management theory to put in place the right processes using the right quality improvement principles.

EDUCATION AND EXPERIENCE

Education and experience varies in the global market. Most firms desire a minimum of a bachelor's degree, with most wanting some sort of further education, such as a master's, or significant work experience. Educational focus should be representative of business quality methodology, business degree, healthcare degree, or engineering. Experience for global positions is significant with many wanting upward of 7 years relevant work experience in the healthcare field and knowledge of the country to be placed.

CORE COMPETENCIES AND SKILLS

- Exceptional verbal and written communication skill
- Outstanding analytical ability and skill at solving complex problems
- Exceptional interpersonal skills with diverse groups of customers
- Significant skill and ability in Six Sigma and Lean Methods
- Knowledge and understanding of human factors engineering
- Skill and demonstrated experience in change management
- Proven ability to work independently in rapidly changing environments
- Significant experience working overseas with many different cultures
- Knowledge of global marketplace and regulations
- The ability to speak, write, and understand languages other than English
- Presentation ability and ability to speak with diverse groups

COMPENSATION

The compensation for Global Services Quality Managers varies greatly. Depending on the location of the project and the size of the organization, they can earn anywhere from $45,000 to $200,000 or more. Salary is very dependent on previous experience and the type of work being done. Larger companies have top C-Suite positions for Global Services Quality Managers who oversee multiple sites and have increased salaries due to their increased responsibilities.

EMPLOYMENT OUTLOOK

Increases in medical tourism and doctors being trained in the United States and other countries have resulted in an increased demand for

Global Services Quality Managers who have been trained in the Western style of continuous quality improvement. They can take these skills to developing or established countries in order to improve their processes. There is also opportunity to learn from these healthcare facilities overseas. As travel continues to improve, people will begin to desire healthcare options that are on par with some of the top performing hospitals and care facilities.

FOR FURTHER INFORMATION

- Medical Tourism Association (http://www.medicaltourismassociation.com/en/index.html)

14 ■ CAREERS IN HEALTH ASSOCIATION MANAGEMENT

95. DIRECTOR OF GOVERNMENT AFFAIRS

JOB DESCRIPTION

The Director of Government Affairs is a member of the executive team of the association and is primarily responsible for acting as the liaison between the association and local, state, and federal government elected officials and government agencies. The Director is expected to critically analyze current and proposed government legislation for its effects on the association. The Director is also called on to monitor legislative and regulatory activity and develop positions that should be taken by the association in response to that activity.

EDUCATION AND EXPERIENCE

The Director of Government Affairs typically requires a bachelor's degree in business administration, health administration, public administration, or political science, although a master's degree is frequently the preferred educational preparation. Most Directors of Government Affairs have 5 to 7 years of experience in government affairs.

CORE COMPETENCIES AND SKILLS

- Outstanding interpersonal skills including the ability to effectively communicate with current and potential members and other stakeholders along with persons throughout their organization
- Excellent verbal and written communication skills
- Relationship management, strategy development, problem solving, and change management skills
- Ability to motivate volunteers to further the mission of the association
- Outstanding motivation and organizational skills

- Ability to stay calm and composed even under difficult circumstances
- Experience with lobbying and influencing elected officials
- Demonstrated ability to work with staff members of elected officials
- Ability to quickly learn and understand the field in which the association members work
- Demonstrated ability to use standard computer software programs, including Word, Excel, Access, and PowerPoint

COMPENSATION

Health management association Directors of Government Affairs typically earn between $75,000 and $200,000 per year, depending upon the size of the association. This salary does not include annual performance bonuses.

EMPLOYMENT OUTLOOK

Effective Directors of Government Affairs are highly valued members of the association and, while turnover in these positions is relatively low, they are frequently a position that is promoted into senior management roles in the association.

FOR FURTHER INFORMATION

- American Society of Association Executives (http://www.asaecenter.org)

96. PRESIDENT AND CEO

JOB DESCRIPTION

Health management associations represent individuals who practice healthcare management or organizations who are otherwise related to the field. The role of the association is to provide a venue for members to pursue professional development, create best practices, and speak with one voice about issues of concern to their constituency. Additionally, health management associations help to define the field of healthcare management by working to link members with the practice-based organizations in healthcare delivery, finance, manufacturing, consulting, and others. The role of the President and Chief Executive Officer (CEO) is to lead the association and represent the membership with a wide variety of external stakeholders. The President and CEO are responsible for all strategic, operational, and financial activities of the association.

EDUCATION AND EXPERIENCE

The association President and CEO typically requires a minimum of a master's degree in business administration or health administration along with at least 10 years of progressively responsible experience in association management. The Certified Association Executive (CAE) credential is highly preferred.

CORE COMPETENCIES AND SKILLS

- Outstanding interpersonal skills including the ability to effectively communicate with current and potential members and other stakeholders along with persons throughout their organization
- Excellent verbal and written communication skills
- Relationship management, strategy development, problem solving, and change management skills
- Skill in directly managing staff members
- Ability to motivate volunteers to further the mission of the association
- Demonstrated experience in developing partnerships and coalitions with other organizations and stakeholder groups
- Ability to read and understand standard financial documents
- Experience with lobbying and influencing elected officials
- Ability to quickly learn and understand the field in which the association members work
- Demonstrated ability to use standard computer software programs, including Word, Excel, Access, and PowerPoint

COMPENSATION

Health management association Presidents and CEOs typically earn between $150,000 and $500,000 per year, not including annual bonuses based on performance. Base salary is frequently a function of the size of the association.

EMPLOYMENT OUTLOOK

While there are many opportunities in health association management, there is very limited turnover of Presidents and CEOs. The typical President and CEO stays in the job a decade or more and when these jobs open up, there is usually very intense competition.

FOR FURTHER INFORMATION

- American Society of Association Executives (http://www.asaecenter.org)

Name:
BRUCE SIEGEL
Title: President and CEO
Organization: National Association of Public Hospitals and Health Systems

1. **Briefly describe your job responsibilities.**
   I head a Washington-based National Hospital Association that focuses on Safety Net Health Systems. We advocate for resources to care for vulnerable patients and to promote the finest care for all Americans.

2. **Please give an example of what you would consider to be a "typical" day for you.**
   A typical day would include going to the Hill for meetings on Medicaid and the federal budget, working with our staff on how we communicate the economic impact of our member hospitals in their local community, and then discussions with member CEOs about challenges they may face. Often I am on the road in a community with a Safety Net Health System.

3. **What education or training do you have? Is it typical for your job?**
   I am a physician, board-certified in Preventive Medicine. That would not be typical. I am also a former health system administrator; that is more typical for people in this job.

4. **What is the most challenging part of your job?**
   Maintaining constant communication with a broad array of audiences and hundreds of individuals.

(*continued*)

Name: BRUCE SIEGEL (*continued*)

5. What do you consider to be the best part of your job?

I am privileged that I have a job where I can advocate for what I believe every day, and use all the skills I have developed over my career.

6. What path did you take to get to the job you are in today?

I started out in public health administration, then hospital leadership, followed by a decade in academia. The only theme: serendipity.

7. What advice do you have for someone who is interested in a job such as yours?

Life pitches curveballs: that's a good thing. There is no one path; what really matters is a core set of management skills and the ability to articulate a vision and a horizon.

15 ■ CAREERS IN GOVERNMENTAL AND NONGOVERNMENTAL REGULATORY BODIES

97. SURVEYOR

JOB DESCRIPTION

The job of the Surveyor is to conduct site surveys of healthcare organizations throughout the United States on behalf of nongovernmental regulatory bodies. The Surveyor applies systems analysis skills and inductive reasoning skills to determine the healthcare organization's degree of compliance with applicable standards and functionality of care delivery systems. The Surveyor engages healthcare organization staff in interactive dialogues on standards-based issues in healthcare in order to assess compliance and to identify opportunities for improving compliance, quality, and safety. The Surveyor prepares management reports that clearly link individual standards deficiencies with potential systems vulnerabilities and related organization risk points. Finally, the Surveyor effectively communicates this information to healthcare organization leadership in a constructive and collegial style.

EDUCATION AND EXPERIENCE

Surveyors typically possess a clinical degree in nursing, behavioral health, or other clinical area coupled with at least 5 years of work experience in healthcare delivery. Management experience in healthcare delivery is highly recommended.

CORE COMPETENCIES AND SKILLS

- Outstanding interpersonal skills including the ability to effectively communicate with current and potential customers along with persons throughout the organization
- Excellent verbal and written communication skills
- Outstanding critical thinking skills along with teamwork skills

- Demonstrated skills in managing difficult and potentially confrontational situations
- Strong data analysis, evaluation, and problem-solving skills
- Ability to use standard computer office software

COMPENSATION

Surveyors typically earn $75,000 to $100,000 per year depending on their level of experience.

EMPLOYMENT OUTLOOK

The employment outlook for Surveyors with nongovernmental regulatory organizations is stable. Organizations like the Joint Commission have a continuing need for new and replacement Surveyors.

FOR FURTHER INFORMATION

- Joint Commission for the Accreditation of Healthcare Organizations (http://www.jointcommission.org)

Name:
SHRUTI GOEL
Title: Quality Improvement Consultant
Organization: Delmarva Foundation of the District of Columbia (Medicare Quality Improvement Organization)

1. **Briefly describe your job responsibilities.**
Functioning as the Quality Improvement Organization (QIO) representative to the community is the most important aspect of this role. The major responsibility is to develop and proactively manage relationships with stakeholders at participating organizations, such as federally qualified health centers, as well as small and large private physician practices. The Quality Improvement Consultant (QIC) travels throughout the state to provide staff education and training, and patient education materials to participating organizations. The QIC is also expected to perform project management activities in successfully administering the Center for Medicare and Medicaid Services (CMS) QIO contract. This includes working with an interdisciplinary team to plan and develop strategies to meet contract objectives, ensuring timely deliverable submission, and working with the analytics team to develop and maintain comprehensive databases tracking clinical quality measures related to the project.

2. **Please give an example of what you would consider to be a "typical" day for you.**
A typical day for me consists of following-up with my clients on any ongoing concerns or questions regarding our project. Sometimes, I interact with an Electronic Health Record (EHR) vendor's support team to learn about a new functionality within their EHR and later share that information with clients. We have a number of standing meetings with CMS and our National Coordinating Center every month to report on project progress and outstanding issues. We have numerous stakeholders in the

(continued)

Name: SHRUTI GOEL *(continued)*

state, including American Heart Association, American Cancer Society, State Medical Societies, and many others, and we are frequently engaged in partnering with them for planning events, webinars, and teleconferences. I also dedicate at least 1 day in a week to researching regulatory issues and hot topics relevant to my clients and disseminate it to them in various formats.

3. What education or training do you have? Is it typical for your job?
I have a Master's in Health Services Administration from the George Washington University. I completed my management training at Johns Hopkins Bayview Medical Center. Yes, this is the typical education required for my job but the most important aspect is experience in working with physicians.

4. What is the most challenging part of your job?
The most challenging part of my work is engaging physicians to undertake quality improvement initiatives. They are very interested but pressed for time, particularly in primary care.

5. What do you consider to be the best part of your job?
The flexibility of working both in the field and in the office has been great for me. When I work in the office, I make sure to research and keep myself up-to-date on the topics that are of importance to my clients. Then, when I am in the field, I share that valuable information with my clients, which strengthens our relationship and helps my clients succeed.

6. What path did you take to get to the job you are in today?
I followed my interest in Health information technology (IT) cultivated through projects at Johns Hopkins to my position here at the Delmarva Foundation. I found that focusing on your areas of interest rather than a particular job title will help you decide what kinds of opportunities to seek.

Name: SHRUTI GOEL

7. What advice do you have for someone who is interested in a job such as yours?

Experience in working with physicians is the most sought after skill in my job. So my recommendation to an incoming student is to make sure at least one of their internships exposes them directly to working with physicians. You can work or volunteer at a physician office or at a clinical department in a hospital. Be sure to work on at least one project where you need a physician's buy-in to complete the project.

8. What is a QIO?

QIOs are private, mostly not-for-profit organizations, which are staffed by professionals, mostly doctors and other healthcare professionals, who are trained to review medical care and help Medicare beneficiaries with complaints about the quality of care and to implement improvements in the quality of care available throughout the spectrum of care, including hospitals, physician practices, and nursing homes.

By law, the mission of the QIO Program is to improve the effectiveness, efficiency, economy, and quality of services delivered to Medicare beneficiaries. Based on this statutory charge, and CMS's Program experience, CMS identifies the core functions of the QIO Program as:

Improving quality of care for beneficiaries;

Protecting the integrity of the Medicare Trust Fund by ensuring that Medicare pays only for services and goods that are reasonable and necessary and that are provided in the most appropriate setting; and

Protecting beneficiaries by expeditiously addressing individual complaints, such as beneficiary complaints, provider-based notice appeals, violations of the Emergency Medical Treatment and Labor Act (EMTALA), and other related responsibilities as articulated in QIO-related law.

Name:
TAQUEENA A. HALL
Title: Claims Compliance Auditor II
Organization: ERN/The California Council of Reimbursement Advocacy

1. **Briefly describe your job responsibilities.**
   As a compliance auditor, I advocate passionately for medically appropriate healthcare by restricting third-party payers from making improper denials and medically inappropriate decisions on behalf of both the patient and healthcare professionals (providers). Preparing compliance audits, enforcement campaigns, and filing regulatory complaints with the Department of Managed Healthcare are supplementary responsibilities to assist in advocating on behalf of patients, physicians, and other healthcare professionals.

2. **Please give an example of what you would consider to be a "typical" day for you.**
   A typical day as a compliance auditor is challenging, yet intriguing. Not a day passes by without a lesson being learned. Healthcare is forever changing and within this line of business, my goal is to become an authoritative leader/a warrior in America's fight for appropriate healthcare for its citizens, as third-party payers are restricted from improper decisions of reimbursing medically necessary services and care rendered in good faith by healthcare professionals.

3. **What education or training do you have? Is it typical for your job?**
   I'm a recipient of both a Bachelor of Arts in Chemistry (prepharmacy) and a Master's in Health Service Administration.

   I believe that the training that I have had in pharmacy and health administration has prepared me for this healthcare

Name: TAQUEENA A. HALL

environment, that is, in management, customer service, and the importance of developing relationships with physicians/healthcare professionals.

Are my skill sets typical for my job? Not necessarily; my current position as a compliance auditor focuses on the statutory law that mandates timely reimbursement and identifies insurers who engage in unfair payment patterns. Within my area of compliance, currently, I'm the only individual in Administrative Healthcare; the others are Juris Doctors (lawyers). However, I do believe individuals with my skill set will be a great influence within this niche of healthcare compliance.

As I continue to develop within this elite group of healthcare professionals, I will continue to function in the administrative role and fight, as managed care reform is a daily fight.

4. What is the most challenging part of your job?

Speaking with representatives of health plans who aren't willing to assist their leaders/businesses back into compliance is very challenging. It reminds me of children who don't listen to adults, who are looking out for their best interest.

Not only do I advocate for healthcare professionals and patients, we at ERN, as a courtesy, alert third-party payers of their noncompliance and offer them an opportunity to self-initiate remediation prior to regulatory compliant filing with the appropriate state departments, that is, Centers for Medicare and Medicaid Services, Department of Managed Healthcare, Department of Insurance, and so on.

5. What do you consider to be the best part of your job?

Every day is a compassionate day, as I assist in saving lives. Each outstanding claim not reimbursed due to improper denials represents a life; if providers violate the law and fail to provide medically necessary services to patients, who depend on providers for reimbursement, the United States would be in more trouble than what it presently is.

(*continued*)

Name: TAQUEENA A. HALL *(continued)*

Furthermore, I educate and train whomever I may speak with, as each call is a compliance call; the statutory law should be known by those who are in violation of it.

Lastly, I stand as an authority in the "gap" where many aren't able withstand.

6. What path did you take to get to the job you are in today?

As a student of The George Washington University–School of Public Health and Health Services, I became an Administrative Resident at Tehachapi Valley Health District Hospital, where I met an amazing Chief Financial Officer, Mr. Joseph Demont.

Mr. Demont introduced me to Mr. Ed Norwood, who provided Tehachapi's business office with seminars on how to foster and increase knowledge of, and proficiency in, insurance law compliance and protect a patient's right to access of care. Mr. Norwood gave me an opportunity to learn a different angle of healthcare.

7. What advice do you have for someone who is interested in a job such as yours?

Always work hard, even if you're not sure what it is you want to do. Having true compassion for this field is what it takes to become successful. Success is not measured by money; success is measured by how many lives that have been touched and overturned.

Name:
LEON HARRIS
Title: Healthcare Business Analyst
Organization: NCQA

1. Briefly describe your job responsibilities.

Support the physician recognition process by researching and synthesizing background information and pertinent data. This includes the following:

Researching background information on questions regarding recognition measures and requirements

Analyzing and summarizing results of research, surveys, and outcomes assessments—including quantitative and qualitative analysis, and preparing responses and reports for discussion at internal meetings

Develop various documents for communication to customers; including management of Frequently-Asked-Question (FAQ) products

Assist in the maintenance and update of program materials and tools, including draft and final standards, systems instructions, and other program requirements

Reports, brochures, and presentations

Track changes, corrections, and clarifications and integrate suggestions from staff and internal workgroups

Initiate and participate in quality assessment and improvement for data, materials, and tools

Serve as an internal expert and liaison on product tools, including supporting integration of new products and tools from product development and IT to operations

(*continued*)

Name: LEON HARRIS *(continued)*

Lead training activities on new products and tools

Support internal and external training efforts, including developing materials and responding to questions from internal and external customers

Participate in and support multifunction teams and internal workgroups involved in the process of physician recognition, issues clarification, and program enhancement

Support internal and external workgroups or organizations involved in the process of new program delivery and initiatives

Manage meeting scheduling/logistics (in conjunction with administrative support staff)

Develop and work with others to develop agendas and materials (e.g., written analyses of issues, staff reports, written summaries of meetings)

Assist in the enhancement of techniques for internal and external communication and data processing

Manage ongoing communications with committee/team members

2. Please give an example of what you would consider to be a "typical" day for you.

Well, a typical day consists of responding to e-mails from internal staff at National Committee for Quality Assurance (NCQA) and external customers/stakeholders; attending meetings related to the recognition programs department; maintaining our database and providing technical support to customers and internal staff members.

3. What education or training do you have? Is it typical for your job?

I have a bachelor's degree from Winston Salem State University in biology/chemistry. I completed my Master's of Health Services

Name: LEON HARRIS

Administration (MHSA) degree from The George Washington University. Also, I completed a Health Information Technology Certification from The George Washington University.

4. What is the most challenging part of your job?
The most challenging part of my job is assisting our customers with technical and logistic issues. Also, assisting internal staff members with simple technical issues can be mundane and burdensome at times.

5. What do you consider to be the best part of your job?
Well, I love helping people, so resolving an issue for our customers and internal staff members is always a plus. Also, I do a lot of work with our Patient Centered Medical Home department, which is a big initiative in the United States and the promise for this new delivery of healthcare is rewarding. Knowing that I work for an organization that created this program and being able to see the positive results it has made in healthcare organizations across the country is the best reward anyone working in healthcare could ask for.

6. What path did you take to get to the job you are in today?
Well, I have always worked in healthcare and I knew I wanted to make a career in this industry. I began working as an andrologist for a Reproductive Science Center in the Washington, District of Columbia, metro area. I went back to graduate school to further my education and applied for this position after speaking with a recruiter at a career fair that was held at The George Washington University, School of Public Health and Health Services.

7. What advice do you have for someone who is interested in a job such as yours?
I will say that you must be technically sound and understand how IT plays a major role in streamline processes. Also, you must have

(*continued*)

Name: LEON HARRIS *(continued)*

a strong background in analyzing data and the ability to use MS Excel, MS Access, and a basic understanding of SQL. Being able to communicate with computer programmers and web applicators/developers is key in this role. Also, being able to deal with people is very important. Whether it is fellow coworkers or customers, the key is that you must have the tenacity to communicate effectively. Being a team player is also a critical piece in this role.

16 ■ CAREERS IN HEALTHCARE MANAGEMENT EDUCATION

98. INTERNSHIP/RESIDENCY COORDINATOR

JOB DESCRIPTION

The role of internship and residency coordinator is to work with undergraduate and graduate healthcare management students and provide direct assistance to them and their programs to identify and secure administrative internships, residencies, and fellowships. The internship and residency coordinator must work with program faculty, alumni, and local and national practitioners in order to develop a current inventory of practice sites. The internship and residency coordinator also works with program leadership to make sure that all field experiences are in compliance with the stated goals of the program and regulations of the university.

EDUCATION AND EXPERIENCE

Internship and residency coordinators typically have a master's degree in healthcare management and at least 3 years of experience as a healthcare practitioner.

CORE COMPETENCIES AND SKILLS

- Outstanding verbal and written communication skills
- Demonstrated ability to effectively work with all students in the program
- Skill in developing and maintaining networks of professional organizations
- Proven ability to work effectively with multiple stakeholder groups
- Demonstrated ability to advise students on academic and professional questions

- Exceptional interpersonal skills
- Ability to use both standard computer software and specialized programs depending on need

SALARY AND JOB GROWTH

The salary for internship and residency coordinators depends on whether this person is hired as a staff or faculty member. The typical internship and residency coordinator earns a mean salary of $65,000. Every certified undergraduate and accredited graduate healthcare management program requires a field experience for their students and most mid-size and larger programs all have their own internship and residency coordinator.

FOR ADDITIONAL INFORMATION

Association of University Programs in Health Administration (http://www.aupha.org)

99. PROFESSOR (INCLUDES ASSISTANT/ASSOCIATE/FULL PROFESSOR RANKS)

JOB DESCRIPTION

The role of professors of healthcare management is (primarily) to educate undergraduate and graduate students who wish to study this discipline and either initially enter the field or grow and advance their professional skills. While many healthcare management programs have practitioners teaching their students, most universities employ full-time faculty members to serve as the intellectual core of the academic program. These faculty members have three areas of responsibility: teaching/advising, research/scholarship, and service. Depending on the type of student, teaching will typically be done in person or online. Student advising requires the professor to help the student attain their professional career goals and may include the supervision of master's or doctoral theses. Research and scholarship are activities centered on the creation and dissemination of new knowledge. Service can include membership in department, college, and university committees; participation in local, state, regional, national, or international healthcare management organizations; and service to the community broadly. The distribution of effort in each of these three roles is negotiated between the professor and the department in which the person works. Most professors enter the profession at the assistant level and within 6 years of employment are given the opportunity to be promoted to the associate level. Promotion to full professor is reserved for associate professors who have demonstrated ongoing excellence in teaching, scholarship, and service.

EDUCATION AND EXPERIENCE

Professors of healthcare management typically require a doctoral degree in ether healthcare management or a related discipline. While prior experience in some level of healthcare management is highly desirable, it is not required. Many new assistant professors are hired directly out of graduate school once their doctoral degree is completed, although some schools will hire a new assistant professor if their degree is not yet done. In some more research-intensive universities, a year or two of postdoctoral training in research is strongly recommended.

CORE COMPETENCIES AND SKILLS

- Outstanding verbal and written communication skills
- Demonstrated ability to effectively educate students using a variety of different technologies
- Skill in quantitative and/or qualitative research methods
- Proven ability to share research findings in many different venues and formats, including peer-reviewed manuscripts, books, professional meetings, and scholarly seminars
- Demonstrated ability to advise students on academic and professional questions
- Exceptional interpersonal skills particularly with faculty colleagues
- Ability to use both standard computer software and specialized programs depending on need
- Ability to apply for and receive funding for research through governmental and nongovernmental sources

SALARY AND JOB GROWTH

The salary for healthcare management faculty members is a function of at least three variables: academic level (assistant professor, associate professor, or full professor), the academic home of the program (typically healthcare management programs in schools of business pay higher salaries than do programs in schools of public health, but this is not universally true), and the size and governance of the university (public or private). According to the Association of University Programs in Health

Administration, in 2010, the median salary for assistant professors was $65,800, the median salary for associate professors was $74,600, and the median salary for full professors was $123,400. All of these salaries assume the person holds a 9-month contract and does not include potential summer salary support. The job growth for professors of healthcare management is expected to be very strong. There is expected to be a number of job openings for assistant professors due to retirement of existing faculty and the continued growth in the number of university-based programs teaching healthcare management.

FOR ADDITIONAL INFORMATION

- Association of University Programs in Health Administration (http://www. aupha.org)

17 ■ CAREERS IN EXECUTIVE SEARCH FIRMS

100. RESEARCH ASSOCIATE

JOB DESCRIPTION

Executive search firms conduct senior personnel searches for a variety of organizations, including hospitals and health systems. The Research Associate's primary role is to support candidate identification and database and business development for associates and partners in firms both local and nationwide. In addition, the Research Associate will assist associates and partners in generating names of potential candidates using the phone, print materials, and online information resources. As a vital member of the search team, the Research Associate assists the firm in designing search strategies, develops company target lists, and works to identify potential business opportunities.

EDUCATION AND EXPERIENCE

The Research Associate requires a minimum of a bachelor's degree in health or business administration. Research Associates typically possess experience in a recruiting or research function within an executive search firm.

CORE COMPETENCIES AND SKILLS

- Outstanding interpersonal skills including the ability to effectively communicate with current and potential customers, as well as with persons throughout their organization
- Excellent verbal and written communication skills
- Outstanding customer service skills
- Attention to detail and the ability to successfully follow through with assignments
- Ability to work effectively in a team-oriented environment and provide healthcare industry-specific information to members of the firm working in the healthcare sector

- Skill in conducting ongoing information audits to determine relevance of the information that is generated
- Ability to build and maintain strong client relationships
- Exceptional learning skills; able to quickly develop industry, company, and functional expertise
- Excellent multitasking and time management skills
- Demonstrated ability to use standard computer software programs, including Word, Excel, Access, and PowerPoint

COMPENSATION

Research Associates generally earn a base salary of $45,000 to $65,000. This salary will vary depending on the size and geographic location of the executive search firm.

EMPLOYMENT OUTLOOK

The employment outlook for Research Associates in executive search firms is good. This is an entry-level position in this industry, and talented and skilled Research Associates are frequently promoted to Senior Associates. There remains a high level of demand for the services of executive search firms, as healthcare organizations seek to fill vacant senior-level management positions.

FOR FURTHER INFORMATION

- Association of Executive Search Consultants (http://www.aesc.org/eweb/StartPage.aspx)

101. SENIOR ASSOCIATE

JOB DESCRIPTION

Executive search firms conduct personnel searches for a variety of organizations, including hospitals and health systems. The Senior Associate's primary role is to manage the initial candidate identification and development process. In addition, the Senior Associate will assist consultants and shareholders in generating, managing, and/or executing search assignments, including potential candidate development, screening and presentation to clients, cultivating, and/or maintaining client and candidate relationships. As a vital member of the search team, the Senior Associate has the ability to network with professionals and assist them in achieving their career objectives in organizations committed to improving quality of life, assess a candidate's skills against a client's needs, and collaborate with colleagues across the firm.

EDUCATION AND EXPERIENCE

The Senior Associate requires a minimum of a bachelor's degree, with preference given to those with a Master's in Health Administration. Senior Associates typically possess 5 or more years of experience in healthcare executive search, with preference given to those with direct healthcare experience.

CORE COMPETENCIES AND SKILLS

- Outstanding interpersonal skills including the ability to effectively communicate with current and potential customers along with persons throughout their organization
- Excellent verbal and written communication skills
- Ability to participate in and/or lead the search process, including, but not limited to, working with clients and search committees, sourcing, interviewing, conducting references, negotiating, and closing assignments
- Demonstration of an understanding of the full search process
- Proactively network and seek out candidates in an expeditious and cost-effective manner
- Participate in candidate development. When appropriate, manage candidates through the search process, including candidate interviews, candidate presentations, and referencing
- Ability to build and maintain strong client relationships
- Ability to develop an effective and compelling presentation to market the role and client company to prospective candidates. Communicate position profile to potential candidates
- Relationship management, strategy development, problem solving, and change management skills
- Demonstrated ability to use standard computer software programs, including Word, Excel, Access, and PowerPoint

COMPENSATION

Senior Associates generally earn a base salary of $88,000 to $125,000. In many cases, bonus compensation in the form of cash is made available to associates who successfully place candidates with firms.

EMPLOYMENT OUTLOOK

The employment outlook for Senior Associates in executive search firms is good. There is a high level of turnover in executive-level healthcare positions, and many hospitals and health systems turn to executive search firms to help identify candidates for these jobs. There are a limited number of large, national firms and competition for the best Senior Associates is fierce.

FOR FURTHER INFORMATION

- Association of Executive Search Consultants (http://www.aesc.org/eweb/StartPage.aspx)

III ■ THE FUTURE OF HEALTHCARE MANAGEMENT

18 ■ TRENDS THAT WILL IMPACT HEALTHCARE MANAGEMENT

For years, many experts were predicting that universal health insurance was "just around the corner" but when the 2010 Health Reform Law actually happened, in some ways it seemed quite surprising. The future is so affected by unknowns. And, of course, local markets are different from national markets. Our experience is limited by where we have been, what we have read, and whom we know. We are going to examine futures in healthcare management as follows: What are the key drivers of expected change? How do these drivers affect healthcare management? And, where (and where not) we think the jobs for healthcare managers are going to be. We shall be examining the period from today (we wrote this in January 2012) through 2016.

WHAT ARE THE KEY DRIVERS OF CHANGE?

All kinds of questions surround us concerning the economic challenges the country now faces. What kinds of changes will be made to bend the healthcare cost curve? How will Medicare be cut back? How will providers be paid under Medicaid? What can Safety Net Providers do when they consistently lose money on operations? Who will pay what for healthcare for immigrants? Most providers agree that everyone will be cutting back. Some say that if healthcare organizations need only take out the waste in their processes (this includes interventions shown not to be effective based on best available evidence, and inefficiency, for example, as a result of hospitals and physicians requiring staff to bill and collect from 1,000 different insurance carriers, with multiple coverages and formats).

To sum up, we predict the following 3- to 5-year trend forecast as follows:

- The 2010 Health Reform Law will evolve considerably. Coverage will increase. Payments to providers will no longer rise at a much faster rate than the general cost of living. There will be more accountability and transparency demanded from providers.

- Electronic medical records will be implemented more widely. All Americans, including immigrants, will receive some basic form of medical coverage (this may only be allocated through increased funding to Safety Net Providers).
- A two- or three-tiered health system will continue to develop, as it has in the airlines. The market for high-end services is growing rapidly because the rich in the United States have a greater share of the economic pie and are willing to spend whatever it takes for first-class accommodations and technology, as they do for transportation or hotels. "Second-class" care for those with commercial insurance will be increasingly competitive in cost and quality. And "third-class" care for those with Medicare (providers are dropping out of the program) and Medicaid will resemble regular coach fare on the airlines. Patients will get safe care, pay for extras (which used to be provided free), and be cared for in volume.
- More health resources will finally move into primary care, public health, and prevention. It would seem that the foundation of any accountable and transparent local healthcare delivery network will be based on a relationship between a patient and a regular provider of care, interacting with community organizations (such as schools and churches) on the one hand, and, on the other hand, after the patient is diagnosed and treated by the regular primary source of care, with a network of specialists and specialist organizations.
- Fewer resources will flow into inpatient-only hospitals and medical specialists, such as cardiologists and radiologists. This may not be an absolute decrease but a relative decrease in share. There will be a decrease in the rate of growth for diagnostic services, such as magnetic resonance imaging (MRI), and for treatment services, such as replaced hips.
- Healthcare will become more like other service industries, such as banks, car repair, education, and beauty care. Taxpayers and consumers will be increasingly price conscious, as they have to pay more out-of-pocket (or more than they would like to pay in taxes), while families and purchasers at the same time become more quality conscious, as they become increasingly conscious of what quality care is.

HOW DO THESE TRENDS AFFECT HEALTHCARE MANAGERS?

More organizations are going to be part of larger systems. More clinicians are going to work as managers. Employers will place higher value on graduates of accredited healthcare management education programs. Skills, experience, and fit matters. This applies whether the organization is hiring new graduates or promoting existing managers. Skills required vary by job. The manager for community development needs a different skills set than the manager of information technology. In the larger organization, preference is given to the manager who has worked in the organization for a while because the learning curve as to how to work effectively in that organization will not be as steep. Managers require increasing knowledge of compliance issues, and data analysis and marketing using electronic skill sets.

- Focusing accountability for results

Organizations will be increasingly held accountable, even by their own trustees in the case of not-for-profit organizations, for results with regard to quality, cost, and access.

Managers will have to be fluent with the relevant metrics and process analysis to come up with these results. Their performance will increasingly be benchmarked against managers in their own organizations and in comparable organizations.

- Investing in management training and development and in management research

The assumption is that as organizations become more accountable in more transparent ways for outcome and output, they will invest more resources in learning how to develop human resources who can deliver results, with increasing emphasis on succession planning, and on process management.

- Customers will increasingly travel to get higher quality medical care. Healthcare will become less local, as patients and their families become aware of different outcome results and lower prices farther from home. Wealthy New Yorkers may travel to the Mayo Clinic for a workup. State Medicaid programs may send clients to other countries because surgery is cheaper there (and quality just as good), even including transportation costs.

- Managers must achieve results by supporting doctors and nurses who directly take care of patients. Internal marketing is a high priority for organizations, because when primary care physicians and nurses feel they can provide care as they were trained to provide it and are proud of working where they work, customers and patients get to feel the same way about the organization and tune competitors out.

WHERE THE JOBS WILL BE AND WON'T BE

There will be more jobs in larger organizations, whether these will be hospital systems, vertically integrated health systems, physician group practices, insurance companies, or visiting nursing organizations. Healthcare will resemble other sectors of the economy and there will be more movement by managers across sectors and across ownership boundaries of government, nonprofit, and for-profit.

- More jobs in operations

These are jobs closer to the physicians and nurses who take care of patients. Managers will need to be experts in process management and in motivating and supporting first-line providers.

- More jobs in specialized functions

As firms grow larger, they need more specialized experts in marketing, operations, quality, human relations, and other functional areas. These managers can be functional experts educated in business school, as the health context, although it has to be learned, is usually learned more quickly than are the specialized function skill sets.

- More jobs in entrepreneurial organizations

These opportunities are typically found in organizations that sell outsourced functions or departments to hospitals and other organizations—ranging from emergency services to housekeeping. Also, many of the new primary care and accountable organizations are entrepreneurial in nature and need managers versed in start-ups and government compliance.

- Fewer jobs in stand-alone smaller traditional hospitals and in traditional hospital financial departments

Smaller, less nimble organizations will increasingly go bankrupt. Payment systems for hospitals and other organizations will become simpler. Increasingly payers, or internal stakeholders are asking questions about "what do we get for our money" and "how does budgeting coalesce with strategic priorities?" and financial managers will increasingly have to learn new skills.

SOME FINAL WORDS

Our book title is *101 Careers in Healthcare Management.* One of the authors (AK) has had at least eight different jobs in healthcare, most of these very different from each other. They have included nursing home administrator, hospital administrative resident, assistant hospital administrator, neighborhood health center administrator, senior health consultant to the United Autoworkers Union, administrator of a group practice in a department of medicine, hospital consultant, hospital trustee, national director for demonstration programs of several large foundations, and program director in healthcare administration. AK defines this as *one* career in healthcare management. His advice to younger managers and would-be managers has always been: Work for a growing organization, work for a boss who will take an interest in your professional development, build up your resume with results each year, and update an exit plan specifying under what conditions you will no longer stay at this job, having generated a supportive network to facilitate your next move.

■ JOB SEARCH BLOG

These are fictional notes about one individual based on true stories illustrating the underside of the difficulty of getting employment in healthcare management, even after attending a master's program in this field. They are diary notes of 5 days searching for employment, while finishing up a degree in a graduate program of healthcare management.

DAY 1

I have spent the last week trying to line up a management internship for the spring semester. The placement office has been helpful to me with leads, information, and advice about my resume. I interviewed today with human resources at an academic medical center. I gave them all my information and they said they will get in touch with me. If I should ever be interviewed by anyone, I don't know if they will use me appropriately, and whether I should accept the position without knowing whether I shall be appropriately used. I also interviewed with my faculty advisor. He told me he was not an expert on getting someone a job, he didn't know where the jobs were, but he gave me the names and e-mail addresses of four of his former students whom he said would talk with me, just based on his name. These were a hospital administrator, a manager of a neighborhood health center, an associate project director at a large visiting nurse service, and a mid-level manager at an insurance company.

DAY 2

All the persons the faculty member referred me to responded to my e-mails, and I set up appointments with each one of them. I will summarize in days 2 through 5 my conversations with these individuals. The hospital administrator told me that she had no jobs available for someone like me at her hospital. There was no money available for jobs and she doubted that such a job would open up soon. She said she might be able to offer me an internship with no pay. After reviewing my resume, she asked me what my skills were, and I told her that I had some experience as a billing manager in a doctor's office. She said this was good and asked whether I had looked into positions in finance and billing. I said that was not what I was interested in or why I had gone to graduate school. I wanted to help patients and improve healthcare, and work on the program side to improve service and quality, and access and contain costs. I told her that I was intelligent, had performed well at school, and that I was a hard worker who needed little direct supervision. She said she would keep me in mind, wished me well, and would think further if she had any work she needed done that would benefit from a nonpaid management intern.

DAY 3

I met with the manager of the neighborhood health center. He was extremely sympathetic and seemed interested in me. He didn't know if he could help and he had no open jobs. If I wanted to work as a nonpaid management intern, he had plenty of work for me to do. I could help the team working on a grant proposal for becoming an accountable healthcare organization, or with another team examining the process for recruiting physicians and nurses to the staff of the center. I said either of those projects was desirable, and I could learn skills by doing that work that I could put on my resume and help me get a paid position. I said I would get back to him within a few weeks after I had completed interviewing for a position.

DAY 4

I met with the associate project director of the visiting nurse service. After examining my resume, she concluded that I didn't have the skills to get the open job doing what she was doing in her operations management department. She had excellent quantitative skills and some consulting experience that I lacked. Besides, I was not interested in primarily doing staff work that required quantitative analysis. She suggested that I meet with someone in the human resources office. A graduate of my master's program in healthcare management, she said that she had received excellent training at the school and lauded my faculty advisor in particular for being realistic and helpful.

DAY 5

I met with the mid-level manager of a large insurance company. He worked in a department dealing with provider payments and said that maybe my billings experience would be useful for employment there, but he was unaware of any current vacancies. Besides, I should take some additional courses either at the business school or at our school in third-part payment and financial analysis. He thought there would be jobs available in hospitals and group practices dealing with billing and reimbursement and that even for jobs in operations, faculty practices were more likely to be growing and looking for administrative people than traditional hospitals. He said that looking for a job through the Internet had not worked out for him, although this was definitely superior to contacting people blind through e-mail or writing letters and attaching my resume. He suggested that management internship was indeed a good idea—some of them even paid—although it was, of course, a gamble in that some places didn't know how to appropriately use a management intern or didn't care how you were used so long as "the work got done."

POST SCRIPT (6 MONTHS LATER)

I have finally been offered a job in project management in network contracting for a large insurance company. I got this job primarily through networking and following the advice of a senior faculty member. He told me that I would get the lead on an appropriate job through the other members of my class and that's what happened here. A classmate working at Blue Cross started the ball rolling and his contacts led to other contacts. At the suggestion of adjunct professors, I did a lot of shadowing of program graduates 5 years after graduation, learning in this way about what graduates do and how they had obtained employment.

INDEX